To Jane,

The Tony Conigliaro Story

By

Bruce Fitzpatrick

"He who triumphs over himself is greater than he who conquers a city."

- Old Proverb

I hope you love the read!

Best,

Bruce Fitzpatrick

* Cover photo courtesy of Tony Conigliaro and Julie Markakis
** Additional copies of this book can be obtained by going to:
www.createspace.com/3738481

- The Tony Conigliaro Story -
Endorsements

Major League Baseball Hall Of Fame :

"The Tony Conigliaro Story is highly recommended, particularly for those of Red Sox Nation."

> *- Bruce Markusen,*
> *Sr. Executive, Writer,*
> *MLB Hall of Fame,*
> *Cooperstown, NY.*

ESPN :

"I loved it! So much I didn't know. What a crazy story. You did a terrific job with it. I wish more young fans today knew exactly how good he really was! Thanks again!"

> *- Jay Crawford,*
> *Sports Anchor,*
> *ESPN*

Fenway Nation:

This is a must-read for every Red Sox fan—those who lived through it all or those who need to know how it happened. Bruce Fitzpatrick does a masterful job of letting us all recall the amazing life of Tony C. We recommend the book highly.

> *- Ernie Paicopoulos, Executive*

Julie Markakis:

I finished the book this morning. I want to express my gratitude for such a great read. You truly captured Tony's life. I'm sure he is smiling down on you. I hope you sell tons of copies.

> *- Julie Markakis*
> *Childhood Sweetheart,*
> *Lifelong Friend*

- Acknowledgements -

I would be gravely remiss were I not to give thanks and appreciation to those whose direct and indirect contributions made this novel what it is. In doing so, I have also tried to accurately represent that which was so generously passed along to me. In keeping with the integrity of those facts, and in an effort to honor Tony's life and legacy, I now present what for me was a sheer labor of love from beginning to end.

I would first like to express my thanks to the Conigliaro family. They were the personification of the Italian-American family unit. Billy and Richie opened up their lives, their hearts and their memories of a closely knit, loving and moral family who clung together during the best of times and the worst of times, of which there were many.

I next need to thank the Markakis family. Julie, Lou, and Alex all contributed their insights and recollections of Tony, his Red Sox career and his time spent away from the bright lights, cheering crowds, cameras and microphones. Without their poignant enlightenment this book would not have become what it is.

I want to extend my thanks to the Boston Red Sox and Tony's former teammates. They generously took time to recall their days on the team with him, the contributions he made, and all that he did to personify the ultimate professional. Carl Yastrzemski, Johnny Pesky, Jerry Moses, Mike Ryan, Bill Lee and George Scott all added their own personal Technicolor to the year of The Impossible Dream. So did Manager Dick Williams.

I thank David Cataneo and Jack Zanger, writers whose works gave me further insight to the world and people among which Tony lived. I thank Jerry Maffeo, who was a stalwart in Tony's life, as were Frank Carey and Tommy Iarrobino. Each of them contributed significantly to this work. I also thank Donna Heath whose recollections of her teenage hero worship of Tony were both uplifting and deeply touching.

Another of my interviews involved Jack Hamilton, the pitcher whose errant ninety mile an hour fastball struck Tony in the face on August 18, 1967. He was open, forthright and contrite with his memory of that fateful night. I heard the regret reflected in his voice. In his own words, had he known what was destined to happen that night he'd never have shown up at the park, and I thoroughly believe that.

I must also mention Bobby Martini, Mike Phillips, Jimmy Cummings and Dorothy Aufiero who originally invited me to write this story. Cumulatively, they contributed each in their own way to me getting to participate in a project that ultimately morphed into the dream of a lifetime.

In closing I believe that no matter how great a life a person leads, it's those who were there, and who recall and detail it for those of us who write such stories, and for those of you who read them, who deserve major kudos for your contribution.

And for that, I thank you all...

- Prologue -

August, 1950

The vacant East Boston sandlot was the perfect setting for a rag-tag five year old and his forty year old uncle to develop their baseball skills. Young Tony Conigliaro wasn't concerned that his shirt was half out of his sagging, baggy pants, or that his baseball cap was tilted far to the side. It didn't even matter that the laces on one of sneakers were untied. His only concern was the baseball his Uncle Vinnie had lofted toward him from twenty-five feet away. The late afternoon sun that had begun to cast a golden hue over the surrounding neighborhood was behind him now. As long as he could follow the flight of the approaching ball, his world was in order.

Tony watched as it came closer, closer...until he devoured it in the glove he wore on his left hand. *Thwap!*

Uncle Vinnie, himself a sturdy, former aspiring athlete, whose dream of becoming a pro ball player had been cut down by a knee injury, triumphantly raised his hand over his head as Tony gathered the ball into his glove.

"Yeah! That's the way to do it!" he yelled. He encouraged his young protégé every chance he could. And when he did make a mistake, he patiently explained what Tony had done wrong, and then showed how to better handle the situation the next time. It was part of how he'd begun vicariously living his own missed opportunity through the yearnings of his sister's first-born son. It filled a deep need while also giving him a sense of purpose. He'd never seen someone that young committed to playing baseball as was Tony. What had begun as a casual pastime between them had blossomed into a penchant that now consumed fifteen to twenty hours a week. He loved this little guy, and would do anything for him.

"I really love this, Uncle Vinnie!" Tony proclaimed. "I want to do this forever!"

"You? You're gonna be a star some day. All we got to do is keep practicing just like we been doing."

"Good, because I—"

A familiar voice interrupted them in the midst of charting Tony's future.

"Anthony! Anthony, time to come home."

Tony frowned, looked across the street, then back at his Uncle Vinnie. "That's my mom, I think she's coming."

"Uh-oh! You know what that means."

"But we're not done. I want to keep playing."

A moment later Teresa Conigliaro, in her late twenties, appearing very lovely and very Italian, joined them. Blessed with dark hair and a rich, Mediterranean complexion, she bent down and scooped the ball from Tony's glove.

"Ma, what're you doing?"

"I'm taking you home. The neighbors already think I'm a bad mother for letting you play so much baseball with your Uncle Vinnie."

"But it's what I want to do, and he's teaching me!"

Placing her hands on her hips, she patiently looked down at this three-and-a-half-foot love of her life. "He can teach you later. Right now you need to eat."

Uncle Vinnie, understanding Tony's disappointment, yet wanting to do right by him, intervened. "Go ahead, we'll come back later."

Frowning, Tony looked up at his mother. "What's for supper?"

"Spaghetti and meat balls."

Tony mulled that over for a moment. Then, "I guess that'll be okay..."

Feigning relief, she said, "Why thank you, Anthony. I'm so glad you approve." With that, she winked at Vinnie, took Tony by the hand, and led him back toward the house.

- Chapter One -

Eleven Years Later

Tony Conigliaro, now a six-foot, rangy-looking high school sophomore watched with intense interest from the bench. For him there were no average games, no average at bats, no average moments. Not even in high school. Every play brought its own opportunity, its own challenges, and its own unique learning experience. One only need be an apt pupil. Even as a high school sophomore, he had long since become a student of the game. That, combined with his abundance of natural talent, was why he'd made the varsity team as a freshman. He'd been noticed. But then, he had expected to be noticed. Well aware of his abilities, he had labored tirelessly to develop them, and had never doubted he'd start as a varsity player.

The dual about to take place between the batter and pitcher would be extremely helpful to him. The batter, Tommy Iarrobino, his close friend, would be the perfect benchmark by which to plan his strategy. Like Tony, Tommy was a solid hitter, had good power, and hit for a high average. He was a known quantity around the league, and the manner in which they pitched to him was usually indicative of what he himself might expect when he stepped to the plate. Today he'd step in against Danny Murphy, the highly touted phenom from St. John's Prep. He'd heard about Murphy, but this was the first time he'd actually seen him. So far, Murphy appeared as overpowering as Tony had heard. But Tony was also convinced he'd never faced anyone with his own skills and tenacity, and by day's end, were it up to him, Danny Murphy would learn a thing or two about Tony Conigliaro.

Tony glanced at the crowd. Many of them were scouts from various professional teams, there to see Murphy, who was considered to be among the best in the country. Tony was loathe to admit it, but that rankled him. He didn't like being upstaged. They wanted to see something special? No problem, he'd give it to them. See what they said then. Moreover, his family was there, and no one – *no one* - was more important to him than they were. He'd make them proud of him. Unlike the average player, he had a special need deep inside him to excel, and ten Danny Murphy's weren't going to stand in his way. If anything, it served to fuel his determination. He'd show them all where the real talent was. By the end of the game they'd be talking about *him,* not Danny Murphy.

He held a long-standing conviction that he, Tony Conigliaro, had a special destiny. He had first become aware of it as a four-year old boy, and it had never diminished. His mother had trouble getting him to come home because he'd dedicated his every waking moment to working at this labor of love that he could neither explain nor understand. Before he was old enough to go to school, he'd pull on his sneakers, have his mother tie them for him, then bolt out the door to the ball field across the street from his house, in Revere, Massachusetts, where he'd remain all day. Even as the sun was setting and dusk was full upon the playing field, he had to have a baseball, a glove or a bat in his hands. At day's end his mother would have to retrieve him. Such was his passion for the game, and the passing of time only further cemented his commitment to it. Though his father had encouraged him to try his hand at other sports, and he had excelled in all of them, they had ultimately agreed that baseball was the sport for which he'd truly been born to play.

He watched Murphy look in for the sign, then stand erect, pausing before delivering his pitch. The ball arrived so quickly and slapped into the catcher's mitt with such velocity as to be heard by all of the one thousand people who had come to see the game. Tony took note and nodded begrudgingly. Murphy was good. No wonder the pros were scouting him.

"Strike one!" came the call from the plate umpire. Tommy Iarrobino stepped out, and glanced at Tony as if to say, 'Good luck with this guy.' After collecting himself,

Tommy stepped back in to face Murphy again. The next pitch was a fastball that just missed the outside corner of the plate for ball one; the pitch after that was another blinding fastball that was called a strike. The following pitch was a fastball that Tommy fouled off, and the next pitch was the one that gave Tony a piece of valuable information. Having the count in his favor at one ball and two strikes, Murphy next delivered a much slower, arcing curve that tied Tommy up in knots because of the radical difference in speed and the angle from which the ball arrived. Tommy was already leaning into the pitch while the ball was still five feet away. So effective had Murphy been with his fastballs, Iarrobino had become conditioned to them and was lucky that he was able to foul it off, despite the pitch having handcuffed him. This told Tony that not only had Murphy been endowed with physical attributes, he was also cagey, and that when he faced him he'd be unable to assume anything. Tommy stared out at Murphy, as if to say Murphy couldn't fool him. Thinking it would be another slow breaking curve, Tommy stepped in a little closer to the plate and was promptly plinked by a Danny Murphy fastball that moved in on him and hit him on the back, dropping him. After a short delay, Iarrabino trotted to first base, staring daggers at Murphy every step of the way.

With Iarrabino on first, Frank Carey, himself a solid hitter and close friend of Tony's came to the plate as Tony moved to the on-deck circle. Tony watched closely as Murphy went to work on Carey with another scorching fastball, which Frank stood and watched. Frank had often told him that he liked to see what a pitcher had before he took him to task. Apparently feeling he'd seen enough, he swung at Murphy's second offering and flied out. Tony had hoped for a better look at Murphy, but the encounter had ended almost as quickly as it began.

Tony now stepped in against the player the pros had come to see. He couldn't put it into words, but he felt a rush of adrenalin surge through him, especially with a runner on first. Murphy's opportunity to shine would now become his. His nerves were taught and his entire world was suddenly reduced to two people: himself and Danny Murphy. Tony's focus and fierce determination removed from him almost everything that was human, leaving only his concentration and that part of him that was pure machine. The two of them stared at each other, each regarding the other. During the silent exchange, they acknowledged each other's worthiness as opponents. And it was in that moment that

Tony knew that Danny Murphy had heard of him, too. It gave him a special satisfaction, not in a boastful, conceited way, but rather that he was becoming known beyond his hometown.

Murphy's first pitch came at him like a comet. Just as Frank Carey had done, he had studied the first pitch to see what Murphy looked like from the batters box. The ball blew past him in a blur, boring into the catcher's mitt with a loud *thwap.* Everything he'd heard about Danny Murphy was true. He had an arm like a cannon and was without a doubt professional material.

"Strike one!" yelled the home plate umpire. Tony stepped from the batters box, used the bat to tap the dirt from his cleats, and then looked at the ump. "He's pretty good, huh?" he asked, with a smile bordering on a smirk.

"That's why the pros are all here," answered the umpire, trying not to show partiality.

"Then maybe I'll give them more than they bargained for," answered Tony. He thought he saw a look of mild confusion pass over the umpire's face as he stepped back into the box. Tony found it hard to suppress the smile he felt within him. He watched as Murphy prepared to deliver his second pitch, and this is where he felt having studied Murphy earlier would be helpful. If he wanted to throw a curve, let him; he'd wait for one of Murphy's inevitable fastballs. If it looked right he'd launch it to a faraway place it had never been before. He was glad that his Uncle Vinnie had spent so much time with him helping him to develop his ability to select the right pitch to hit. It was rare that he swung at anything outside the strike zone, and by waiting for Murphy to throw the pitch he wanted, he would neutralize Murphy's element of surprise. He'd not distract himself by trying to anticipate what Murphy would throw; he'd simply wait until he got the pitch he wanted.

Murphy's next pitch was the same arching curve ball that he'd delivered to Tommy Iarrabino. Having seen it before, and seeing it drift out of the strike zone, he let it pass.

With the count now at one ball and one strike, Tony's confidence grew. Murphy would likely come at him with a fastball, and that was Tony's bread and butter pitch. His eye had developed to where he could pick up the spin on an approaching baseball when it was within ten to twelve feet from the plate. It told him what type of pitch it was, and whether or not it would be a strike. Murphy took his stance, got the sign, and fired the fastball that Tony had been waiting for. With incredible focus and blazing bat speed, Tony came around on the pitch and lofted it over the left field fence for a two run homer. As the crowd erupted, he gave Murphy the briefest glance as he trotted down the first base line. It pleased him immensely to see Murphy staring curiously after the ball as it became lost in the late afternoon haze. Tony's gaze then shifted to the scouts who were there, curious as to their reaction. His satisfaction nearly turned to giddiness as he studied their astonishment. Their jaws were slack, and their faces appeared frozen in time. Who was this kid who had just launched a Danny Murphy fastball into the next county? As he continued his trot around the bases he soaked up the cheers from the crowd, and finally let his gaze come to rest on his family. Younger brothers Billy and Richie, along with his mother and father, and his Uncle Vinnie, who had spent so many hours helping him develop his skills, were on their feet, going out of their minds, loving it. It meant more to him than all the pro scouts in the country.

Nor would the day end there. By game's end three more at bats would produce two more hits, giving him a three-for-four day against Murphy, including two home runs. At the end of the game, his family and friends surrounded him, congratulating him. Even Danny Murphy came over to give him a pat on the back. Murphy also used the moment to remind Tony that he had returned the favor by hitting a Tony Conigliaro fastball over the fence and into the parking lot, something that Tony grudgingly acknowledged.

Presently, his uncle Vinnie, who worshiped the ground Tony walked on, came up to him on his way out of the park. It was Uncle Vinnie, who while president of the Little League of Revere, used to pitch batting practice until Tony's hands bled. It was Uncle Vinnie who devoted every spare moment he had to helping Tony learn how to swing properly, and with authority until his hands became like vice grips. As a child Tony had developed calluses on his hands. Even with bleeding hands and calluses, Tony couldn't get enough practice time to satisfy him, and Uncle Vinnie had always been the one who had been there. His father had had a huge impact on him too, but it was under Uncle Vinnie's tutelage that Tony had begun to develop the sense of power and exhilaration he got from hitting baseballs so far they often had trouble finding them. There had been something surreal about it, and Tony had come to suspect he was developing skills at something that would become a lifelong pursuit, and that if he stayed with it he'd become better at it than almost anyone else. Now, Uncle Vinnie, six feet tall, stocky, and limping slightly, his face aglow, ran to him from the stands like a runaway train.

"Look at you!" he beamed. "*Look at you!* The home run king of Saint Mary's High School. Not only that, you guys beat 'em! You turned some heads today, Tony. You watch, all the time we spent practicing will pay off." Tony shook his outstretched hand and hugged him. To Sal, Tony's father, who was watching them, Vinnie added, "I'll take Teresa and the kids back to the house and drop them off. It's a proud day for us, Sal. Three out of four against Danny Murphy. Unbelievable. I'm glad I was here to see it."

"You should be proud," Sal said, patting Vinnie on the shoulder. "You had a lot to do with it."

Tony smiled as Vinnie walked off, the bounce in his step was unmistakable. As the crowd ebbed, Tony looked at several men who were still in the stands. He knew who they were, and wondered how they felt now that they had seen him in action. Al Lopez from the Chicago White Sox, Milt Bolling from the Red Sox, and two other scouts from the Detroit Tigers and the Baltimore Orioles were looking at him with speculative eyes. He was disappointed when the scouts from Baltimore and Detroit made several notes, and shook hands with Bolling and Lopez before departing. His spirits rose, however, when Bolling and Lopez put their pads away, and began walking toward him. Tony, who now stood alone with his father, watched them approach.

"Hello, Tony," Bolling began, shaking Tony's hand. "I'm Milt Bolling from the Boston Red Sox."

Tony shook Bolling's hand, smiled and said, "I know. You're a scout for them now, but you used to be their second baseman. You did a real good job for them, too."

Bolling smiled, unable to conceal his appreciation for this kid's brash honesty. "Well that's good, Tony," Bolling said, laughing. "I'm glad you approve of the job I did."

"Come on, Mr. Bolling, you know what I mean." As part of his rich Italian heritage, Tony had been rigorously schooled in the areas of protocol and manners. You showed respect to everyone you met, even people you didn't get along with. But Milt Bolling? Tony wanted to get along with Milt Bolling. A lot.

Bolling continued. "This is Al Lopez. He's a scout for one of those teams way out west in Chicago. You know, a faraway place where it's really cold and windy. You wouldn't want to play that far from home, so I wouldn't be talking to him for too long."

Lopez laughed. "He's just trying to get the inside track on you, Tony. I think we can give you a lot of reasons to play in Chicago when the time comes. For now, I just wanted stop by and say hello, and tell you how well I thought you did today. Just watch out for these Red Sox guys, that's all."

Beaming, Tony wanted to jump right out of his skin. Playing baseball was something he wanted to do the rest of his life. It was something he'd always wanted to do. For him nothing else mattered. And the thought of two pro scouts taking time to come and talk to him, even for a moment, was exhilarating. He'd have quit school right then and there and go try out for them if he could have. The year before, he'd commented to Tommy Iarrabino, Frank Carey and several other kids for whom he was holding court, that he'd like to face Whitey Ford, the great New York Yankee pitcher, who many believed would be in the Hall Of Fame some day. He was convinced that even as a high school kid he'd be able to get a hit off him. They laughed back then, but now they weren't so sure. Tony's power and skills were increasing enormously. "Thanks, Mr. Lopez, I appreciate it," Tony answered. "By the way, when it comes time for us to talk you'll be talking with my father more than me. Meet Salvatore Conigliaro, he's my dad."

- Chapter Two -

Bolling and Lopez regarded Sal. Though shorter than Tony, the man had an appearance that suggested dignity, authority, and a pleasant demeanor. At the same time, nowhere did it suggest belligerence, unreasonableness or false bravado. He was a man with the appearance of both father and mentor. Prior to that day Tony's name had come up on occasion as a potential future prospect, but not much more than that. After all, he was only a high school sophomore. But after today's performance, they realized he was worthy of a much closer look. And whereas Tony had presented himself with abundant confidence, even cockiness, his readiness to defer to his father made an unspoken declaration: the senior Conigliaro was the man to be dealt with, and it appeared that a game plan for the younger Conigliaro turning pro one day had already been formulated.

And well it had. Like any loving parent, Sal wanted Tony to have a better deal than the one he'd been dealt back when times were hard in America. Sal Conigliaro, a self-styled entrepreneur, had held jobs shoveling horse manure at the Boston Rodeo for a dollar a day; building music stands for orchestras; running his own bakery and donut shop; had had an in-the-back-yard chicken farm; and most recently had begun working in a zipper factory. The factory job paid sixty dollars a week; the chickens cost thirty-five dollars a week, and his family lived on the rest. In time it became obvious that the math wasn't working in the family's favor, so the chicken farm had been scrapped. But because Sal had paid his dues along the way he had a finely tuned appreciation for life and the values and ethics that brought ultimate success, despite having never basked in conventional luxury. What he had done, however, was ingrain within his three sons a hard and fast uncompromising belief that life could afford what people wanted most if they were willing to work for it. Especially if it were in a nurturing family environment, and not knowing the meaning of the word quit. As the oldest son, Tony had been taught that right from the beginning, and had integrated those qualities into his work ethic, especially when it came to baseball. In addition to those came the respect he had always maintained for his father, both as mentor and head of the family. Therefore it was only natural that he readily defer to Sal as the voice of authority. And now, in a matter of seconds, both Lopez and Milt Bolling's vigilant eyes had accurately surmised that.

Extending his hand to Tony's father, Bolling said, "How do you do, Mr. Conigliaro? Your son caught my attention today, and I thought I'd stop by to tell him so."

"He may have been overlooked before now," added Lopez, "but I suspect those days are over."

"My pleasure," answered Sal, clasping both men's proffered hands. "I'm sure you're busy men, and that there are many young players that you're watching. We're honored that you'd do that."

"True," answered Bolling, "but none of them ever turned in a performance against Danny Murphy like the one Tony did today."

"He was very impressive," Lopez echoed.

Tony's heart was in his throat as he watched his father engage two of the league's top guns. How many countless nights had he laid awake in bed, fantasizing this magical, mystical moment?

"That's great, fellas," Sal responded. "We think we have a special boy in Tony, and we hope you'll continue to watch him."

"If today was an example of his capabilities, he may have the right goods," said Lopez. "We'll let time answer that."

They shook hands, then Bolling and Lopez left. Tony's eyes were bugging as he watched. Two pro scouts had just said he had the goods. At the same time, he felt a sense of desperation as he watched them walk off and get in their cars. He turned to his father in bewilderment.

"What's the matter, Choo?" Sal asked. "What's wrong?" 'Choo', the nickname his father had given him, the one that always brought Tony back to ground zero. He'd given it to him when he was barely more than an infant. The rapid manner in which Tony had crawled across the floor on his hands and knees reminded Sal of a 'choo-choo train'. Over the years the name had stuck, and had become a special term of endearment they shared between them.

"Why you letting them walk away like that?" Tony asked. "I mean, they're getting away. We should invite them over the house, have Ma cook supper for them. Maybe we can cut a deal over lasagna."

Sal shook his head and smiled. Tony was always a hundred yards ahead of the rest of the world. Get it done here and now. Quick, before time runs out. He rested his hands on Tony's shoulders and looked up at him. "Listen to me," he began, patiently. "You just pay attention to developing your skills. Do that, and a lot of people are going to come around making comments like they just did. You got something special going on, but you can't afford to get distracted by anything. And I mean *anything*. That includes guys like them, girls, hanging out with your friends, skipping school, *anything*. Focus on getting better at baseball, and becoming a decent human being – no matter what – and all these other things will come to you. Trust me on that. Just make sure you keep the main thing the main thing. Okay?"

Tony exhaled long and slow, his disappointment and the fear of having missed a once-in-a-lifetime opportunity beginning to subside. "Sure, pop. But it's hard, letting a couple guys like them just walk away, that's all."

"I understand. But trust me, there's going to be a lot of guys like them that'll come into your life. And when they do, we'll let 'em slug it out with each other to see who gets you. In the meantime, let's go home. You've earned one of your mother's great home cooked meals."

****

Teresa, Tony's mother, greeted him with her customary kiss on the cheek as he entered the house. "You did good today, Anthony. Your father and I are very proud of you." She paused, and took a closer look at his uniform, which was covered with dirt and grass stains. "When you were a little kid you used to get pretty dirty every time you played. But now that you're a teenager I think maybe you get even dirtier. I feel sorry for the girl you marry some day if you don't change your ways."

Sal chimed in from the next room. "Never mind about girls and when he gets married, he's got a baseball career to pay attention to. He can get married when he retires, maybe even hire a maid to do his laundry."

Tony smiled that smile that warmed his mother's heart. "See ma? We got it all figured out. Besides, it's not my regular clothes."

She frowned in mock consternation and waved her wooden spaghetti spoon at him. Nodding, she said, "You do that to your regular clothes, I'll take this spoon to you just like when you used to skip school to practice baseball."

He leaned over and kissed her on the cheek. "Put the spoon away, Ma. I promise to be careful."

"Good, now go get cleaned up so we can eat."

As Tony was about to go upstairs, his eight-year-old brother Richie came down from his bedroom. "Hey, you," Tony said. "What's going on?"

"Nothing," Richie answered.

"Nothing? Like nothing at all?" Tony knew Richie had been at the game. For the locals it had been much more than a game, it had been an event. What normally might have drawn a few hundred people had drawn a thousand. Danny Murphy was a marquis player; everyone knew he was destined for big things. People who loved high school baseball were flocking to see him play. But Tony was also getting a reputation, and everyone had wanted to see what would happen when the two collided. Richie was too young to attain celebrity status, but it didn't hurt having an older brother who was getting written up in the local press. And in many ways Tony was Richie's best friend. Most teenage boys were loathe to take their 'kid brother' anywhere. But not so with Tony; Tony and Richie had gone places and done things on countless occasions. Richie was the one he took with him when he wanted to go somewhere alone without being alone. He could be himself with Richie, who never made demands on him. For Richie's part, he loved having someone older who could answer questions, teach him things, and be a role model, especially when it came to sports. At eight, Richie viewed becoming a teenager as some strange, faraway place at the other end of the rainbow; but he loved asking Tony what it was like. Moreover, Richie and Billy were both showing a lot of promise athletically, and as the oldest of the three, Tony was the one who naturally paved the way. Not only did Tony find it fun to drag answers from Richie by pressing him for them, he secretly enjoyed Richie's admiration.

"You saw the game today, right?" Tony asked.

Richie, having trouble suppressing a smile, said nonchalantly, "Yeah, so?"

"Whatta ya mean, 'so'? What'd you think?"

"It was okay."

"Think your friends will ask you about it at school tomorrow?"

The smile on Richie's face got broader. "Yeah, I guess so."

"So maybe they'll think I'm a star, and maybe they'll even pay you to get my autograph. Maybe they'll even think you're a star because you're my brother and you live with me."

"Yeah, right. What's for supper?"

Billy, Tony's thirteen-year old brother, had entered the dining room and was about to sit down for dinner. Billy wasn't as outgoing as Tony, but his quiet determination was just as committed. Billy was the brother who reminded everyone that still waters ran deep. Not that he was quiet or unassuming; he just maintained a lower profile. Hearing the exchange, he said, "I don't think he's going for it. He's getting pretty smart for an eight year old kid."

"That's because I give him lots of practice. How about you, you want to sell autographs for me?"

"Forget it, I got my own career to think about."

"That's right, you do," said Sal, entering from the living room. "Any kind of luck all three of you guys will be in the pros some day."

"That happens, we'll chip in and buy you and Ma a new house," Tony said.

"Worry about graduating from high school first," Teresa said. "Now go clean up before dinner gets cold."

- Chapter Three -

November, 1961

Just as girls had never been strangers to Tony, Tony had never been a stranger to them. Having matured over the past year-and-a-half, he was now six-foot-three, had filled out physically, and was one hundred seventy-five pounds of solid muscle. This lent him the physical attributes required for three of his passions beyond baseball. One of them was girls; the others were hockey and football. The girls his father didn't mind as long they didn't get too close. Even so, he realized Tony was still a teenager, and it was natural that he should be interested in them.

It was the other two that he and his father had discussed. Sal readily admitted he wasn't pleased by Tony's attraction to football, but hockey really bothered him. "Listen to me, Choo. I'm not going to force you to do anything, and I know you're a hell of a skater. But if you play hockey in high school you risk ruining your opportunity at having a future in professional baseball. If you feel the need to play something else for now, let it be football." Therefore, football had been chosen as the lesser of two evils, at least until baseball season resumed in the spring. Tony hadn't appreciated his father's advice, but he was willing to trust his father's judgment, and had acquiesced.

As quarterback for Saint Mary's High School, Tony had been noticed yet again. He had an arm like a rifle, a sixth sense for reading defenses and changing plays at the line of scrimmage, and he was hard to bring down. Give him a chance to break free and run for a touchdown, he'd try it every time. Again, the need to excel was the force that drove him, especially when the game was on the line.

His skills and presence on the field had given his small, unassuming, little-known high school what it might otherwise never have had: a reputation. And on this particular day the opposition was Lynn, a much larger, more highly regarded city school; it was also their traditional Thanksgiving Day rival. But this year had been different; this year St. Mary's had put together the best record in the school's history, and this year Lynn had no guarantee that they'd come away a winner.

A light rain was falling and a chill had descended over The Manning Bowl, in Lynn, Massachusetts, and the two thousand people who packed the stadium couldn't have cared less. Just like the Danny Murphy confrontation, the same air of anticipation raced through The Manning Bowl. People had turned out to watch what promised to be a special event.

Tony had taken an intense interest in beating Lynn. This year they were a combined team of Lynn's three high schools, and they had been openly ragging on St. Mary's, calling them pansies. Earlier in the week Tony had gone to the St. Mary's dance in his father's 1959 Cadillac, a gorgeous car that his father loved. In the middle of the dance a police officer had come inside and informed him that someone had smashed all the windows in it. When Tony and the police officer had gone outside he'd seen all the shattered windows where bricks had been tossed through them.

After the police officer had taken Tony's information and had gone back inside, Tony had noticed a couple of tough looking kids off to one side giving him the evil eye, and he had recognized them as members of the team he'd be playing on Thanksgiving Day. One of them had said, "Hey, Conigliaro, don't think it's going to end here. We know how to bust more than just windows."

Tony, normally level headed and easygoing, had gone into a rage. "Oh yeah? You want to go, we can go right now!"

One of them had raised his hand to stave off Tony's advance. "Not here, down at Lynn Beach."

Tony had been born at night, but it hadn't been that night. He knew what they'd do. Lynn beach was where they and all their friends hung out, and going down there would be tantamount to putting his head in a meat grinder. He'd have gotten 'stomped'. And now it was game day. His family was in the stands with the rest of the crowd, three thousand strong. Even so, when Tony walked out onto the field, he was still angry about the incident and wanted revenge. His nerve endings were wired, and adrenalin was coursing through his veins. What normally would have been a high school football game had turned into a personal vendetta. And it showed. His passes were like rifle shots and thrown with deadly accuracy, hitting on nine of eleven attempts, one for a touchdown. He'd also carried the ball on four occasions for a total of sixty-two yards.

Now, just before halftime, he had worked the team to within field goal range. Looking up at the clock, which had been stopped while the sideline markers were being moved, he gauged the odds of scoring a touchdown with only twenty-two seconds left and no time outs. He smiled to himself; this was the kind of situation he lived for. Moreover, it was an opportunity to rub some more mud in the opposition's face; especially the guys who had chased him home earlier in the week. There was an obstacle, however, and it was a formidable one: his coach. Tony looked to the sideline and saw that the coach was already gathering the field goal unit around him. As the coach glanced at him, Tony urgently waved his arms back and forth, begging him not to send them out there. His coach, a man who had seen Tony do some amazing things during his four-year tenure at quarterback, paused, scowled, and stared out at Tony, then up at the clock.

Aware that the chains were almost in place, Tony yelled, "One chance, just one chance! I promise, I won't let the clock run out. One chance for a touchdown!"

His coach looked at him, then back up at the clock, more in prayer than to check the time. Part of him wanted to give Tony free reign, yet the sensible part of him said go for the sure three points. After a short deliberation, his heart won out. "One try, then we go for the field goal. Make me look bad, and you'll spend the second half on the bench."

Several players from Lynn had tried to make his life miserable; now it was his turn. He motioned his teammates to huddle. "Alright, we all know what these guys have been saying about us for the last two weeks. We got any 'pansies' in this huddle?" His question was met with a chorus of 'hell no's' and 'no ways'. "Good, now let's show 'em who the real pansies are. Twenty-five slot left, fake tailback draw, staggered count, on the third hut." Turning to Frank Carey, his baseball teammate from the Danny Murphy game, he added, "Frankie, when you break the front line go like hell on a deep post. Don't let up until you're in the end zone. If everything goes right, there'll be a little present waiting for you when you get there. Let's go!"

The huddle broke, and everyone assumed their positions for the play. As Tony stepped to the line, he perused Lynn's defensive set. As he did, he made eye contact with two of the opposing linemen who had chased him. A third player, one of their linebackers, was one of the kids who had been there the night his father's windows had been smashed. He'd have loved to say something to them, but feared he'd draw a penalty for unsportsmanlike conduct. Mindful of the bigger picture, he settled for blowing them a kiss.

Up in the stands, Sal and Vinnie were trying to make sense of Tony's actions. "What the hell's he doing out there?" Vinnie asked. "This is supposed to be a football game, not some kind of mating thing."

"I think he's sending a message to the kids who smashed my car windows the other night. Let's hope it don't cost him a broken leg."

Down on the field Tony had become deadly earnest as he called the play. "Twenty-five left twenty-five right, hut, hut. *Hut!*" The center snapped the ball and the linemen teed off on their opponents. Frank Carey faked taking a hand-off, then bolted through the crush of offensive and defensive linemen, and took off toward the goal post in the end zone as if the devil were chasing him. For his part, Tony faked the hand-off, hid the ball behind his thigh, then dropped back and scrambled, trying to avoid the two Lynn players who were chasing him. Mentally, he counted to three, avoided a would-be tackler, and arced a rainbow that came down in the end zone...right into Frank Carey's outstretched hands. Not only had the completion upped the score to twenty-one to six in favor of Saint Mary's, it gave Tony an opportunity he couldn't resist. Rising from the turf where he'd been driven by two of the players who had smashed his father's windows, he pointed toward the goal post. "Ball's in the end zone, fellas. And from now on, stay away from my family's property." He then sauntered to the sidelines and accepted the congratulations of his coach and teammates.

The extra point was successful; St. Mary's had run up twenty-two points by the end of the first half, and was en route to their biggest Thanksgiving Day success in the school's history.

In the second half, however, the unexpected happened. Late in the third quarter, with the score unchanged, Tony had removed his helmet to get some air while the referee called for a measurement. The measurement produced a third down and short yardage situation, and he called for an end sweep. Tony leisurely approached the line, pulling his helmet down over his head. He looked left and right to make sure everyone was in place. In doing so, his gaze darted to the opposing team's sideline where their cheerleaders were at the edge of the playing field, cheering for Lynn to hold St. Mary's. It never ceased to amaze him how cheerleaders never gave up on their team, no matter how far behind they were. One of them, however, caught his eye in a way no other girl had ever done before. Not only had she caught his eye, he had caught hers. Her movements suddenly went from enthusiastic to mechanical, and 'cheering by rote'. As she raised her arms, she let go of one of her pom-poms, which landed on the field. Her left foot instead of her right rose to kick in unison with the other girls, and accidentally kicked the girl in front of her squarely in the butt. The ripple effect of that unscheduled move went down the line of cheerleaders, and it quickly began to look as if they were cheering blindfolded.

So magically disruptive was their moment that both of them had forgotten where they were, and what they were supposed to be doing. Still smitten, Tony began yelling a snap count that hadn't been called in the huddle, and none of his teammates were prepared for it. Worse, he had lined up behind one of the guards instead of the center. Only when the man in front of him didn't snap the ball on his third request did Tony suddenly become aware of his mistake. Embarrassed and panic-stricken, he yelled, "Screw it, just give me the ball!" The center awkwardly flipped it to him over his shoulder, the play fell apart, and Tony got mugged.

Tommy Iarrabino ran over to him. "What's wrong with you? You trying to let them back in the game, or what?"

Tony got up and brushed himself off. "Sorry." Looking over at the cheerleader that had caught his eye, he asked, "See that girl over there, third from the end?"

"Yeah, why?"

"You know her?"

"I've seen her around. Her name's Julie."

"Good. After the game, I want you to tell me everything you know about her."

"Tony, she's just a girl. Not only that, she's from the other team."

"Hey, I don't care where she's from, I got to meet her. Can you arrange that?"

"You sound like you're in love with her already."

"No girl ever made me feel like she just did. I'd kinda like to return the favor, that's all."

As he and Tommy walked back to the huddle, he paused to look across at Julie. What had this girl done to him that he absolutely *had* to meet her? And if he did get to meet her, how would he explain it to her? It didn't seem right that a girl – *any* girl – could affect him like this.

He never saw the consternating, yet curious, glance she gave him as she trundled out onto the playing field to collect her pom-pom.

This boy...who was this boy...?

- Chapter Four -

Tony had never been shy about anything. Always brimming with confidence and enthusiasm, something that had often been misinterpreted as cockiness, he took life pretty much in stride. Other than the occasional situation that arose unexpectedly, he felt ready for almost anything. But today was different. He and Tommy Iarrabino had come to the Lynn Public Library on the chance that 'Julie' would be there. Tommy had seen her there on several occasions, none of which had included the same boy more than once. Tony's hopes had been bolstered when Tommy had told him about 'never with the same boy more than once'. She was pretty, to be sure, and no doubt lots of boys chased her. But it appeared none of them was going steady with her. Now, as he and Tommy made their way down the library's main corridor toward the study area, he was irritated at feeling restless with anticipation. To his way of thinking, he was too cool and self-assured to be restless. Restlessness was one more thing for pansies; and he wasn't a pansy. So why was he feeling this way? Hard as it was to admit, he wanted her to be there, he wanted her to like him, he wanted her to not have a boyfriend, he wanted to ask her out, and he didn't want anything to interfere with that. Most of all, he had no idea why these things were suddenly so important.

He'd reluctantly admitted to Tommy that she wasn't just another girl he wanted to date. The prospect of having her saying no made him ache inside. Yet, there was something about that that was indescribably exciting; he hadn't even met her, and she already had the ability to make him ache. What kind of girl *was* this? It was like the agony and the ecstasy. There was the part of him that found this interesting and unusual, a new horizon to look forward to; then there was the other part, the agony of not knowing what she'd be like, or what she'd say when she met him.

Tommy, a half foot shorter than Tony, was trying hard to keep up with him. When it finally got to be too much, he said, "Hey, slow down will ya. I feel like I'm running a marathon trying to keep up with you. And I know what'll happen if she's here; you'll end up talking to her, and I'll have to find a ride home."

Tony stopped, and looked at him. They'd been friends since he'd moved to Swampscott, having first met on a baseball field. They'd noticed each other's formidable skills, and when they'd discovered their mutual Italian heritage they had become quick and close friends. Tommy and Frank Carey had been through many of Tony's antics with him. They had also witnessed many of his sporting glories.

"What do you think," he asked. "A guy's going to leave his friend with no way home?" Handing over the keys to his old 1956 Chevy, he smiled, then winked and added, "Just make sure you fill the tank, that's all."

Tommy scowled at him. "Yeah, right. Let me know if she has any nice looking girlfriends. Then maybe we'll talk about gassing the tank." He took a couple of steps, then turned to look at the kid he'd come to regard almost as a brother. "Good luck with her."

"Luck? I'm praying about this one."

Tommy shook his head. "I was right, you got it bad."

As Tony entered the study area he caught a glimpse of Julie as she rounded a corner and walked in between two rows of stacked books. Her purse was on the table, and her jacket was draped over the back of her chair. A pencil and several papers were strewn across the table. Seeing her drop from view, he decided humor would be the best way to break the ice. It would help him relax, too. Approaching the table, he reached for the three-ring binder near her seat. Another girl, apparently a friend of hers, gave him a troubled look, as if to question what he was doing.

"You with Julie?" he asked.

"Yes," she answered, not sure what to make of him.

"Good," he answered, flashing her the smile that most girls seemed to like. He wanted her to know he meant no harm. Holding out his hand, he introduced himself. "Hi, my name's Tony."

She seemed to soften, then took his outstretched hand, and smiled. "I'm Roseanne. You a friend of Julie's?"

"Sort of, but not as much as I'm going to be. I'll say one thing though."

"What's that?"

"If you're anything like the rest of her girlfriends, she got some real nice girlfriends." And he was right. Roseanne would catch many an eye during an average day, including his. But not today; today his eye was on Julie.

She grinned, then broke into a broad smile. "I think maybe Julie's going to like you."

"I think she will, too. I sure hope so." He'd felt nothing pretentious about what he'd said, and it had gotten the reaction he wanted; she had smiled at him, completely disarmed. "What are you guys doing here?" he continued.

"We're studying for a History test."

"Good, because that's what I want to do. I want to make history with Julie. Help me have some fun with her. Okay?"

He pulled a sheet of paper from Julie's binder, drew a picture on it, and scribbled a note beneath the picture. He then folded it into something akin to a paper doll and stood it on the table beside Julie's books. Raising his index finger to his lips, he added, "Just play dumb and go along with me. I want to see what happens when she reads this." He then walked do a distant table, sat down, picked up a magazine and pretended to read it.

A moment later, Julie emerged from between the rows of books and sat down. As she placed a large History book on the table, she reached for her pen and notepad. Seeing the paper doll, she paused, trying to remember how it got there. Unable to, she frowned and turned to Roseanne. "Where did this come from?"

"I don't know, some guy dropped it on the table, and ran out of the library."

"Some guy? *What* guy?"

"I don't know, just some guy. He asked me to have you read it, and went back the way he came. I don't know what it is."

Julie looked at Roseanne, as if she were crazy. All Roseanne could do was shrug and go along with Tony's plan. She took a deep breath, picked up the paper doll, and said, "Okay, I can play that game, too."

She opened it, and stared at the picture Tony had drawn. It was the caricature of a spooky little Halloween mask. She then read aloud the note scribbled beneath it. "Better watch out, there's a real scary guy over there watching you."

She looked at Roseanne, then quickly glanced around the library. Her gaze darted everywhere, and then abruptly went back to a face she'd seen before, a face that was presently laughing at her, almost hysterically.

Pointing at her, Tony said, "Gotcha!"

He got up and casually started walking toward her. Standing, she asked, "What's that for?"

"That's for making me look stupid in front of three thousand people in The Manning Bowl Thanksgiving Day. Now we're even."

"Even? We're not even, we may *never* be even," she answered, trying hard to be mad at him, but finding it impossible. Aside from being drop-dead Hollywood handsome, he had the dreamiest smile she'd ever seen. His movements appeared to be *in slow motion*. His eyes were filled with so much warmth she wanted to dive into them. Fearing she'd melt, she rested her hands on the edge of the table in case her knees buckled. "Surely this boy's name must be Adonis," she uttered.

"I heard your name is Julie," he said.

"That's right. What's yours?"

"Tony."

"What's your last name?"

"Conigliaro."

"Italian."

"That's right. What's yours?"

"Markakis."

"A Greek girl."

"Pretty much. Except my mother's Spanish."

"Cool." He stepped a little closer. Being six three, he was a foot taller than she was. She looked up at him without taking a backward step. Up close, his eyes were mesmerizing, almost hypnotic. His name might not be Adonis, but Tony would do.

His tone softened, and his words sounded as if she was the only girl in the world they were meant for. "So how come we'll never be even?" he asked, smiling down at her. They were standing only two feet apart, and even that felt too far away.

"Your team beat my team on Thanksgiving Day," she uttered, trying not to lose herself in him. "That wasn't very nice."

"That's because you were cheering for the wrong team. Besides, you almost got me killed. I lined up in the wrong place when I saw you, and the guys on your team stomped me. Made me look like some kind of dope."

"How do you think I felt when I kicked one of the other cheerleaders in the ass, then threw my pom-pom out onto the field where everyone could see? I'm supposed to be the head cheerleader, and I blew it. That was your fault. I was paying more attention to you than what I was supposed to be doing."

"You were supposed to be paying attention to me."

"You sound pretty sure of yourself."

"I am."

"Going to tell me why you came here today?"

"You kidding? No one's ever done to me what you did. I had to come and see you. Is that okay?"

"I guess so."

"You *guess so?*"

She tried to stifle the smile she felt creeping into the corners of her mouth. "Yeah, I'm glad you came."

"You better be. Got a steady boyfriend?"

"No. How about you?"

"Me? What would I want with a steady boyfriend?"

They burst into laughter. The tension evaporated, and the magic from the previous day had returned.

His laughter slowly subsided, and his gaze came to rest on her eyes. She saw something there she hadn't seen in any boy before him. If she had seen it before, it must not have mattered; with him it did. There was something about him, something mystical, as though she'd been waiting her whole life to meet him.

"What are you thinking about?" she asked.

"I'm thinking about you, and how much I want to get to know you," he answered. "I'm thinking about all the things I want to ask you, and all the things I want to tell you. You're a pretty cool girl, Julie Markakis, and I want to get to know you."

Looking up into his eyes, she surrendered without making any attempt at restraining herself. Nodding slowly, she answered, "Me, too."

Roseanne, who had quietly watched the exchange, had seen all she needed. "I think I'd better get going." To Julie, she added, "Call me later." She collected her books, then turned to leave. After a couple of steps, she paused. "Wait a minute, we came here in your car. How am I supposed to get home?"

"There's a kid outside named Tommy," Tony said. "He's seventeen, about five ten with blondish hair. He'll be climbing into an old blue Chevy. If you hurry, you can catch him. Tell him I said to give you a ride. Not only that, but he's a good guy, and he isn't going with anyone right now. Maybe you'll like him. And hey, thanks for going along with me, I really appreciate it."

She smiled. "Yeah, right. Look what I started."

When she was gone, Tony asked Julie, "Let's go get an ice cream, my treat."

"How about a hot chocolate, instead? *My* treat."

Winking, he said, "Like I said, you're a pretty cool girl."

- Chapter Five -

Tony had escorted Julie to a table in the corner of the ice cream parlor. She'd been pleasantly surprised when he'd held the door for her as she got out of the car; he'd held it again when they entered the parlor. As she prepared to sit, he had pulled out her chair and held it for her while she sat down. He was either very smooth, or very much a gentleman. *God, please let Adonis be a gentleman,* she thought.

Having ordered, they now sat facing each other in the corner, alone and content to seal themselves off from the outside world.

Tony smiled at her from across the table, something that made her both curious and amused. "What?" she asked, dying to know what was running through his mind. She had already determined that he was one of those boys who would bear watching.

He shrugged. "How come you had to do this to me?"

"Do what?" she asked.

"You know what," he answered.

"No, tell me," she retorted, thoroughly enjoying herself. She sensed he was experiencing something with her to which he wasn't accustomed. That was a good thing. "What did I do?"

"How come you had to steal me away from all those other girls that wanted to go out with me?" He knew he was talking like a dope, knew that she knew it, and knew they were both loving it. Yet, it was an honest question; he really did wonder how she could affect him like she did.

Deciding to indulge him, "It's my job to do that to you."

"Your job?"

"Sure. How could I get you to ask me out if I didn't steal you away from them?" She paused for a moment. This was one of those times she wished she was a grown-up. Grown-ups always seemed to have the answers; at present she had more questions than answers. At the same time it was fun. "So how did I do?"

He was becoming lost in her. He'd heard the definition of the word 'smitten' during one of his literature classes, and was only now coming to understand the full implication of its meaning.

"You did pretty good. I mean, I'm here, right?"

"So were a lot of other girls," she answered, calmly. "And I don't want to be just another one of them."

He slowly shook his head from side to side. "You're not," he answered, softly. "If I thought you were just another girl, I wouldn't have come to the library." He paused for a minute, and his mood seemed to change. He stared down at the table, as though collecting his thoughts. Finally, he asked, "What grade are you in?"

"I'm a junior. What about you?"

"I'm a senior, I'll be graduating in June."

"Going to college?"

"No, I don't think college is for me. What about you?"

"I'm not sure," she answered. "I know I'm only a junior, but they don't have what I want. Not in high school, anyway."

"No? What do you want?" This girl was becoming more interesting by the minute.

"I want to be a dancer. You know, a professional."

"That's cool. What kind of dancer?"

She looked at him closely, trying to read his sincerity as she gathered her resolve. She'd answered this question before, and had received a variety of responses, few of which had been encouraging. "I want to go to New York, and dance with The Rockettes."

"You're kidding."

"No," she answered, stiffening her resolve. "I love it, and it's what I want to do with my life."

He thought he detected mild frustration, as though she felt the need to defend herself. And having been there himself, he understood. He remembered an instance earlier in the year when one of his teachers, a nun, who for lack of a better word could be described only as hateful, had delighted in being especially hard on him. His aspiration to become a professional baseball player had come up in class one day, and she'd asked him to describe why he thought he could do it. As matter-of-fact as possible, he had done as requested, after which she had said, "Mr. Conigliaro, I doubt you'll ever make it; one, because you're no good, and second, because you just plain don't have the guts." She had then begun keeping him after school instead of allowing him to go practice with the team. On another occasion during his Sophomore year, he had worked particularly hard on a science project, and had thought he had done a great job on it. Science was difficult for him, so he'd put a lot of extra time and effort into it. That same nun had given him a 'C', and had gone on to humiliate him in front of the class, using the words 'wop' and 'guinea' in front of them, which had infuriated him. After telling his mother about the incident, she had gone to school to speak with his teacher. The nun had been exceedingly polite to her, telling her he needed to study harder, and should perhaps devote less time to sports.

Another time, he'd sustained a football injury. That same teacher had called him a phony, and when he'd tried to show her the injury, she'd cut him off and told him to sit down and shut up, and to stop feeling sorry for himself. All these memories came rushing back, just by hearing the urgent tone in one girl's voice as she spoke of her dream and aspiration of becoming a dancer.

"You know what?" he asked.

"What?" She waited for the other shoe to drop. It always did; she'd heard it before.

"I think that's a great idea. You know, dancing."

She sat trance-like as the waitress delivered their order. Her trance was quickly broken, however, when she got a look at his order. "What do you call that?"

"A banana bucket. It's got three scoops of ice cream, a mound of whipped cream, nuts, and a banana. Why?"

"You're not afraid it'll make you fat?"

"Nah, you could empty a cement truck into me and I wouldn't gain an ounce. And with how hard I work out? No way." Before leaving, the waitress shrugged at Julie as if to say some people are just plain lucky.

When they were alone, she asked, "So are you serious? You like it? You know, about me becoming a dancer?"

"Of course. Dreams have to begin some time, right? Might as well be now."

"These dreams didn't begin today," she answered, her zeal suddenly fired. "They began a long time ago. I've been taking dance lessons since I was three. It's what I live for, it's part of why I became a cheerleader."

Her eyes narrowed as he smiled at her. Why does he have to do that, she wondered? Didn't he know what it did to her? That's probably why he did it; he knew what it did to her. "Why are you smiling at me like that?" she asked.

"Because you just answered something I was wondering about," he answered.

"What's that?" she asked, mildly suspicious.

"You said you've been dancing since you were a little kid. No wonder you look so hot."

"Don't make jokes, I'm serious about it."

"So am I," he said. "I think you *are* hot." He then did something she found curious. He reached across the table and took her hand. At first she thought it was meant to be romantic, but quickly realized there was more to it than that. And she made no effort to disengage from him.

He then put his other hand over hers. With her hand in between his, he slowly began rubbing them back and forth. At first it felt like her hand had been sandwiched between two slabs of rough stone. They were hard and calloused, and felt extremely powerful. Yet, she didn't feel unsafe with him, but the effect was unsettling. It seemed so uncharacteristic of what she expected from this handsome, soft-spoken boy with all his charm and manners. She'd never experienced anything like it.

"My God," she said. "Your hands, what's wrong with them?" She found it almost shocking.

"You're following your dream. This is from me following mine." Reassuring her, he continued. "You began dancing when you were three, I began playing with bats and baseballs when I was five. I practiced for hours, all year round. I still do. Even though there are lots of other things I could do with my life, this is the only thing I've ever dreamed of. It's all I want to do; it's all I'll *ever* want to do. My hands are rough from practicing something I've been in love with since I was born. And it's why I understand how you feel about becoming a dancer. If it's a dream, and it's all you've ever wanted, that's what you're supposed to do as long as you're willing to work for it. And that's why I'd never laugh at you for wanting it. I understand how you feel. It's how I feel, too."

She felt a torrent of relief wash over her, laying to rest all her trepidation. She had stopped talking about it a long time ago because she'd grown tired of all the disparaging remarks. It was hard to believe she'd told him about them, and that somehow he'd understood. What else might she be able to tell this boy that he'd understand?

"I'd like to get together again and talk some more," he said. "What do you think?"

"We can do that," she answered, stunned at how easy he was to be with, and how trustworthy he seemed, especially about her dancing. He hadn't made fun of her, or tried to talk her out of it.

The waitress brought their check. He reached for it, but Julie placed her hand over it before he could take it.

"You're pretty quick," he said, appearing impressed.

"I'll have to be if I'm going to be spending time with you," she answered.

"So when can we do this again?" he asked, already looking forward to it. This had been reassuring for him. He'd never been afraid of girls turning him down, because there were always other girls to take their place. But this girl? For this girl there was no replacement.

"Soon, maybe over the weekend," she answered, her voice become just a little coy. This was going to be nice, different from what she'd experienced with other boys.

"Cool." He pointed to the check. "Going to let me pick that up, or what?"

"No. I told you I was paying. Remember?"

He took a fifty-cent piece from his pocket. "I'll flip you for it. How's that?"

She looked at him with mock impatience. Then her face softened, and she said, "Okay, Mister Gambling Man, if that's what you want. Heads, I pay; tails, you pay."

"Deal." He tossed the coin into the air. Suddenly, her hand shot out like it had been launched from a slingshot, grabbing the coin on its way down.

Cupping the fifty-cent piece in her hand so only she could see it, she looked at it and announced, "Heads, I pay." She then dropped the coin on the table, adding, "We'll leave that for a tip."

He leaned back and folded his arms. "I can tell you're a girl I'm going to have to watch closely."

"Good, I hope you do."

- Chapter Six -

It had been two months since they'd met, and what had developed between them was beyond his wildest dreams. Now, as he climbed out of the old Chevy, he looked up at the house, and made his way up the stairs, brimming with contentment and anticipation. The contentment came from having spent himself to the point of exhaustion earlier that day in his cellar. He'd given his all, poured himself out entirely. There was nothing more he could have done. The anticipation, on the other hand, was from knowing he'd be with Julie. Though still a teenager, he realized he was living a special time of his life. He sensed he was mature beyond his years, both physically and emotionally. He could appreciate things that a lot of other kids his age couldn't. For him it was a great time to be alive, to have a special girl, a car to take her out in, and a few dollars in his pocket to spend for an enjoyable night hanging out together. He also appreciated having a good relationship with her family. Her brother Alex, two years older than him, was becoming a close friend. So were her parents. He appreciated that, and knew it kept Julie from having to feel the heat from going with someone they didn't like. Besides, he loved this girl and they might all have a lengthy future together. All in all, life was good.

He knocked on the door, waiting for her pretty, smiling face to greet him. They'd been practically inseparable in their spare time, and he hadn't grown tired of it. If anything, the more he saw her, the more he wanted to be with her. They had split a half-dozen pizzas and a couple of banana boats, much to Tony's delight. A girl that wasn't afraid to eat was a requirement if she was going to spend time around the Conigliaro household. His mother was accustomed to feeding small armies, which would now include Julie.

If there was a problem, it was his father's growing consternation toward her consuming so much of his time and interest. "Choo," he'd said, "you got to make sure you keep the main thing the main thing. And that's baseball. Julie's a nice girl, but she's not what you've spent your whole life preparing for. Remember that." For the first time, Tony had felt a pang of anxiety, and hoped to God he'd never have to choose between her and baseball. And why did his father have to make such a big deal out it in the first place? Why couldn't he have both? It rankled that he should even have to think about making a choice.

His thoughts were interrupted when she answered, saw him, and with no one around, threw herself at him. He scooped her up off her feet with those incredibly strong but gentle hands, pulled her to him, and kissed her long and deep. Oh, the things he did to her. She wasn't sure how long she'd be able to restrain herself. This boy made her feel things that were dangerous.

"You ready?" he asked, glowing. One of the things she loved most about him was his total lack of pretense. He wasn't afraid to show himself to her. He wore no masks, maintained no personas, or hidden agendas. What she saw was what she got. And right now that was the happiness reflected in his eyes every time he was with her.

"Are you kidding?" she asked. "I've been counting the minutes. You said you had a surprise for me. What is it?"

"I don't know, we might have to find out if you can handle it first," he said, teasing her.

She pulled him close. "Try me," she said, her voice suddenly husky.

"Well," he began slowly, "I've been thinking. You know, about us."

"And?" She loved it when he played this game with her, but tonight it felt like something important was in the air. He had a special, wistful look about him.

"We've been going together since Thanksgiving, and I was wondering how you felt about us going steady. It's something I'd really like to do."

He took out a small box and handed it to her. She opened it and looked at the gold friendship ring that lay within. "I love it!" she said, beaming. "Put it on my finger."

He took the ring out of the box and slowly eased it onto her finger. "Now everybody knows you're my girl. And I want it to stay that way forever."

She looked at it a moment, admired it, then wrapped her arms around him. "I love you, Tony."

"I love you too, and I want us be together for the rest of our lives." Then he pulled back and looked down into her eyes. "There's something I got to say, though."

"What's that?"

"You do things to me inside that are sometimes hard to handle."

"I know," she answered. "I've thought about that, too. But for now we'll have to wait. It's just not time yet."

Reluctantly, they walked to his old Chevy and got in. Even as he fired it up, he paused for a moment to take her into his arms and kiss her again. After a long embrace he looked at her.

"I have to ask you something," he said.

"Ask whatever you want," she said, nuzzling against his shoulder.

"How many boyfriends have you had?"

"A couple," she answered, softly.

"Did you ever cheat on them?"

Wounded, she pulled back and looked at him. "I'm not like that. I'm disappointed you'd even ask."

"I'm sorry, but I had to. I never felt like this about anyone. I love you more than I can describe, and it would kill me you ever did that to me."

She settled back against his chest. "It's all right, baby. I'm not that kind of girl."

"I didn't think so, either. But I had to hear it just the same." He kissed her again, and they drove off.

- Chapter Seven -

SEPTEMBER, 1962

"Choo," his father began, "this is a very important day in your life." They were alone in the living room, a place where Sal had often spent time teaching his sons life's lessons. The gravity in his father's voice on this occasion, however, told him this wasn't going to be an average conversation. Despite having heard that tone before, he sensed today would be different.

"We've discussed many things over the years from the standpoint of preparation; now the time has come to live it. You're not in high school any more. This American Legion team you've been playing on all summer just played its last game, and I don't have to tell you who's been hanging around watching you for the last two-and-a-half years. Fortunately, they have laws that keep these guys away from you while you're too young to know what's going on. Now, even that's over. This is the part where things get real. You're going to be eighteen in a few months; in the eyes of the world you'll be a man." This was something Tony had contemplated and longed for all his life. He loved the idea of being independent and making his own decisions, of calling his own shots, free of parental encumbrances. He would finally get to discipline himself, instead of being disciplined by the nuns at school, his parents' house rules, and everyone else who had controlled his life. He'd always looked forward to being his own man, and was excited at the prospect. He knew how well he'd been prepared by his father, his Uncle Vinnie, his coaches and other people - even his brothers - and he'd be forever grateful for it. He'd always been close to Billy and Richie, and the competition among them had greatly contributed to their development. He was the oldest, the one from whom the most had been expected. Moreover, he was the standard bearer, the one who had gone through the maturing process first. And now his childhood was over, and it was time for him to shed his adolescence and assume the responsibilities of adulthood. Skipping school as a boy to play baseball had been fun, and skipping out on his mother's errands had been defiantly childish, but he could no longer hide behind the mantle of being a 'kid' any more. The world would require him to climb down out of the high chair, take off the little boy pants, put on some long ones, and start walking like a man. And the world wouldn't let him do that on his terms; he'd have measure up to life's uncompromising circumstances. As much as he loved them, 'mom and dad' would now become his mother and father. And, like them, he'd be expected to conduct himself accordingly.

Yet the exhilarating challenge of becoming an adult wasn't nearly as daunting as embarking on his baseball career. It occurred to him that his lifetime of dreaming and preparing had kept the future at a safe distance, tucked away in some far off time and place. Those days were over. The future was now, and the time had come to find out if he was ready for it.

"This is it," Sal continued, "your last game as a kid is over. They're all out there today. They've watched you closely, made their final notes, and calculated your worth. But remember this: the dollar amount they've assigned you has no bearing on your worth as a man. I'm proud of you, I love you, I've *always* loved you and I always will." He paused as the impact of his own words took hold of him, grateful that he'd always had the openness to tell all three of his sons how he felt about them. It was his hard and fast belief that any fathers and sons who couldn't speak to each other in such a manner cheated themselves.

Breathing deeply, he continued. "So where do we go from here? We'll have to let that play itself out. One thing's for sure: I wrote to all the teams in both leagues. Fourteen of them have expressed an interest in you, and they'll be here today. Any minute, they'll be forming a procession outside the house; they'll come in one at a time, and make their offer. As the day progresses we'll get a good feel where you stand and who you'll be playing for. We know the Red Sox are the local team, and we'd like to play for them if we can. But they may not make the best offer. If that happens you may have to consider playing somewhere else. Remember, at this level it only looks like a game. The reality is that it's business. They don't care what a great kid you are, how hard you tried to get A's in school, or how you respected your mother and me. They don't even care how nice you are to other people. They're looking at you as an investment, a business proposition, a potential moneymaker. They know there are a million other kids out there who'd love to take your place, and so do we. But you have something they want, and you have more of it than all those other kids, or they wouldn't be here today. Okay?"

Tony shrugged, nodded. "Sure, dad. But I was wondering about something. Danny Murphy, Billy Madden, and Tony Horton all got hundred thousand dollar deals; Bobby Guindon got a hundred twenty-five thousand. Think I'll get a hundred? Maybe a hundred twenty-five? I mean, I think I'm better than all those guys."

"I think you are, too. But hey, to them maybe you're not. It doesn't matter what we think, it's what they think that matters. We'll have to play poker with them and see where we stand at the end of the day. You ready?"

Tony took a deep breath. Good question, was he ready? After a brief pause, he looked up at his father. "Yeah, let's get ready."

They heard a car pull up out front. Sal leaned over, peered outside, and yelled to Teresa, who was in the kitchen, "Here they come."

****

The first interview began at 9AM. Tony and his father sat across from Chicago's Bill Carter. Tony's interests lay not in whether he'd make the team, but how much he'd be paid to sign. The question wasn't so much financial as it was determining their opinion of him. Sal, on the other hand, was more interested in getting Tony signed. Period. He knew his son had professional ability, but the thing that mattered most was making the team. Salary meant nothing if he didn't make it to training camp. Sal was equally as confident as Tony, but the objective was to get signed, not price one's self out of the market. Sal wasn't an expert in the sports arena, but he knew his way around the business world. He worked in an executive capacity for the tool and dye company that employed him, and negotiations were part of his job. Once he had determined how serious a team was about acquiring Tony, he'd begin grinding them over money.

After Carter was seated, Teresa brought in coffee and pastry, and then quietly left...to go pray. She knew how important it was to Tony and Sal, as well as to Billy and Richie, and she wanted more than anything that Tony be accepted into the ranks of professional baseball.

"Well," Sal began, "before I say anything else, I want to thank you for coming here today. You're a long way from home, and I'm sure there's a lot of other things you could be doing." The fencing match had begun.

"We think it's worth the trip," he began, pleasantly. "As you're well aware, we've been watching Tony for about two years, and we like what we see. So much so, that we'd like to offer him a professional contract."

Tony wanted to jump out of his seat and start screaming. He was going to be a pro! A quick glance at his father's calm, non-committal face, however, brought him back to ground level. He knew why his father was staying calm. No terms or conditions had been agreed upon, nor had the subject of money been broached. He father, ever the rational businessman, wanted to hear the rest of the offer.

"It's a long way to Chicago," Sal began, "but we'll consider it for the right deal. Needless to say, there's a dozen teams who would also like a crack at Tony."

"Understood," answered Carter. "So I'll lay it out as plainly as possible. We'd like to sign Tony to a two-year deal. He'd report to spring training, after which we'd determine which of our farm teams would be best for his development. We'd also require that he first attend the Instructional League later this fall. Depending on his performance in those two places, we'd take a closer look at where he'd go from there."

Sal and Tony glanced at each other. Agonized longing and anticipation shown in Tony's eyes; softer, gentler contemplation from Sal's. "That sounds reasonable enough," Sal responded. "What is the team prepared to pay him for a salary?"

"We think we've worked out a fair offer," Carter answered, matter-of-factly. "We're prepared to give Tony eight thousand dollars the first year, and if things work out he'll get ten thousand the following year."

Tony's eyes couldn't have reflected more alarm if he'd been told he had a terminal wasting disease. Did he really hear what he thought? Had it been eight thousand, or eighty? Even eighty would have been too little, and he wasn't about to give himself away like that. Obviously, these people weren't really interested in him. Not with an offer like that.

"You're not serious, are you?" he asked. "Only eight thousand?"

"Actually, we are," Carter answered. "We've calculated your market value, and eight thousand is the right number."

Sal hurried to stem the emotional bloodletting before it developed into a hemorrhage. "Look, Mister Carter, we appreciate your coming here. If that's your best offer, it's your best offer. Like I said, we're early in the process, and still testing the waters. We're not in a position to make any decisions right now."

"I understand," Carter said, rising. "I'll give you my card and you can call me when you've made a decision." He then shook hands with Sal and Tony, and left. As the door closed behind Carter, Sal peeked outside to see how many more team representatives had arrived. There were now no less than eight cars parked along the street, and many of the team reps were standing around talking to each other as if they were limo drivers. What might they be discussing?

Looking at Tony, who was a portrait of quandary and shock, he said, "Choo, don't worry. A lot of other clubs still have to come. By the time we get to the end of the day we should be doing pretty good. Just sit and listen, answer their questions, and no more jumping out of your seat. These things have been worked out long before they arrived here; these guys are little more than messengers for their teams. Let's see what the rest of them have to say."

But as the other clubs marched in and out the money didn't get much better, and Tony and Sal were slowly coming to the sad realization that they wouldn't. They'd not be receiving the big money they'd been expecting. Every representative had unanimously stated that the new rules instituted that year had changed the dynamics of signing young players like Tony. It was now very difficult for them to throw around money as they had in the past. Most clubs were saving the big money for the one hot prospect they had in their sights, and that the remaining signing bonuses had been scaled back sharply. Sadly, it was no longer the seller's market it had once been.

- Chapter Eight -

The Red Sox were the second to last team Tony and Sal were scheduled to meet. Neil Mahoney and Milt Bolling arrived, and Tony and his father greeted them with as much enthusiasm as they could muster. There had been no hundred thousand-dollar offers; there hadn't even been an offer for fifty or twenty-five. Tony's despondency weighed heavily, but as each disappointing offer was made he had sense enough to be as ingratiating as possible, and careful not to alienate anyone. Though several teams, most from out west, had mathematically eliminated themselves with sub-standard monetary offers, he didn't want to burn bridges with any of them. Who knew what the future might hold a year or two down the road?

Bolling extended his hand as he entered. "Good to see you again, Sal. Hello, Tony. I think you and your dad know Neil Mahoney. He's our Director of Scouting, and he's had some really nice things to say about you." Sal shook hands with them, as did Tony, who hoped against all odds that Bolling's comment was an indication of the offer that would be forthcoming. He wanted to play pro ball more than anything in the world, but the thought of being worth less than ten percent of Bobby Guindon, Tony Horton or Danny Murphy was an outrage. *He'd gone three for four against Murphy!* Surely the Red Sox could appreciate his worth. Not only that, he was a local player, someone people in the area had already heard of.

All of them sat down as Teresa brought her thirteenth tray of the day, with coffee, condiments and Italian cookies. Maybe she should open a restaurant? She knew things hadn't been going as hoped for, but this was the Red Sox; maybe they would pay her Tony what he should get.

When they were alone, Milt Bolling came right to the point. It was one of the many things Sal liked about him; he could be pleasant and friendly, yet businesslike without creating an air of tension. "So tell me Sal, how's the day gone so far?"

"We've been considering offers all day, and I think I'll be dreaming about numbers tonight. Except for the teams out west, everyone's coming within a few thousand dollars of each other. I sometimes wonder if all you guys conspire out there while you're waiting your turn."

Mahoney laughed, heartily. "Us? *Baseball guys?* We wouldn't do a thing like that. Used car salesmen maybe, but we're competing with each other. You know, sell to the highest bidder." His tone was sincere when he added, "The fact is, we'd really like Tony to join us. I mean that."

"We think we know him and appreciate him more than anyone," Bolling chimed in. "He's a local guy, we're the local team. It's been a joy watching him develop."

"I don't have to tell you that Tony's first choice would be the Sox," Sal answered. "I mean, he only lives fifteen minutes from the park. It's a natural. He already has a name in the area. And if he comes in and starts making noise with his bat – especially if Boston's having a good year – he'll fill the place. But the deal has to make sense."

"I understand," said Bolling, "and I agree with everything you've said. But even though Tony's a potential star in the local area, he's still an unknown quantity on the professional level. We can't get too far ahead of ourselves this early in the process. We'll have to get a good look at him before we start blowing the padlock off our bankroll." One way or another, the conversations had gone like this all day, and Sal had become more adept at cutting right to the quick. This was the home team, Tony's first choice, and the one he would love to play for.

He looked at his son and nodded. "Everyone's telling the truth here, Choo. Let's get the number and decide."

Tony shrugged, hoping against hope.

"Okay, Milt," Sal said, "What have you got?"

"We'd like Tony to sign a one-year contract," he began. "We'll want him to do the customary Instructional League tour in the fall, then report to spring training. In addition to the usual fringe benefits, we're prepared to pay Tony twenty thousand dollars, including his signing bonus. That's our offer."

Sal and Tony looked at each other, exchanging poker faces. It was better than any of the other offers they had received, but there still remained Baltimore, who was said to be very high on Tony, and they were the last team who would bid. The unspoken exchange was also an unspoken agreement.

"Thanks Milt," said Sal. "It's a generous offer, but we'll still have to think about it."

This time Tony couldn't restrain himself; he had to speak up. "Why do you feel I'm only worth twenty thousand, Mister Bolling? There's so much I can bring to the team. *My* team. I thought I was worth a lot more than that. You've been watching me play for three years; you know how good I am. Bobby Guindon and Tony Horton got five times that much, and I'm as good as they are."

"Tony," interjected Mahoney, his voice filled with empathy, "I know you're disappointed. But we have certain concerns about how prepared you are for the majors. Tony Horton has a lot more power, so does Bobby Guindon, and they're more prepared than you. They're also older and more mature. Give us – and yourself – a chance to see exactly where you stand, and we'll talk again. Right now, our offer has to stand at twenty thousand."

Tony knew he was as far as he was going to get with Boston. His heart ached at the prospect of not getting what he felt he deserved, and it ached even more at the prospect of not playing for Boston. Still, he felt he owed it to himself to see what Baltimore's offer would be. He knew his father felt the same way.

Extending his hand, he said to Bolling," Thanks, Mister Bolling. It looks like my father and I will have to talk things over."

"That's okay, Tony," said Bolling, shaking Tony's hand. "It's business, and we understand."

After leaving his card, Bolling and Mahoney left. When they were gone Tony looked at Sal. "I don't know what to think, Dad. I really want to play for them, but I don't think their offer is good enough."

Sal shook his head in agreement. "And that's the good news. The bad news is that if they wanted to make a better offer they'd have made it."

"Why do you say that?"

"They'd never give Baltimore a shot at you, which is exactly what's going to happen a minute from now." He glanced outside. It was getting dark and only one more car remained in front of the house. A man got out as Bolling and Mahoney reached it.

They all shook hands, chatted a moment, then Bolling and Mahoney got into their car and drove off. When they did, the lone occupant of the last car made his way up the walk.

"Get ready," said Sal. "Here comes our last shot."

Rob Timmons knocked at the door, and was welcomed inside by Sal. He greeted Tony, and was invited to sit at the dining room table, which had seen more activity in one day than in the past month. After serving coffee and pastries, Teresa quietly excused herself and left the men to discuss their business.

"I'm sure it's been a long day, Mister Conigliaro," Timmons began, "and I'm sure you've heard every manner of offer known to baseball, so I'll come right to the point. I know that most teams have the same benefits and perks, and that the two biggest things that separate most offers are the length of the contract and the amount for which the player can be signed."

"Sounds like you've been doing this for a while," Sal answered, grateful that this wasn't going to be a long, drawn out affair. "Give us the numbers and we'll get on with it."

"Very well," Timmons answered. "We think very highly of Tony, and we'd like to have him join us. We hope our offer will accomplish that. We'll give Tony a one-year deal for twenty thousand dollars, including his signing bonus. If things work out, we'll proceed from there."

Sal was amazed that Baltimore and Boston had arrived at precisely the same offer, both in terms of dollars and length of contract. He found it hard to believe that all the scouts who had shown up weren't out there talking about the offers their teams would put on the table. He'd never heard of a Psychic Baseball League. They had to be talking among themselves, not just outside the house, but elsewhere too. Some day maybe someone would do something about that, and things might change in favor of the players. Tony was watching intently for his father's reaction. There seemed no reason for him to go to Baltimore for the same deal he could get from the home team. And how was it that they had come up with precisely the same deal?

Sal decided to come right to the point, just as Timmons had done. "Mister Timmons," he began, "we'd love nothing better than strike a bargain with you. But here's the problem: you've offered the exact same deal as the Red Sox, and there's no reason why Tony should play away from home for the same money he can get playing here. So...I'll make this offer to you: give us five thousand more, and you can have him."

Timmons stared at the table, thinking. Finally, he said, "I'm only authorized to give you twenty thousand. If I'm to do better than that I'll need the approval of my boss, Bill DeWitt. May I use your phone?"

"Sure, it's in the next room on the lamp table."

Timmons left to make his call, leaving Sal and Tony to ponder matters. Sal extended his palms to Tony, as if to say, *Hey, we've been hearing this all day.* All Tony could do was shake his head and hope.

A moment later Timmons emerged from the living room. Sal tried to read his expression, but could find nothing to indicate what was coming. "What did he say?"

Timmons shrugged. "My boss says that twenty thousand is our best offer. It looks like you'll be playing in Boston." They shook hands, Timmons left.

An hour later the house was filled with Billy and Richie Conigliaro, Uncle Vinnie, his wife Phyllis, Milt Bolling, Neil Mahoney, and attorney Joseph Tauro, who was also a friend of the family. The deal had been closed, Tony would be playing for the Red Sox.

Uncle Vinnie, who knew Tony's true value perhaps better than anyone, sat on the couch next to Neil Mahoney as champagne was being served. Mahoney, having seen Vinnie at many of Tony's high school games, raised his drink, for a toast. "This is a good night for all of us," he said.

"A good night?" Vinnie exclaimed. "You call this a good night? You guys should be sent to jail."

"For what?" asked Mahoney. In his heart, he thought the team had done well by Tony; everyone should have come away happy.

"For kidnapping. You just stole our kid." Vinnie paused for a moment, then lifted his glass and smiled at Mahoney. "I'm just glad it was you guys. Anyone else, I'd be mad at you."

"Hey," Mahoney said, "he's still Sal's boy."

From across the room, Sal answered, "Not any more. His name's on your contract, he's yours now."

Milt Bolling nodded in agreement. "He is, and we're going to do some great things together as soon as he develops more power. But that'll be our job, we'll take care of that."

"You won't have to, Mister Bolling," Tony said, his face beaming, his disappointment gone. He was a professional ball player now. "I'll get my power up to what you need, and I'll be knocking baseballs all over Lansdowne Street. They'll still be looking for 'em ten years from now. You wait and see."

After everyone had gone, Tony and Sal sat quietly in the living room, completely spent. For them it had been an excruciating day. They'd worked years to achieve this goal, and now it had happened. Looking at his father, Tony smiled and said, "I finally did it, I got my chance to play for the Boston Red Sox."

Sal raised his glass to Tony, and said, "Hey, don't forget the twenty grand they'll be paying you. How's it feel to be a millionaire?"

They burst into laughter. Indeed, they had every right to celebrate. It was a golden moment in their lives.

- Chapter Nine -

- Training Camp, Bradenton, FL -

They would be staying at the *Hotel Dixie Grande,* which looked like an enlarged version of the hotel from the movie *Psycho.* It was hardly what he would have imagined for a professional baseball team. His image of pro ball had included fine food, adoring girls, big money, limos, game winning home runs and delirious crowds chanting *'Tony! Tony! Tony!'* He'd never heard that professional baseball had a mundane side, too.

"I guess this is what you meant," he said to Mike Ryan, who was to be his roommate, as they dropped their bags onto the beds. "They didn't tell me this part when they were patting me on the back, and telling me how much they wanted me to join the team."

"Don't worry," said Ryan a muscular young catcher, casually removing Tony's bags from the bed nearer the window, which was also the larger of the two beds. "There was a lot they didn't tell you about minors that wasn't in your contract."

Tony was miffed by the removal of his bags from the bed. Their accommodations had given him a wake-up call, but the thing with the beds was a new mystery, a mildly irritating one at that. "Mike, what are you doing?" he asked. "I wanted that bed."

"You'll have to earn that bed." Tony noticed there was no humor or apology in Mike's voice. He'd meant what he said.

"What're you talking about? I like that bed."

"So do I," Mike answered. "And because I'm a second year player and you're a green pea rookie, I get the larger bed. And I get to shower first, and I get my choice of towels. Why? Because I've earned them." Seeing Tony was struggling with the minor league facts of life, he added, "It's called dues. Around here, you have to pay dues. That's the way it is."

"I don't know if I like that so much," Tony answered, disgruntled.

"That's the other part. They don't ask you to like it, they just expect you to do it. Period. Let's unpack, we'll be taking the field tomorrow, and out there they don't take excuses from anyone about being tired. Get some rest, there's a lot for you to learn."

****

A couple of nights later, laying in bed, Tony contemplated his new life. The combination of being homesick and not being able to see Julie had given him an ache he'd never felt before. He missed her terribly. He was seized with a mixture of overwhelming fear and depression. If he felt this way so soon after getting there, what would it be like a month from now? Again, he had to plant himself on firm ground, reminding himself that this was something for which he'd been preparing a long time. Besides, this was supposed to be his destiny. Right? He'd known it since he was a little kid. So where were all these crazy feelings coming from? He wondered if Mike and the other guys went through this. None of it had been mentioned in his contract. He was beginning to suspect there was a lot more to being a man than simply growing tall enough to look like one.

Conventional academic studies were never his strong point. Were it up to him, he'd have learned the basics of reading, writing and arithmetic. The rest of his life could have been devoted to baseball, and he'd live long and happily. But there was one subject that he'd always been drawn toward for reasons he couldn't explain, and that was English Composition. He liked to write. There was something about expressing himself on paper and then examining what he'd written that he found fascinating. It gave him insight into himself and how he felt about certain things, and that also intrigued him. Now he was grateful more than ever that this had been so. He couldn't speak with Julie at that precise moment, but it didn't mean he couldn't express himself to her. He got out of bed and sat down at a small desk, took out a pen and paper and began writing.

Dear Julie,

I wanted to write before now, but they've been working us so hard I've been too tired to do even that. There are so many things I want to tell you, especially the fact that I love you with all my heart and soul.

So far we have had three workouts in the boiling heat. Today we worked out from 10:30 – 2:30, and I'm doing real well. I'm rooming with a guy named Mike Ryan from Haverhill, who's a real good kid. After the workout he and I went to the beach, better known to you as the Gulf of Mexico. The country down here is beautiful. Yesterday, during the workout, I had some fresh fruit that was picked right off the trees.

You don't realize how much you love a person until you leave them for a while. It's only been four days, and I miss you so much I could cry.

There aren't too many girls down here. To tell you the truth, I wouldn't care if there were millions. I am grateful to you for waiting for me, because baby, you're the girl I want to marry. I have a picture of you hanging on my bedpost. I look at your pretty face and I could cry. In fact, I did cry my first night here.

Let's face it Julie, I will be here for a while and I will have to take it. When I get back I don't care if my father, mother, brothers, and the whole family is there. I'm going to wrap my arms around you and give you the biggest and best kiss I have ever given you before.

I'll write to you again soon. Please write to me as much as you can, because I live on hearing from you.

He reached into his pocket, took out several small items he had retrieved from the beach and placed them in the envelope that would contain the letter. Picking up the pen again, he added,

Here are some shells from the Gulf Of Mexico. I'll be good, so you do the same. I trust you.

Love,

Tony

He sealed the envelope, kissed it, and slept well that night. Even though only seventeen, and one of the youngest players there, he felt confident that things were going to be okay. He'd work hard at his end of it; the rest would be up to God and fate.

****

Tony was relieved to learn that sitting on the bench wasn't necessarily bad news. They simply wanted to get a good look at everyone in camp, and that meant everyone took their turn on the bench. It was explained to him that the Instructional League wasn't the same as Spring Training; it was merely a chance to see who had what strengths and weaknesses, and what would be the best strategy for developing a player. Hearing that had raised his spirit, and he found it easier not to read so much into every little thing that happened.

During high school, his positions had been pitcher and shortstop. Now, it appeared that the outfield would offer the best opportunity. Carl Yastrzemski, who had taken on the almost impossible task of filling Ted Williams' shoes, had nailed down left field. But the other two spots appeared attainable once he retooled himself. Despite the cold, he spent a fair amount of time training outside, catching fly balls hit by his brothers and a couple of friends. As had been the case in high school, enduring temperature extremes and the elements were helping to develop his mental toughness, which was a big part of the sport.

He soon discovered that there was more to playing outfield than he'd anticipated. He now realized this was actually a melting pot for all the minor league Red Sox players, and like the Instructional League, the level of competition was intense.

However, being assigned to one of the minor league teams didn't mean he'd be playing for them that season. Each player would have to prove himself beforehand, so the assignment was only temporary. And occasionally, a player was deemed ready for the big leagues, and was assigned to the parent team immediately.

Initially, he was assigned to Wellsville, which was in the single-A league. They were situated in one of the more desolate regions of upstate New York, something he didn't look forward to. But his off-season weight training regimen had begun showing its worth. He was hitting for higher average and had now begun hitting much longer home runs, the kind that got players noticed. At the end of the season he had hoped that his performance would get him assigned to the Double-A team in Pittsfield, Massachusetts, which would have left him less than a hundred miles from home.

****

But the Red Sox had seen things differently. They left him with the Wellsville club, and the trip was a ten-hour ride from home. Because of that, he'd been able to convince Neil Mahoney, the scout who had recruited him, to take a detour to Swampscott, and pick up his car, a white 1963 Ford Galaxie convertible, complete with a big 390 cubic inch V-8. He cherished this, his first new car, which he'd bought with his signing bonus, and to which he lovingly referred as his 'dream cruiser'. Though Mahoney had given him permission, he had also cautioned him about the importance of arriving at Wellsville in time to start the season. He'd have to be there in three days.

Over the course of one particular day he'd spent much of his time painstakingly hand washing and paste waxing his car. His plan was to surprise Julie by picking her up after school, and taking her for a ride along the coast. After that he planned on having a romantic supper with her at a quiet restaurant overlooking the ocean in Hampton Beach, New Hampshire. They had already made plans to go to her prom in June, and this was to be an added bonus with what limited time they had left together.

As she walked out the front door of the high school, Tony began beaming. She lit him up every time he saw her. It was great to have a steady girl, especially one he loved as much as he did her. Upon seeing him, she broke into a smile, and then into a run. Ever the gentleman, he got out of the car, rounded it, and was holding the door open for her by the time she reached him. After a quick kiss and a hug, she climbed inside. A moment later, he was sitting next to her.

As he was about to pull out into traffic, someone she knew, Dave Massey, a large, muscular kid about 6'3" and over two hundred pounds, stepped in front of the car and started screaming at him.

"You're a punk, Conigliaro!" he yelled. "You got no business coming over here and dating a Lynn English girl! Get out of the car, and I'll beat your ass! Come on, get out! *Get out!*"

Tony turned off the car and reached for the door handle. "That guy can't talk to me like--" He was cut short by Julie, who reached over and grabbed his arm to keep him from getting out of the car.

"Tony, *don't!* Please! He's just a guy I know, and he likes me, that's all," she urged. "Just leave him alone. Please, do it for me."

"You hear what he said to me?" Tony shot back, infuriated. "You hear what he said in front of all those people? He needs to be taught a lesson!"

"Tony, please. It'll only make it worse!"

"Worse? Are you kidding me? Look at the kids that are watching! They're going to think I'm afraid of him." Actually, the opposite was the case. He wanted to get out of the car and give this kid an overhaul in front of everyone to make sure they knew he *wasn't* a coward. Bad enough to get ragged on in front of all those kids, but if word got out that Tony Conigliaro, who played for the Red Sox, chickened out of a fight with some high school kid? He'd never live it down. Exercising every shred of self-restraint he had, and knowing he and Julie had little enough time before he left for Wellsville, he ground his teeth, started the car, and screeched away from the curb, but not without giving Massey the finger as he did. He wondered if this kid knew how lucky he was.

Even so, his plans changed as he drove Julie back to her house. This had spoiled everything; the polished car didn't matter, going to a restaurant for a romantic meal had lost its appeal, and the night was blown as far as he was concerned. The trip home was made in tense silence.

As he pulled up in front, she turned to him. "Thanks for doing that for me," she said, leaning over and kissing him. "I appreciate it."

"Yeah, sure," he answered. His heart wasn't in it, and she felt it. She suddenly wondered if she'd made a mistake, even though she'd helped him avoid getting into a fight. "Who did you say he was?" he asked.

"Dave Massey, he's just a guy," she answered. "He's the captain of our football team, and he kind of likes me. He wants to go out, but I told him I was your girl, and it made him angry."

He leaned over, and kissed her. "I have to go."

"You're not coming in?" she asked, surprised.

"No, I have to be someplace. I'll call you later."

As she walked toward the house and watched him pull away, she knew more than ever that she'd made a mistake.

- Chapter Ten -

Not only had his mood been sour, he hadn't opened the door for her, or walked her to the front porch. He then spent the next twenty minutes driving around, aimlessly. The incident at Lynn English was gnawing at him like a crazed termite. He had let Massey talk to him like that, and hadn't done anything about it. He'd let him off the hook. Guys cut other guys slack once in a while, but not when it came to the type of thing Massey had done. He'd let the kid treat him like a pansy in front of over a hundred kids. How long would it take for word to get around? An hour? Two hours? By tomorrow it would be all over the school. Worse, it would only be a matter time before somebody called the local papers and told them about it. Then the whole world would think he was some kind of trembling coward. He couldn't allow that to happen.

He pulled over to a pay phone, got out of the car and dialed a number. When a male voice came on the line he was relieved, because the number he'd dialed was Julie's; the person he wanted to speak with, however, was her older brother Alex, who had become a close friend.

"Alex, it's Tony. What are you doing?"

"Right now? Nothing. Why?"

"You know who Dave Massey is?"

"Yeah, why?"

"Know where he lives?"

"Yeah."

"Good, I'm coming over."

****

Julie's brother, Alex, was a couple of years older than Tony. Of medium build and height, he was laid back, and had become one of his best friends. He now sat beside him in the dream cruiser as they drove along the Lynnway. "You sure you want to do this?" he asked.

"You kidding? Does a bear crap in the woods? After what he did in front of all those kids, I won't sleep at night until I go over there and straighten him out." Then on a more solemn note, he added, "The only thing is, if I get knocked out or something, I want you to put me back in the car and drive me home. Okay?"

"Yeah, sure," Alex answered. "Take this left, it's the street he lives on."

Tony took the turn, then asked, "What if he hits me?"

"Hit him first, and maybe that won't happen," Alex advised. "But if you're going to hit him, don't fool around about it. Do it right, he's a big strong guy"

When they reached the house, Tony parked, got out of the car and went up the front steps. Taking a deep breath and gathering his resolve, he knocked on the front door. Through the screen, Tony saw Massey spot him, and he saw the look that crossed Massey's face. He knew why Tony was there, and appeared just as eager to engage Tony. He came right out the door and they locked up immediately.

Standing on the first step, Tony had the advantage of being in position when Massey came outside. As he approached, Tony drew back just like he'd seen John Wayne do in the movies, and delivered a colossal punch from down around his ankles, connecting squarely with Massey's nose, which exploded. Having used all the same power and intensity he used when hitting baseballs, the sheer force of the blow knocked Massey down. The sight of all that blood drove Tony to further rage, and he ran into the house and began screaming at Massey's mother.

"If your son *ever* uses that kind of language around me and my girl again, I'll come back and do this again!"

"What did you do to my son? *What did you do to my son?*" She had a rolling pin in her hand and now, enraged, began chasing him, swinging the rolling pin while screaming. "Get out of my house! *Get out!*" She began pummeling him with the rolling pin to emphasize her point.

As he burst through to door to escape the fusillade of blows, Tony tried to scramble past Massey, who was still down on his hands and knees, holding his nose while bleeding profusely. To his credit, Massey made another attempt to fight Tony by grabbing him around the hips, and trying to drag him off his feet. Tony wrestled free of him, just as his mother was about to bounce the rolling pin off the side of his head. As he ran toward the car, he noticed that his chinos, once white, were heavily smeared with blood, as though he'd just come home from a day at the slaughterhouse.

Alex ran up onto the porch and dragged Tony back to the car, jumped in, and screeched away from the house. "You okay?" Alex asked.

"I feel great!" Tony answered. "Now see what they say when they get a look at Massey's face. That'll change the story. By the time this gets around people won't know what to think. One thing's for sure, his face will say a lot more than anything I could say."

As he watched Alex lean into the big V-8, he felt all the tension drain from him...for about ten seconds. It was then that he noticed the throbbing in his thumb. Taking a closer look, and his eyes bulged. A bone was sticking right through the skin, and he couldn't move it.

He was suddenly frightened. "Alex, I've broken my thumb in half. What the hell's my father going to say when he sees this? I sure as hell can't tell him what happened. He'll kill me"

"He's the least of your worries," Alex said. "What are you going to tell the Red Sox? You're supposed to report to Wellsville the day after tomorrow."

"What am I going to tell them? If they ever find out about this, I'm dead!"

"Know any doctors that work privately?"

Tony thought for a minute, as he fought off the growing pain. It was really begun to throb. No way could he play ball with a thumb like that. "Yeah, I know one who might help. Let's go see him."

- Chapter Eleven -

Two hours later they emerged from the doctor's office. Tony's thumb had been set with a splint that reached all the way from his thumb to his elbow. Not only could he not hit or throw, he couldn't even move his arm.

"Figure out what you're going to tell your father yet?" Alex asked.

"Yeah, I'm going to ask him please not to kill me."

"For now, the best thing you can do is figure out what to tell them on the way home. And get rid of those clothes, you look like you just killed somebody."

****

The ride home after dropping Alex off had been a time of introspection. How could he have done what he did? All his life he had fought tooth and nail for his big chance. Now that it was here he'd broken his thumb in a fight with some high school kid who mouthed off to him in front of a bunch of high school kids. Was it *that* important? Was it worth blowing a once-in-a-lifetime opportunity that most people would give their right arm to have? Moreover, he had gone to Massey's house, beat him up in front of his mother, and had dragged Alex into it. That all by itself would earn him a year in Julie Purgatory. Still, there was that part of him that felt good about what he'd done to Massey. He deserved it. Too bad breaking his thumb had been part of the package.

He wondered if Alex had already told Julie. That was something else he dreaded. Even though Julie was sweet and pretty and nice, she had no reservations about dressing him down when she thought he was out of line. And this particular incident would be ranked among the worst. She had practically begged him to let it go, and he hadn't.

After pulling into the yard he tentatively entered the house, not relishing the prospect of facing his family. But that's what grownups do; they faced life on life's terms, even when it included facing the music for indiscretions. As he slowly made his way down the hall toward the dining room he was relieved to hear that everyone sounded in good spirits. He stood there, quietly listening to them for a moment before he went inside.

"It'll be good, it'll be bad, papa," Teresa was saying. "Tony will be a professional, but he'll be away from home a lot. I don't like that."

"Maybe he can get us free tickets!" Richie was saying.

Tony loved Richie's enthusiasm. *There will be free tickets,* he said to himself. *Especially, for you guys... provided the Red Sox don't can me for breaking my thumb.*

"It's a proud day for the Conigliaro family," Vinnie was saying. "I'm telling you, that kid's gonna put us on the map. I can't wait to see him play his first game in Fenway. The whole family will be there."

"I hope he blasts one," Richie said. "And that I catch it!"

"Where you going to be standing?" Billy asked. "On Lansdowne Street?" Billy teased him from time to time, but let one of the older kids pick on him, watch what happened next. The Conigliaro family was the personification of clannishness.

"You know what I mean," Richie said.

Billy ruffled his hair and smiled at him. "Hey, maybe some day I'll hit one out of there, and you can catch that one too. How cool would that be?"

None of this was making it easier for Tony to face them. A lot was hanging on his future with Boston. He hadn't even made the big team yet and his family was already dreaming dreams of glory. He took a deep breath, and headed for the dining room.

As he entered Billy was saying, "Wow, that'd really be something, Tony and me playing together for the Red Sox as teammates. Maybe we'll even get to—" He abruptly stopped in mid-sentence, and all activity at the dinner table seemed to suddenly die. Initially, Tony was glad that his Uncle Vinnie was there; so was Albert Martelli, his grandfather. He found his grandfather's presence a source of immediate relief. Aside from being wise and patriarchal, his mother's seventy-four year old father had a very calming influence. His presence would diffuse much of the heat he otherwise might suffer.

Or, so he thought. His initial relief turned to grinding angst when he saw the stunned look he got from them. His mother, especially, appeared alarmed. The terrified look on her face was one of complete shock. She wasn't even looking at his cast; she was looking at his pants. It then occurred to him that he'd not changed them, and the abundance of red smears and dried bloodstains were there for everyone to see.

"Tony...*Tony!! My son! Who stabbed you?*" she screamed.

His grandfather, himself gravely concerned, waved her to silence as he closely studied Tony. "Are you all right, Anthony? Were you in a car wreck?" His tone was sane and rational; but even so, it couldn't overcome the horrified looks he was getting from everyone else.

"I'm okay, grandpa," Tony answered, as he slowly entered the dining room. "I just got into a disagreement, that's all."

Uncle Vinnie wasn't seeing it that way. Quietly, he rose from his chair, trying to comprehend Tony's appearance. "A disagreement? What kind of 'disagreement' leaves people covered with blood with a cast on their arm?"

Suddenly Tony wondered if calling ahead might have been the better idea. Prepare them for what was coming. He hadn't expected his family to go this far over the edge.

"I'm sorry, Uncle," he said, softly. "I didn't mean for it to be like this."

Vinnie hung his head for a moment, thinking of the countless hours they'd spent practicing. Now he was faced with reconciling the reality of Tony's condition; nothing like this had ever been part of their plan. He quietly regarded him, then walked over to him and gently hugged him. "I'd rather have both my legs broke than for this to happen to you, especially now," he said. He pulled away from Tony, and looked him up and down all over again. "I don't know where we're gonna go from here, kid."

Sal on the other hand, had been quietly watching, performing internal damage control. This nightmare, this pants-covered-with-blood, arm-in-a-cast-at-the-worst-possible-time nightmare, was a complete bewilderment to him. He'd already begun dreaming of Tony's imminent glory as a player for the hometown Boston Red Sox; now a single enigmatic portrait framed in the dining room doorway had suddenly dashed everything to pieces.

The best he could utter was, "What happened?"

"I got in a fight."

"A fight? Over what?"

"Over my girlfriend."

"You're getting ready to play baseball for the Boston Red Sox and you got into a fight over a girl? What are you, *crazy*?"

"Dad, there was this guy—"

Sal cut him off. "*Guy*? I don't care about any guys! I been telling you about no girlfriends for a long time. Now look! I don't believe it!"

"But dad, you got to understand. I—"

Sal wasn't feeling sympathetic. "What's to understand? Look at you, standing there covered with blood and a cast. Getting into a fight with a pro ball career on the line? What are you, some kind of little kid? I'm sick. You have so much more at stake than the kid you fought with. Now what are you going to do? I can't believe you did something as stupid as this." He stared at Tony, his mind reeling. This son of his, who he loved more than he could ever describe, and of whom he was so proud, might have just thrown away all his dreams and aspirations. Tony could have been a star athlete and Red Sox slugger; and he could have boasted about his son, and being the proudest father on the planet.

Vinnie tried to keep things from getting worse. "The Red Sox aren't going to like this, Tony."

He didn't need his Uncle Vinnie to tell him that. It had been on his mind all the way to the doctor's and back. "I know, Uncle. I'm sick about it."

"We can't let them know about this," Vinnie said. "We got to come up with some kind of reason for this."

Teresa had her own maternal view of the situation. "Listen to you, all of you. Looking like that, he could just as easily be lying in the morgue right now. We should be grateful he's not dead." Then she paused, frowned at him, and asked, "You didn't hurt anyone did you?"

Tony nodded his head. "No, just you guys."

Sal was still angry. Picking up on Vinnie's comment, he said, "We'll be lucky if the Red Sox even speak to him after this. Broke his thumb over a girl."

Tony's grandfather intervened. "Calm down, Salvatore. He's still a boy, and boys will do boy things. How bad is the injury?"

Tony looked at his cast. "The doctor says I can't play for six to eight weeks, provided it heals right."

"And when are you supposed to report?" his grandfather asked. Tony sensed there were wheels turning inside that seventy-four year old mind.

"In three days."

Tony's grandfather looked to Sal and Vinnie. "This could interfere with his career. Obviously, we'll have to tell them something."

"How close are you to Neal Mahoney?" Vinnie asked.

"We're pretty close," Sal answered. "Why?"

"Why not tell him I was pitching Tony batting practice, and broke his thumb?"

Sal thought about it for a minute, then shrugged. "They might go for that."

"Hey, what can they say? A broken thumb is a broken thumb, right?"

Tony's grandfather motioned him to his side. When Tony bent down to him, he grasped Tony's shoulders. "No more being stupid. You can't be a boy any more; from now on you must be a man. The world expects it of you." He paused for a moment, and his next statement almost drove Tony to tears. "Besides, I want to see you play baseball in Fenway Park some day before I die. *Capisch*?"

Tony nodded slowly. He was grateful for the love of his family, and that they had found a possible solution. "Thanks, grandpa." Then, looking around, he added, "Can I eat now?"

Richie looked at Tony, and frowned. "How you going to eat with that on your arm?"

"Let me worry about that. Just hope you don't get one." Richie lowered his head and quietly went back to his supper. Sometimes older brothers had a way of saying things.

- Chapter Twelve –

It was May. The weeks had come and gone, and one by one most of his problems related to the incident had been solved. Somehow, the media had not gotten wind of anything, Massey and his mother had calmed down, and things between him and Julie were better than ever. He was given a clean bill of health by the medical community, and for all intents he should have been excited at finally being able to hop into the dream cruiser and head for Wellsville. But he wasn't. There was an awkward residual that had hung in the air between him and his father, and it was obvious to both of them. Neither wanted it to remain like that, especially now that he'd be going away for the spring and summer. They'd not experienced anything like this since his childhood, when he and Billy had refused to do an errand for their mother. She'd called Sal and told him about it, and he'd promptly come home and given both of them an old fashioned whipping. Tony had hated him for that, but in time they had reconciled. Now they were both in the adult world and, wanting the love they had for each other to be untainted, they made a point of meeting alone for a moment before Tony left.

Tony came downstairs, bags in hand, and looked at Sal, who was waiting to say goodbye to him. "I guess this is it. This is where I go out there and make something of myself."

Sal, ever the stoic patriarch, restrained himself as long as he could, then welled up and broke into tears. Going to Tony, he hugged him, and said, "I'm sorry I've been so hard on you. I'm sorry about what's happened, but you know how much I want you to make good."

Tony dropped his bags and embraced his father. "I love you, dad."

"I want to forget about what's happened too," Sal said, hugging him, tightly. "I want you to go there and play the hell out of that league. We both know you can do it. I wish you the best of everything, always."

They embraced for a moment longer, letting the recent past drain from them. As Sal walked Tony to the car with Tony's bags, Tony knew right then that he'd go to Wellsville and make the big leagues for him *and* his father.

****

When he pulled into Wellsville, he felt like he'd entered a deserted ghost town left over from the old west. The first thing he missed was civilization. Living without an abundance of humanity or modern conveniences would be his incentive to do well and play his way out of there.

When he reported to the team the next day, he wasn't very encouraged. All three outfielders were hitting over three hundred. That, combined with nursing his thumb back to health, made playing time look doubtful at best. Fortunately, the manager for the team was Bill Slack, whom he'd met in Ocala. Aware of Tony's broken thumb, Slack's first comment was for him to stay ready and not get down. One never knew in this game.

The town was said to have six thousand people, but Tony suspected someone had added an extra zero or two. This he premised on the average twenty-five to fifty people who showed up at the games. Obviously, the town had been chosen because the only thing to do other than look at the sky was to play baseball. Or milk cows.

His initial foray into live action was another distressing experience. In high school he had been a standout, a star. In Florida he had done well, but wasn't a shoe-in to make the big leagues. In Wellsville, he started off batting oh-for-sixteen, hardly the stuff Hall Of

Fame careers were made of. In his first full game he went oh-for-four, and lay awake all night, tossing and turning. The only good news was that his thumb no longer hurt.

Then came his first road trip, and he got a close-up of where the term 'minor league' got its name. Big Leaguers traveled by jet, sitting in first class with air conditioning. At Wellsville, road trips were taken in an old school bus that should have been junked for scrap. It had no springs; just solid rubber tires, and what sounded like a lawnmower engine. He found it impossible to sleep on it, even during the torturous, four-hour trips. They were so deprived of luxuries and conveniences that the manager drove the bus. On a trip to Batavia, a deer ran onto the road and caved in the front of the bus, stalling it. Starting it again proved an exercise in futility. Unable to get going again, they had to forfeit the game.

Being rural, Wellsville was made up of beautiful, mountainous terrain. It was pleasing to the eye, but hard on buses. The next morning they found a mechanic who got them started again, but about halfway to Batavia the bus broke down again. Every time they tried to climb a hill it would stall out. This became inconvenient, not to mention embarrassing. His vision of stardom had not included being one of twenty-four players pushing their transportation up the side of a mountain on their way to a game they had already forfeited.

The crowning blow during that insufferable year had come when his family had traveled ten punishing hours to see him. It was their first visit and he was excited about seeing them. After they shared some of his mother's home cooking, they went to a home game that night, and got to see him hit his seventh home run of the season. They had loved it; so had he. But after the game the reality of their isolated location had set in, and his family had despondently made their way back to their 'hotel in the middle of nowhere'. To them it couldn't have been more remote had it been the distant reaches of Siberia.

The next night he had gone to a team meeting, while his family went to see an Elvis Presley movie. It was the 'only movie' playing at the 'only theater' in town. The next morning his father had come to see him. The long look on his face hadn't been encouraging.

"Look, Choo, we love you very much. You know that. But we can't stand another minute in this place." After which they piled into their car and headed for home.

Said Richie, as they were driving off, "Boy, I guess Billy knew what he was talking about. He stayed home."

So much for visits to Wellsville. After that night's game, an extra innings affair that ended late, he stayed up to write a letter to Julie. His family was probably just arriving in Boston as he sat down at the desk in his room.

Dear Julie,

I just got back from tonight's game, which we won 7-6. I'm becoming more and more tired hon, and I feel real run down. Day after day, these bus trips and games can get a guy real tired. There's only one thing that can pep me up, and that's you. You're what I need right now. People really think that baseball is all fun. When you play pro ball everything's for keeps. It's just like any other job; you have to work hard to keep it. But you know how much I want to make the Big Leagues. It's got to happen, and when it does I want to be one of the best major leaguers that ever played in Fenway Park. I want to be great, and the only way to do that is to work. So I'm working real hard.

It's midnight as I write this letter. Tomorrow I get up and get on the bus around 1:30 in the afternoon, and I'll be back around 1:00 in the morning.

How come Alex hasn't written? I'd like to know how he's doing with his girl. Love is great, isn't it? I don't know how you feel, but I feel good that I have someone to love. Just to know that I've got you waiting makes me feel real good. I've been writing every day lately, and I'll keep doing it because I feel like I'm talking to you. I like to tell you my problems, and I like to tell you when I'm happy. The problem I have now is that I'm tired.

I want you to start working because I want you to invest in some pots and pans. Believe me honey, if everything goes the way it's going, and if God wants, we will be married and we will live with each other and love each other forever. Just be a good girl, and I'll give you everything I have when the time comes. It's not that I don't trust you, it's that the 'hunger hounds' from Lynn worry me. All they want is a good time, and it just happens that you're out of bounds for them. If anyone tries to flirt with you down at Roland's let me know about it.

Well, hon, it's time for bed, so I'll sign off now.

My love is yours,
Tony

The year dragged on, there had been dues to pay, but it hadn't been a waste of time. He finished the season with a .363 average over the course of eighty-three games. He had collected forty-two doubles, four triples, six stolen bases, knocked in eighty-four runs, and hit twenty-four home runs. He had also garnered both the Rookie of the Year Award, along with the Most Valuable Player Award in the New York-Pennsylvania League. The .363 was the highest of anyone in the entire Red Sox organization. What began as a disaster had exceeded his wildest expectations.

Best of all his performance, if it had meant anything, would be his passport out of Wellsville.

- Chapter Thirteen -

It was good to get back to Swampscott and eat some of his mother's home cooking, and to see his father strut around town, proud of 'his son the professional baseball player', especially with the Boston Red Sox. He wouldn't get to stay home for long, however, because he'd been notified that they wanted him to play in the winter Instructional League again. What was really exhilarating was that they had notified him that he'd be reporting to Scottsdale, Arizona for spring training. He'd be part of the big team's forty-man roster. But first there was something else he had to do.

He had made a decision to graduate from his dream cruiser to his ultimate dream car: a new Corvette. To him there was no greater success symbol than that. As a guy who wanted to be recognized, a shiny new Corvette was the perfect car.

He took the Lynnway to the local Chevy dealer. He had decided to sell the dream cruiser privately so that he could get more money for it. Besides, he had enough in the bank to buy the Corvette outright, and didn't need the Galaxie to make the deal. He pulled in, went straight to the short line of Corvettes, and started looking at them. They had red ones, white ones, a green one, and black ones, but no blue. Then, as he was about to get back in his father's Cadillac, he saw a truckload of Chevy's pull into the lot and sure enough, he watched the driver lower the ramps and unload a blue Corvette. He went straight to it, looked it over closely, then hurried to the showroom entrance in search of a salesman. One salesman, a heavyset man smoking a cigarette, was standing near the door.

"You work here?" Tony asked.

The man looked him up and down and slowly nodded. Tony's jeans and tattered sweatshirt didn't seem to impress him. "Yeah, why?"

"I want to buy that Corvette they're unloading from the truck."

"Forget it, kid," the man answered. "Come back when you can afford one." He turned and started to walk away.

"Hey," Tony answered, feeling snubbed, "I can buy one right now if I feel like it. But I want to take it out for a test drive first."

"Yeah, right. You and a million other dreamers just like you. Come back with your mommy and daddy and maybe we'll talk."

"Hey, I don't need them to buy a car," Tony persisted. "I'm Tony Conigliaro from the Boston Red Sox. I can buy whatever I want."

"Sure," the man answered, smugly. "All you need is go for a test drive first. Right? Get lost."

"But you don't understand," Tony pressed. "I really am Tony Conigliaro."

"That's nice. Now take a hike, before my manager calls the cops and has you hauled out of here for trespassing." He then turned and waddled away to join another salesman who was also hanging around, smoking a cigarette. Tony heard him mumble to the other salesman, "Kid says he's Tony Conigliaro from the Boston Red Sox. Who the hell is Tony Conigliaro?"

"Probably just some kid with pie-in-the-sky dreams. Forget him."

Tony had all he could do to contain himself. This guy might not know who he was today, but someday he would. He went to a pay phone and called Alex, Julie's brother.

"Hey Alex, you know anyone on the North Shore who sells Chevy's?"

Two hours later he and Alex climbed into the front seat of Tony's new car, a blue Corvette with slotted magnesium rims, dual chrome exhausts, and a .327 cubic inch V-8 engine. With the top down, the radio blasting, and the wind blowing through his hair it was sheer delight. Best of all, the car was his; he'd paid cash for it and no one could take it away from him. Life was good.

"Where you going to go in it first?" asked Alex, living vicariously as he sat beside him. He also enjoyed the looks they were getting; nothing wrong with that. He loved Tony to death and would have done anything for him, even if he hadn't been a Red Sox player. But the perks that came with being on the team were great.

"I don't know," Tony answered, pondering the question. "I mean the first logical place is to your house to show it to Julie."

"She'll go nuts," Alex answered. He'd heard her express her love for 'Vettes' on more than one occasion.

"Best part is I don't even have to wax it," Tony said, thinking out loud. Then he saw a familiar exit leading from Route 1, on which they were traveling. And as soon as he saw the exit, he knew where his first official stop would be. He swerved across three lanes, scaring Alex half to death, and screeched onto the exit ramp.

"What are you doing?" Alex asked, hanging on for dear life. "This isn't the way to my house."

"I've decided that showing it to Julie is going to be my second stop. There's someone else I want to show it to first." And then he burst into laughter as Alex sat there, wondering if he'd lost his mind.

When Tony got to his destination, he tore onto the lot, spun the car sideways, and screeched to a halt. Sitting up on the back of his seat he looked at the pudgy salesman who had earlier treated him like a loser.

"Hey, remember me?" Tony taunted. "Tony Conigliaro? You know, the guy who couldn't afford a car and needed to go home and get mommy and daddy. Well, guess what? All you had to do was let me take that test drive and I'd have bought it from you. And yeah, I *do* play for the Boston Red Sox! Now come polish my new car and maybe I'll let you sniff my jock strap!"

He then screeched out of the lot with his middle finger held high in the air, laughing as hard as he could.

****

After completing another tutorial in the Instructional League, he returned home in December, bristling with confidence. He couldn't wait for spring training to begin. He could feel it, he could taste it; he had every intention of making the big team and could see himself closing in on the dream. The Red Sox had finished in seventh place that year, and obviously were in need of better players. There were three other young players who had also been invited to spring training, Tony Horton, Dave Gray, and Pete Charton.

He and his father had lingered at the dinner table after supper one evening, soon after he'd gotten home, discussing the possibilities. "I don't know, Choo. I just wonder if you wouldn't be better off by going to the minors next season and playing every day, rather than sticking with the Red Sox and sitting on the bench."

Tony's heart sank. He loved his father and respected him like no one else, but on certain things he had to listen to his heart instead. Waiting one more year was out of the question. He couldn't stand another year of waiting. What if someone had a great year, and he lost the opportunity to play at Fenway? What if he got hurt, and couldn't play without ever getting to play with the big club? What if somehow he got traded, and would forever lose the opportunity to play for the Sox?

"I can't do it, dad. The team is allowed to keep three out of the four of us rookies for the season, or risk losing us to the draft. I really think I'm good enough to make the club right now. Who do I have to beat out? Carl Yastrzemski has his job secured, and that's all. The other guys are Roman Mejia, Lou Clinton, and Gary Geiger. Why can't I go into one of those spots? They're okay players, but I think I can win a job as a starter. I have to give it a shot."

Sal paused for a moment, thinking. His son, the eternal optimist; the 'I can do anything I set my mind to do' kid who had always thought he could conquer anyone or anything if given the chance. "It's your career, you can do whatever you want," he said. "I wouldn't count on it too much. I just don't want you to be disappointed if you don't make it."

"Dad, I'm coming back with the team next spring. I'll make that team, you'll see."

Sal exhaled, slowly. There was no dissuading Tony. He was this close, and Sal knew he'd not be deterred. "I hope so," he said. "But don't get your hopes up too high. You'll only be nineteen, with just one year of pro ball behind you. That's not much."

"I'm going to work hard. I'm going to make that club, and it's not going to be on the bench, either. I don't know who's going to be playing those other two outfield positions, but right field is mine. It has my name on it, you watch and see."

- Chapter Fifteen -

- <u>March, 1964</u> -

Until then, the furthest he had been from home had been Florida. Therefore, Scottsdale, Arizona, with its mountains and desert, its wide-open spaces and cactuses and plant life, its 'big sky' look that was filled with a bright moon and countless stars, was a slice of life he had never seen before. Getting off the plane and taking his first glance at his surroundings had been as exciting as almost anything he could remember. It was so different from what he was accustomed to on the east coast; surely the only way to get to a place like this was by plane. Mixed in among all those things was the knowledge that he was an independent grown up, and was actually embarking on the journey he'd been dreaming about since childhood. He wondered how many little boys - or girls - got to live out their childhood fantasies. One thing was certain: what he said to his father after dinner that night was about to happen. There was no way he'd get this close without finishing the job.

The next taste of success came when he and the rest of the team reached their hotel, The Ramada Inn. It was beautiful and neat, and about a million miles from Wellsville. It even had air conditioning. Tony Horton, who had beaten him out of all the bonus money he'd expected to get, was there, too. As a matter of fact, Horton was his new roommate, and that was all right. But it was also troubling, not because of Horton himself, but because of an issue that had become a recurring theme recently. Before leaving, his father had again counseled him about the danger of having a steady girlfriend, specifically Julie. Although she was nice and they liked her, she was a threat to his future as a professional ball player. In plain English, his father had said she was a distraction. It was a lot easier to think about her than it was to think about taking extra batting practice, extra laps around the track, and paying attention to nothing but baseball. That, combined with his growing interest in other girls was becoming a distraction in itself. Now he was rooming with Tony Horton, who was young, single, and a guy who liked free living. This might be a problem.

Not long after they arrived the team was given some free time while manager Johnny Pesky and his coaching staff worked out some logistical problems. Tony was stretched out on the couch, thinking, when Horton came out of the bathroom, showered, shaved and dressed for a night on the town. "Hey," he said, frowning at Tony. "You're not going to spend the night hanging around here are you?"

"I don't know," Tony answered. "I hadn't made any plans. Why?"

"I'm going to check out the club scene. Why don't you join me? Beats hanging around here all night."

Tony felt uneasiness pass through him. He could stay in the room and hang around, bored to death; or he could go out with Horton and at least get to see the city. Besides, it wasn't like he was going out on a date. His decision made, he said, "Yeah, sure."

Downtown they jumped out of a taxi. As Horton paid the fare, Tony stared up at the large, colorful neon sign outside the club. 'JD's. The music thumping from within welcomed them with its rhythm, the promise of excitement, high energy, and a colorful, charged atmosphere.

As Tony entered, he paused to pay their cover charge, and then looked around the club while he waited for his change. A four-piece rock band was up on stage, laying down some heavy tracks as the light show gave them and the club an ethereal appearance. The lead singer was dressed in a pink tuxedo shirt and black levi's, and hugged the microphone to him as he hammered out the Rolling Stones 'Satisfaction'.

What Tony noticed next made his heart thump. The women outnumbered the men by almost two to one, and he had a hard time finding one that wasn't as pretty as a cover girl. Most of them were dressed in jeans and halter-tops, and many of them were dancing together due to the shortage of guys. It reminded him of his high school days before he'd met Julie, and he had to admit the allure was blatantly seductive. He suddenly remembered how much he liked loud music, gyrating bodies, rhythms and dancing.

He and Horton entered the club area, and began searching for a table. "See what I mean?" Horton asked. "This is a whole lot better than sitting in the room watching the Evening News."

"Can't argue that," Tony said, as he began prowling the dance floor. He watched the women dance, each in their own way issuing an open invitation to join them, which is exactly what he did. Leaning over to Horton, he said, "There's too many of them out there dancing alone, and that's not right. Let's go help them out." A minute later both Tony's were on the floor, gyrating with everyone else.

Several dances later, Tony and the woman he was dancing with were perspiring and, with their clothes literally clinging to them, stopped to catch their breath between songs. His dance partner, a tall, thin, pony-tailed blond with a great figure and a pretty face, stopped and stared intensely at him, then slowly lowered her head and broke into one of the most inviting smiles he'd ever seen.

"What's your name?" she asked.

"Tony."

"I'm Patty," she said, moving closer. She obviously was drawn to this tall, olive skinned, movie-star hunk of a man who had stumbled into her life, and who was now making her wish she was somewhere else with him away from all these people.

"You don't look like you're from around here," she said, with a curious smile. "Where you from?"

"Massachusetts," he said, warming to her.

"You here with those Boston Red Sox guys?"

"Yeah, I am. We're here for spring training."

They stepped closer to each other. "We're not going to stop dancing now that the music has stopped, are we?" she asked.

"We don't have to," he said, glancing at her more closely. Not only was she great looking, she also seemed like a nice person. He felt as if he was being reeled in and couldn't do anything to stop it. The thought of Julie passed through his mind, followed by the rationalization that it was only a dance. What harm could that do? "I got the energy if you do," he said.

"I don't know what Boston girls are like, but girls out here got all kinds of energy." Then pulling him closer, she paused, and then abruptly moved away from him. "My goodness, you're all sweaty," she said. The embarrassed look on his face was quickly put to rest when she added, "And maybe that's a good thing, because that's the other thing western girls like to do, we like to get sweaty."

As she said that, the band slowed things down with their rendition of The Righteous Brothers, *'You've Lost That Loving Feeling'*, a slow ballad that brought the mood inside the club to a soft, mellow drift.

When they began to slow dance, Tony could feel his nineteen-year-old testosterone starting to assert itself. She pulled him close to her. He basked in the musky scent of her perfume, and was soon lost in the mesmerizing softness of her hair. For the moment, his mind wasn't on baseball *or* dancing. His mind began to wander, and his pulse rose. The thoughts that occurred to him were no longer in keeping with what he'd learned at St. Mary's.

She looked up at him and smiled. She had moved close enough to discover the one thing he wanted desperately to hide, but couldn't. Feigning shock, and stifling a smile, she asked, "Oh my, are you going to be all right?"

"Yeah, sure," he blurted, "I'm gonna be fine. Just keep dancing. Okay?"

"Of course," she answered, demurely. "I mean, it's not like I'm complaining."

Mercifully, the slow dance finally ended. They did one more fast dance before Tony thought it best they part company. "I need to get back to my table. My roommate and I have to make curfew, and I don't want to be late. Thanks for everything."

"Can I get your phone number?" she asked, coyly.

This was getting complicated, and a growing inner turmoil began eating at him. What about Julie? He was nineteen, and the situation was developing against his will. Well, almost. At the same time, he was beginning to suspect he might not be as saintly as he thought. The last thing he wanted was to hurt her. Yet, his emerging future in professional baseball was taking on a life of its own. As much as he might not have wanted to, he had to admit he liked it.

Maybe even a lot.

Wrestling within himself, he forced himself to say, "Nah, better not. Got to get up early for practice and all that. Maybe some other time."

With that, he forced himself to turn away from her, not wanting to contemplate what had almost happened.

****

As spring training continued, he'd gotten more opportunities to play. The veterans hadn't been producing, and Pesky had grown tired of fielding losing teams. He made good every chance he got, and was getting a reputation as a hitter with power that was reliable. Writers began asking Pesky if he had any chance of making the team, to which he'd said it was possible, but it was still a long time before Opening Day.

His breakthrough game, which had started garnering him a lot of attention, was one in which he almost hadn't played. He'd been airsick on the flight, spending most of it with his head in his hands. It was in Tucson, against the Indians, and Johnny Pesky had decided to use an all-rookie lineup, with the exception of the starting pitcher, Bill Monbouquette. The Sox had won 5-4, and he'd collected three doubles, two of which had been singles he'd stretched into extra base hits on sheer hustle and heads-up base running. This was getting to be more and more the norm as his confidence and skills escalated. Even the papers back home were mentioning his name on a regular basis. It had been those articles that prompted his father to convince his mother that they visit him. Longing to see them, he had paid for their hotel room.

Another huge thrill had come against the Indians. Gary Bell, who could throw some serious heat, was pitching for them when Tony had stepped in against him. Bell pitched a letter high fastball, which he'd hit to dead center field, and had watched it disappear over the wall for a home run. It was the first time in the history of that ballpark that *anyone* had ever hit a home run to dead center. He later learned that Larry Claflin, a sports writer for the *Boston Record American,* had measured the blast, and had found a couple of witnesses who had seen the ball come down and had shown him where it landed. He had measured it at 572 feet, making it one of the longest home runs in baseball history.

The crowning triumph came just before his parents had left. Sal and Johnny Pesky, now become close friends, were sitting beside the pool chatting, and Sal was squirming around as if he had bugs. Finally, when he couldn't stand it any longer, he blurted, "For Christ sakes, John, what are you going to do about Tony?"

"What do you mean 'what am I going to do about him'? He's my starting center fielder. Put that in your pipe and smoke it."

Later on Pesky had given him the news. "Well, Tony, here's the way it is. Yaz will be in left field, Lou Clinton will be in right, and you're my new center fielder. You'll be out there playing the position when we open in New York against the Yankees."

- Chapter Sixteen -

April, 1964

Tony stepped onto Yankee Stadium's playing field with the awe of a child meeting Santa Claus. The weather was good, so the day's game wouldn't get rained out. It had rained heavily the past couple of days, and the first two games of the series had been postponed due to poor playing conditions. His parents and brothers Billy and Richie would be there; so would Julie and many of his friends from back home. He was grateful for their support, yet was mindful of the pressure he felt to perform well in front of them.

He breathed a deep sigh of relief as he pondered the previous day's events and how he'd almost torpedoed his career before it ever got started. He'd looked out his hotel window and, seeing the continuing rain, had assumed the game would be postponed. Therefore, he had gone back to sleep. The game may have been canceled, but practice hadn't. Don Fitzpatrick, their clubhouse attendant, had called him and told him he was the only player on the team who was missing. He'd then jumped out of bed, made a mad dash to the ballpark, and was promptly fined $10 by Johnny Pesky.

"Listen to me, Tony," Pesky had admonished him. "You got a chance to play, don't screw it up! They wanted you to spend another year in the minors, and I talked them into giving you a shot because I believe in you. Don't make me look bad."

Members of the press had been hanging around with little to do, so when it became known that 'the new kid' had overslept, they were quick to question him about it. "Is that true?" one of them had asked, "You overslept?"

Deciding to stand up like a man, he had said, "Yeah, I did. And I got fined for it, too."

"Oh yeah? How much?" another one asked.

"It was only ten bucks, but it could have been a thousand and I'd have paid it. It also came with a stern warning, which I took very seriously. It's important that the team and you guys and everyone else knows how serious I am about playing for the Red Sox." Fortunately, they had dropped the issue and let it go at that.

He continued this, his first real walk around the stadium. The aura, the heroes, the legends, the ghosts and the myths, the tradition, and the reality of playing in this magical, mystical twentieth century coliseum were on the verge of taking his breath away.

He looked at the stadium walls, with their pennants, the World Series Championship flags representing their dynasties, the echoes of long forgotten crowds chanting the names of never-to-be-forgotten gods of baseball's greatest playing field. He contemplated the memories of past and present gladiators who would live in the hearts and minds of New Yorkers and baseball fans everywhere. He tried to absorb the once-in-a-lifetime, first-time opportunity of stepping onto the same grass where so many of the game's most hallowed icons had played before him. And now he was about to play there, too.

There were still only a handful of fans in the stands; game time was still a couple of hours away. Several players had come early to stretch, warm up, toss balls, jog and mentally prepare for the first game of the season. If his season had to open away from home, there was no better place than on Boston's ancient nemesis' home turf, that most famous park of all, Yankee Stadium, The House That Ruth Built.

His walk along the first base line had eventually led him to one of the most hallowed shrines in all of professional sports. A line of plaques imbedded in marble, stood one beside the next, commemorating many of the greatest players to have performed there. Ruth, Gehrig, DiMaggio, Cobb, all giants of the midway, were among them. He contemplated them, their accomplishments, and wondered what history might say about him some day if he were to play the game long enough. No greater company was there than these, he thought. It then occurred to him that he had another once-in-a-lifetime opportunity. Taking care to make sure he wouldn't be observed, he bent down, dug out a piece of turf and placed it in his pocket as a souvenir. When he got to Boston, he'd pay homage to their heroes, too.

He'd committed himself to getting noticed by as many people as possible, but his first game as a professional almost got him noticed in all the wrong ways. On his first at bat, with the bases loaded, he hit the ball extremely hard. Unfortunately it was right at Yankee third baseman Clete Boyer. Boyer scooped the ball up, stepped on third base, fired a rifle shot to second, and were it not for a slight pause by the second baseman when he threw it to first, he'd have hit into a triple play. The next time he got noticed was on a high fly ball that he almost lost in the sun. Fortunately it plopped down in his glove while he was using it to shield his eyes. Had he not caught it, the hit would have gone for extra bases. The third time up, he got noticed again.

Whitey Ford, the Yankees ace and likely future Hall of Fame pitcher, was pitching to him in the seventh inning. One of the pitches landed several feet in front of the plate, and bounded up into the catcher's chest. When it landed in the dirt beside the plate Tony noticed that the ball had a clump of mud on it. Tony knew what that meant.

Turning to the home plate umpire, he said, "For crying out loud, he's throwing spitters. Make him wipe that stuff off the ball!" The umpire gave him a funny look, took the ball from the catcher, wiped it off, then threw it back to Ford without saying anything. By day's end the incident had made the news from coast to coast, and he'd quickly been branded a brash and cocky young player before even making his first appearance at Fenway Park. What they had failed to mention was this same brash rookie had also gotten his first major league hit off future Hall of Fame pitcher, Whitey Ford.

They hadn't mentioned the clump of turf that was in his pocket, either.

- Chapter Seventeen -

April 14, 1964 – Fenway Park
- Opening Day -

At ten in the morning, he and Julie's brother, Alex, had parked in the special area set aside for players, after which Alex had gone upstairs to get the ticket which had been reserved for him. Nor had Tony wasted any time taking the field after arriving. He was anxious to acclimate himself with the conditions in center field, the walls, the angles and pockets, the warning track. He'd never played at Fenway before, so although it was his home field, he treated like he was a member of the visiting team, there for the first time. In an effort to help him adjust, coach Harry Malmberg hit fly balls to him for about an hour, bouncing them off the wall so he'd better be able to anticipate rebounds and nuances.

When his practice session was over, he'd glanced around the park, which was beginning to show signs life. This was it; this was the dream.

Returning to the clubhouse, he was surprised to find about a hundred letters and telegrams waiting for him from friends and family, wishing him well on his first day on home turf. He'd read a few of them, had almost become overwhelmed with gratitude for the wealth of good people who'd been placed in his life, and had then sequestered himself to mentally prepare for this, the biggest day of his life.

****

By the time he had to go outside for his final warm-ups, he'd done all he could to prepare himself. From that point on, it would be up to God, fate and Joel Horlen, the Chicago White Sox pitcher he'd be facing that day. As game time drew closer, he wished this first, pressure packed day was behind him. But that would have been to cheat himself out of a once in a lifetime opportunity.

He looked around the park and saw that it was packed. Included in that crush were the celebrities, dignitaries and other notables scheduled to attend. He glanced toward the area that had been reserved for them, noted their presence, and quickly put his focus back on the game. If he started thinking about who was in the stands watching him, he'd be distracted beyond reason. Besides, though accomplished as they may have been, they were there to watch him, not the other way around.

Prior to the singing of the national anthem, the crowd was brought to complete silence. "Ladies and gentlemen," the public address announcer began, "today's game is being dedicated to the memory of the late President John F. Kennedy." A resounding cheer rose from the crowd before the announcer continued.

"Please share in a moment of silence," he concluded. Tony glanced at the red, white and blue bunting that had been displayed for the occasion and stood, head lowered, hat on his chest, remembering the day of the tragedy. It had been said that anyone who was alive that day could remember where they were, and what they were doing at the time it happened. He remembered being beside the pool in Florida with several other players when they were told about it. He remembered watching it on television, crying at the loss of such a great man. He remembered his letter to Julie, telling her about it. He now got to share in that loss again, this time with the late president's two surviving brothers and the many thousands of fans who had shown up for Opening Day. He'd remember this day, also.

As they took to the field after Opening Day introductions, he stole a glance at his family. They were all there; they and Julie. His feet felt like they were knee-deep in molasses; every second of every minute was being indelibly burned into his memory. He reminded himself, *This day will only happen once. Remember it.*

He was scheduled up seventh, and his first Fenway at bat came in the second inning with two out. As he was about to leave the on-deck circle, Pesky yelled to him, "Just make contact, that's all. Get the bat on the ball." Tony looked over at him, nodded, and continued on to the plate. Listening to the public address announcer introduce him was breath taking. "Now stepping to the plate, number twenty-five, Tony Conniligliaro." The announcer had pronounced his name wrong, and Tony wasn't exactly sure how to react. Maybe he could do something special so they'd get it right the next time. "Number twenty-five, Conniligliaro." The crowd erupted with an ovation that lasted four minutes. They knew he was there, all right. All he could do was stand there, feeling thrilled and just a little bit foolish. *How do you handle a thing like this,* he wondered. What are you supposed to do? Hell, in his mind he was still a kid, but now they had baseball cards with his picture on it. He glanced at his family and friends. They were going crazier than everyone else. His father and Uncle Vinnie were waving their hands over their heads as if it was the World Series.

Finally, when it looked like the ovation might not stop, the umpire leaned over to him, and said, "I'm glad they all like you, but we got a game to play." Tony understood, and by now was happy to accommodate him.

He stepped in, used his bat to tap the dirt from his cleats, and then raised the bat to his shoulder and took his stance. This was it; this was the *real* Day One...

Horlen looked in, got the sign from his catcher, stood erect, and delivered his pitch. Tony picked up the rotation of the ball about fifteen feet from the plate, realized that it would be a waist-high fastball, and shut out the world and everyone in it, focusing on nothing but the approaching ball. Without giving it any thought, he brought the bat around and hit the ball as hard and true as any pitch he'd ever hit in his life. He knew when it left the bat and began lofting toward the famous Fenway Green Monster that it wouldn't be coming back down in Fenway Park. As his legs began mechanically carrying him down the first base line and the crowd erupted maniacally, he watched it continue to rise and knew its destiny was somewhere over the screen and out on Lansdowne Street.

He put his head down as he circled the bases, forcing himself to put one foot in front of the other. It wouldn't do to hit his first home run then trip and fall, or miss one of the bases. He was shocked, mostly because it had happened so naturally. The ball was there; the bat was there; his will was there; and suddenly the ball was out of there.

He peeked out from under his cap as he made his way down the third base line toward home plate. His family was going nuts, and Julie was in tears. He dared not look at them for fear of tripping. He immersed himself in the roar of the crowd, and did everything within his power to look natural. His teammates congratulated him as he crossed the plate and continued on to the dugout. They were standing, laughing, cheering, and sharing in a rookie's golden moment.

When he finally reached Johnny Pesky, he was grinning from ear to ear. "I guess I got the bat on it," he said.

Pesky, smiling broadly, shook Tony's hand and said, "Great job, kid! Welcome to the Big Leagues. As a matter of fact, welcome to the Boston Red Sox!"

- Chapter Eighteen -

In the clubhouse after the game, he was surrounded by teammates and well-wishers. Everyone wanted to congratulate him and speak with their favorite local rookie who had hit a home run on the first pitch of his first at bat on Opening Day in Fenway Park. It felt like a maelstrom of chaotic joy, and there were moments when he had to pinch himself to make sure it wasn't all a dream. And then he started to laugh as it occurred to him this *was* a dream. *His* dream! But he'd never expected it to get off to a start like this. At one point a sports writer asked him, "Did you go out there expecting to hit the first pitch?"

"No," he answered, "I just went up there with the intention of trying to hit the first good pitch I saw. I don't like giving pitchers any kind of an edge." He paused for a minute, and added, "Besides, with all those VIP's and fans out there I felt I owed them something special just for showing up."

In the midst of the laughter and revelries, he noticed a mailman nearby, holding something in his hand. Tony looked at him for an instant, and went back to answering questions. A moment later he looked over at the mailman again. He paused for a moment, and resumed answering more questions. He looked at the mailman a third time, and now wanted to know what was on his mind.

"Is there something I can do for you?" he asked.

Humbly, the man asked, "I guess I was wondering if you could sign a baseball for me."

"Sure," said Tony, beaming. How many teenagers get asked to autograph baseballs? "Give me the one you're holding. It'll be a pleasure."

"Not this one," the man said, "a new one."

Tony was mildly perplexed, but shrugged and took one from his locker. He signed it and passed it to the mailman. Curious, Tony asked, "Why did you want me to sign the other one instead of that one?"

"I was on Lansdowne Street, doing my route when I heard this loud cheer go up. A couple seconds later this came sailing over the screen. It's the one you hit your first time up. I thought you might want it." He then handed him a baseball.

Tony's face lit up like a bulb. "You're kidding? You're sure this is it?"

"I was out there when it landed on Lansdowne Street. Unless someone else hit one the same time you did, that's the one."

"Wow!" Tony said, "This is great! I don't know what to say, except thank you." Then, laughing, he added, "You keep the fan mail coming, I'll keep hitting home runs."

The man smiled, and turned to leave. Pausing, he asked, "You're not saying there's a connection between home runs and fan mail, are you?"

"I hope so," Tony answered, "because I plan on hitting a lot of them, and I sure love to read."

****

After the game he met with his family and Julie, celebrated with them for a few minutes, and was to go back to the house where Teresa had a feast planned. When they were gone, he assumed he'd be able to put the top down on the Corvette, and that he and Alex would be able to cruise out of the players' parking lot and enjoy a leisurely drive to Swampscott. As they were about to pull out, they were suddenly swamped by a mob of admiring fans, all of whom were begging for autographs and trying to touch him. He was forced to stop, victimized by his honorary traffic jam. Bradenton, Ocala, Wellsville, and Scottsdale combined hadn't given him even a snapshot of what fan adoration was like in professional ball. Add to that his outgoing nature, his Italian handsomeness, a million-dollar smile and his natural charisma, the recipe for his first major league wakeup call was in place. Suddenly, he was an object of desire, especially from a crowd dominated by young women. The screaming, shrieking, and groping were nearly overwhelming. But not quite; he'd take this over Wellsville any day. In the midst of what seemed like an onslaught of excitement and chaos, he signed bats, baseballs, T-shirts, pictures and programs. As insane as it seemed, he loved it. He was in demand, and he'd give them everything he had, if for no other reason than pleasing them and making them feel good. Suddenly they adored him, this handsome young slugger. They wanted more, and now he understood why so many players loved stardom. He had to agree; it *was* great. But the real joy was his love of the game, and getting paid to do something he'd have done for free as long as the team would have paid his bills.

An hour later the admiring fans had dispersed, the autograph seekers were no more, and peace had returned to Lansdowne Street. As they pulled into traffic, Tony said, "Did you see that? That was intense!"

"Intense?" Alex said. "Let me tell you about intense. *I* even signed a half-dozen autographs!"

"See that?" Tony said, laughing. "Opening day at Fenway Park, and suddenly Alex Markakis is a star!"

****

His season continued to accelerate. After the first month his average was .270, he had hit five home runs, a triple, five doubles, and had batted in eleven runs. When it looked like he would fall into a slump, he bounced back with a roar, getting ten hits in his next eleven games. He'd needed that slump, he reckoned, even though he hadn't liked it. But he needed to know that he had the steam to stay strong when it looked like things were taking a turn for the worse. All his life he had overcome adversity, and now that he was playing at this level he refused to let anything deter him.

But there was another lesson to be learned at the professional level. Pitchers were nowhere nearly as forgiving or intimated as they had been in his high school or minor league career. Crowding the plate, which had always been part of his game, carried a risk. Getting hit was a real possibility, and the proof had come early and often. The next month Moe Drabowski had hit him in the wrist, which had resulted in a hairline fracture. It had put him on the bench, healing for a week. A month later he'd been chasing down a fly ball in Comisky Park, in Chicago, when he'd toppled over a short wall into the seats at a dead run, and had knocked himself unconscious. That injury had resulted in bursitis in his left knee, a swollen right hand, and a badly strained back. Things were a lot more serious at the professional level, and everyone had to play in the extreme to keep their job. This latest example had put him back on the bench for nine more days. Even so, he was thoroughly convinced that playing the game at a lesser intensity would earn him a trip to the bench, or worse, back to the minors.

****

He returned to Boston while the rest of the team completed their road trip. He'd done a lot of thinking on the plane, something he'd been doing a lot recently, and believed he had reached a decision. Rather than act on impulse, he sat with it for a while to be sure it was what he really wanted to do.

****

He and Julie had gone out that night, first to watch the Red Sox play, and then to Ritz Pizza, one of their favorite hangouts. After driving around for a while, they had returned to Julie's at the end of the night. It had been an enjoyable evening, typical for what they were accustomed. As they walked up to the front door, Julie thought she sensed something.

"Is everything alright," she asked, wondering if she'd done anything that might have upset him.

He looked at her, and there was no mistaking the pain reflected in his eyes.

"What is it?" she asked.

"I... I have to break up with you," he said, appearing agonized.

"What?" she asked, unable to comprehend such a thing.

"I have to break up with you," he repeated. "I'm only nineteen, and there's a lot of life I have to live, and a lot of things I have to do before I'm ready to get married." He paused, gathered his resolve, and continued. "I've got to pay attention to baseball. There's a lot at stake and I need to concentrate on it. My father thinks it's what's best for now, and I think he's right. I love you, Julie, and I always will, but I have to end it."

By now both of them had begun crying. Down inside he asked himself if this was really necessary, but he'd given it a lot of thought and had decided it was. He turned and walked away; she called after him, but he couldn't bring himself to return and talk to her. It was already painful enough, and he knew he'd not get over this easily. The thought of being married at nineteen, however, the thought of all the things he might miss and wonder about forever, and the prospect of ever dating other women behind her back was too much for him. He couldn't do it. She deserved better than that, and he didn't want to live with that kind of guilt. His father had told him it was either Julie or baseball, and that wasn't a risk he was willing to take.

****

He'd sat in his home, staring at the phone, but didn't dial. Inside he died a thousand deaths, second-guessing himself twenty times a day. He thought he must have been insane to do such what he did, depriving himself of the most enjoyable, loving, fulfilling experience he'd ever known. This was the girl that had made him ache with desire from the day he first laid eyes on her. They had laughed together, cried together, had taken long walks, laying their souls bare to each other. His every waking moment with her had been joyous. Even the times they had fought or disagreed over something had resulted in an uplifting reconciliation that brought them even closer. He'd adopted her family as if they were his own. Even though his father had considered her a threat to his career, they had still embraced her like a daughter. In the beginning his heart had ached with desire, now it ached from longing to be with her. He wondered what possessed him to break off with her. Had it been his father's urging, or had he really believed he had to go out and experience life and all the things it had to offer? Could it offer him even half of what she had given him? He doubted it. Even so, he still couldn't bring himself to pick up the phone and call her. A cloud hung over him like a shroud, a death knell to something he felt deep down inside he might never replace.

Yet, for some strange reason, he still he couldn't make the call...

- Chapter Nineteen -

Tony had always been one to give it his best on the field. Whether he played for a year or a lifetime, he wanted to be remembered well. Noble as it might have been, it also left him highly susceptible to injury. Chasing down a fly ball, he had caromed off the edge of the grandstands and sprained his shoulder when he fell. He'd caught the ball, but had placed himself on the trainer's table for a week, having no chance to play. Now his injury had healed and he was back with the team again. Even so, things took on the appearance of a roller coaster ride in Cleveland, when they were playing the Indians. He'd broken curfew the previous night, had been fined $250 by an angry Johnny Pesky, who was normally an easy going, affable man, and had then hit a three-run homer in the first game of a double header. But in the second game the gremlins struck again.

Happy to be back, and pleased with his three-run homer, he had promptly been hit by Pedro Ramos, this time on his elbow.

As he was writhing in agony, Jack Fadden, the team's trainer, had rushed out to him. "Let me have a look at it," he said.

"Don't waste your time," Tony grimaced, "I've got a broken arm." A trip to the hospital had validated his claim; he had a broken arm, and would be out for six to eight weeks, and possibly the remainder of the season. This he found especially disheartening because the team was playing .500 ball, and he'd been hitting everything that was thrown in his direction. They had put a cast on his arm, and sent him back to Boston. Everything was in the extreme in pro ball, including the risk of injury.

The press hadn't been sympathetic, either. Seeming to ignore the twenty home runs he'd hit, they had devoted more ink to the 'wild nightlife' he was supposedly leading. The night before getting plunked he'd spent the night with friends in Cleveland, had blown curfew, and had been fined. The press had gotten wind of it, and had blamed his broken bone on him having been half asleep at the plate. True, he'd spent the night with friends, and yes they had a sixteen year-old daughter, but he hadn't done anything with her. To the contrary, he'd slept all night and had shown up at the game ready to play. But as usual, his propensity for crowding the plate had gotten him in trouble. It had been a normally safe, inside pitch, but because of how he crowded the strike zone, he'd put himself in harm's way.

Despite being irritated by the media's 'party boy' label, he had to admit there was a growing grain of truth to it. Not that night, but on others. He had made the pleasant discovery that being a member of a professional sports team had certain advantages when it came to the opposite sex. His mesmerizing good looks, being single and having a certain amount of affluence was all well and good, but when combined with the allure of celebrity status in one of life's most appealing arenas, it took on a different aura. He'd also noticed that the Red Sox were not a team accustomed to rigorous disciplinary standards. Their owner, Tom Yawkey, was a man who believed in wearing the world like a loose garment in many areas, one of them being the good life. Yes, it would be nice to have a winning team, but Yawkey had never read anyone the riot act in an attempt to achieve that. Johnny Pesky was one of the nicest people Tony had ever met, but he wasn't known for cracking the whip. He required accountability, but believed in minimal discipline. If a player was going to be out late – or even all night – they were required only to leave a note, telling him as much. Other than that, there was little in the way of player accountability. The organization had a country club atmosphere, and he suspected this had a lot to do with the Red Sox continually finishing near the bottom of their division. The average crowd barely reached ten thousand, and although owner Tom Yawkey might have liked them to be larger, he could live with it. The team wasn't going broke, and it had been almost twenty years since the Red Sox had been a serious contender for the American League pennant. All these years later, Tony was coming to realize that winning another pennant wasn't a particularly pressing team issue. Complacency had quietly built a nest on Lansdowne Street, and the end result was an upper management that didn't press its players to excel beyond mediocrity, so long as nothing embarrassing brought public disfavor to the organization. Maintain that posture, and life would continue to sail along smoothly.

Tony refused to settle for being just another player in a Red Sox uniform. He rigidly clung to the attitude that he would be an impact player who would leave his mark on the game when he finally walked away from it. His problem at present, however, wasn't the quality of his play; it was the lack of playing at all. His broken arm gave him a lot of free time, and having gotten a taste of the good life now that he was free to pursue it had left him in an altered state. Quite simply, the girls were looking better than ever and he had begun testing the waters. But he hadn't gone overboard with it, and didn't consider himself a playboy. He had to admit, however, that he did like the girls, and was coming to enjoy their company more and more.

****

He'd been cleared to return to active play at the beginning of September. Not only did it give him a chance to get back to playing again, it also gave a chance to do something he really liked: taking his brother Richie to Fenway Park to hang out with the players during practice before the game. But there was a price Richie had to pay for that lofty honor: he had to endure Tony's aggressive driving in his Corvette. He drove hard to cut back a twenty-minute ride to ten. Fun for Tony; terrifying for Richie. Mercifully, they had made it safely to Boston, parked in the players' lot, and headed straight for the locker room.

Now, as Richie stepped onto the field inside the park, he looked out at the vast expanse of green grass and the towering Green Monster in left field. Though only twelve, he'd often fantasized about parking one in the left field screen some day, even if it was only during practice. He'd asked Tony about the times he'd done it, and liked hearing what it felt like when the crowd roared as the ball sailed up into the night. He'd told him what it was like to run the bases slowly, savoring every minute of it, letting the joy of the experience fill him up inside. It had made a believer out of him. Though athletic, Richie wasn't sure he wanted to play professional baseball. But if he ever did, he'd like to hit one into the screen just like Tony.

"What are you going to do first?" Richie asked.

"I'm going to jog for awhile," Tony answered. "Why don't you ask some of the guys if you can shag fly balls for them?" The smile that crept across Richie's face was testimony enough. Tony would jog; Richie would shag.

Looking toward home plate Richie was disappointed to see that no one was taking batting practice. But a quick glance toward the first base dugout offered new hope. Tom Yawkey, the team's owner, was playing a game of pepper with Carl Yastrzemski, George Scott and Dick Radatz. He wondered how many team owners played pepper with their players. Probably not too many. He went over to them and stood a short distance away, watching.

Pitcher Dick Radatz, who normally would not take hitting practice of any kind, liked to warm up before he started his regular routine. It gave him a chance to loosen up without the risk of pulling a muscle. He was also a close friend of Tony's and had met Richie on several occasions. They had become friends as the result of Radatz' good-natured teasing, something Richie enjoyed and was proud of. How many kids got to play and hang out with the guys on the Red Sox? It didn't hurt his social standing either; kids in school were always asking who he'd seen lately. His answer was always the same; in a cool, unassuming tone he would say, "Aw, just he usual guys. Yaz and Rico and Scottie. You know, guys like that." Inside he'd be bursting with pride, but was careful not to show it. He didn't want them to think he wasn't cool and couldn't handle it. A guy's image meant a lot in a small town.

Radatz looked over at him. "Hey, where's your girlfriend today? You know, that cute little chick I saw you with last time."

"No way!" Richie blurted. "I don't go out with girls. I'm too cool for that."

"Don't worry," interjected George Scott, "Couple years from now you're gonna want to get un-cool. You just wait."

Yaz jumped in. "I don't know George, look what happened to Mr. Yawkey. He only went out with three girls in ten years, and look what it did to him. Made him look like he's sixty and he's only twenty-five. The kid may be right."

"Only twenty-five? I thought he was about forty-five."

"Don't let them kid you, Richie," Yawkey said. "I'm really thirty-five. I just look sixty, that's all."

"Wow, I'm really sorry to hear that, Mr. Yawkey."

Rico Petrocelli came out from the locker room and joined them. "These guys giving you a hard time?" he asked.

"Nah," Richie said. "They're trying to, but my brother told me all about them."

Suddenly they all stopped and looked at him seriously. "Oh, really? What exactly did he say?" asked Radatz.

Realizing he'd just stepped in something, Richie back peddled. "Nothing, honest! He didn't say anything!"

Tony, seeing Richie cornered, and seeing that everyone was having fun with him, jogged over to them. "I have to play with these guys, Richie. You being nice to them?" he asked. Winking at them, he added, "You're not going to get me kicked off the team or anything are you?"

"No! I'd never do that!"

"You sure? Not even by Mr. Yawkey?"

"No! I told him I was sorry he looked forty-five."

Yawkey laughed and decided it was time to take Richie off the hook. "He'd never do that to you, Tony. Richie's a great kid, and we love having him around."

"You better believe it," Yaz said, coming over and ruffling Richie's hair. "You're always welcome around here. Who knows, maybe some day you'll play here just like Tony."

Richie's relief was visible. The last thing he'd ever want was to get Tony in trouble. He loved these guys and it was a thrill to be around them. Even as a twelve-year-old he knew he was having an experience that only a handful of kids in America ever got.

"I know it, too," Tony said, patting Richie on the back. "Hey, I have to get back to jogging. See you later."

Rico looked at him. "Feel like shagging a few?"

"Yeah, I love doing that. Let's go!" He did love doing that, especially if it got him off the hot seat.

Girls? No way! Getting his brother into trouble? Forget it! Wasn't going to happen. He loved Tony, and he loved the Boston Red Sox. That's the way it was.

- Chapter Twenty -

Tony's return came during the sixth inning that day when Pesky looked down the
bench at him where he sat, watching the game. When he noticed, a look of longing
crossed his face. Johnny knew the look; he had seen it, had even felt it, many times.
He nodded at Tony. "All right, young man. It's time for you to go out there and get
reacquainted with your job."

Tony broke into a smile from ear to ear. "Thanks, John, I can't wait to get
reacquainted with my job." So intent was he on doing it that he went to the plate and
promptly drove a rifle shot into the left field screen. This he did to the crowd's delight,
but not nearly as much as to his own. It was important that everyone knew how much he
wanted to play, and play well. Needing them to know that was one of the driving forces
in his life. Without it he might have been 'just another player', and that would have
mortified him.

After his afternoon homer, he went on to close out the season with twenty-four home
runs, a .290 batting average, and fifty-two runs batted in. Not bad for someone who had
been out of the lineup six times, and had only played in one hundred and eleven out of a
possible one hundred fifty-four games. But the issue of crowding the plate and refusing to
compromise might have cost him in other areas. Indeed, he had closed out the season
with twenty-four home runs, but without all the injuries he might have played more

games and broken the all-time rookie home run record of thirty-eight, set thirty-four years earlier. Lack of compromise exacted a price from the unyielding, and he refused to alter his stance.

Besides, next year was another year, and with it would come new opportunities for him to excel.

****

Late that autumn his first chance to do that had presented itself, and it was in an area near and dear to his heart: money. He didn't view himself as being greedy or miserly, but he did believe in an honest day's pay for an honest day's work. What he *didn't* believe in was leaving money on the table during negotiations. And the negotiating on this particular day was about his next year's salary.

He had met with team General Manager Mike Higgins for a press luncheon, after which they had retired to Higgins' office in the clubhouse at Tony's request.

"How are you, Tony?" Higgins asked, breaking the ice.

"I'm doing good, Mike, and I'm happy to be with the team."

"That's good," Mike answered, stretching languidly before settling into his executive chair behind his desk. "We want you happy. What's that paper you've got? Not your 1965 contract we sent you, is it?"

"Actually, it is," he answered, laying it on the desk.

"All signed and ready to go?" Mike asked, his voice friendly, almost sounding like a patriarch.

"Actually, I haven't signed it yet," Tony said. "I think we need to talk about it. Last year I made $7500 as a rookie, which is the major league minimum. Now that I've proven myself, I think I should get paid more."

"We offered you more," Mike said, remaining pleasant. "This contract is for $9000. What's wrong with that?"

"It's not enough," Tony answered, "especially when you consider last year's accomplishments. I want more money."

"I thought we were pretty generous, Tony."

"To you, maybe it was. But I feel I'm worth more."

Mike's smile had faded and he'd begun to look a little annoyed. "Tony, you still have to prove yourself. You've only had one year up here. Do well next season, and we'll make it up to you. You'll see."

Tony was determined to stand his ground. He thought of Horton, who hadn't even been brought up from the minors; he thought of Guindon, who he felt wasn't on a par with him; and he remembered Danny Murphy, who wasn't exactly setting the league on fire. "I'm not interested in next year, Mike. I had a pretty good year this year, and I feel I'm worth more than $9000."

Higgins got up from his desk and began to pace. His annoyance had now begun to look suspiciously like anger. "Tell you what," he said, "the best we can do – and I'm doing you a favor – is $12000." Then, without waiting for an answer, he turned and called to his secretary, "Mary, make up a new contract for Tony, for $12000."

"Hey wait a minute, Mike," Tony said. "I'm not going to sign for $12000 either. I want more than that."

The tone in Mike's voice indicated that at least one of the kid gloves had been removed. "Look, Tony, if you were working in a factory you'd never get an increase like that. That's $4500 over last year. I can't go any higher than that. Why don't you just settle?"

"Because it's not enough, Mike." He now realized that Higgins had become agitated, and wondered if it was wise to push him any further. He'd been working toward this all his life, and hated to risk blowing it over money. Still...

"Sorry, but I just can't do it."

Seemingly beside himself, Mike asked, "Well, you must have some figure in mind. What is it?"

"I'd be okay with $17500," Tony answered.

Higgins suddenly looked like he had a piece of meat stuck in his throat. "You got to be kidding!" he said. "What are you, insane? There's no way I can do that. The club would object. The *owner* would object!" He paused again and continued pacing. He sat down and began scribbling something on a pad of paper.

When he'd concluded, he looked at Tony, and said, "Tell you what, I'll make it $14000, that's the best I can do." He turned again without waiting for Tony's answer, and yelled to his secretary. "Hey, Mary. Draw up a contract for Tony Conig—"

"Hey, wait a minute," Tony interrupted. "I'm not signing for that."

"That's as far as I'm going to go," Higgins said, now wearing his game face.

Tony's rebuttal didn't change that look. "Come on, Mike. Don't you want me to be a happy ball player? I'm from Boston, people are talking about me, and I'm starting to put people in the seats. If I play well, I'll pull in even more. You'll see."

"Who the hell do you think you are?" Higgins asked, his face glazing over with a crimson hue.

Tony had already shot his load, and Higgins' question had momentarily stumped the panel. The best he could say was, "Look, I'm not signing for $14000. If you want to stop all this arguing, just come up with another $3500."

Higgins got up and started pacing again. He looked steamed, anguished, and sorely put upon. Finally, he said, "I must be crazy, but I'm going to do it." Yelling to his secretary, he said, "Mary, draw up a contract for Tony Conigliaro for $17500." A moment later, in a voice much softer and friendlier, he said, "We're really proud of you Tony, and we want you to be happy. Do a good job for us."

He had tried to look casual while the contract was being drawn up, but inside his heart was thumping like a drum. When they had concluded their business, he ran downstairs, got in his car, rolled up the windows, and began screaming at the top of his lungs.

****

He had his new contract, his Corvette, and he was young, single and free to pursue the things he loved. At the same time he was still haunted by the memories and the questions that still lingered regarding his break-up with Julie. Their mothers had even spoken with each other, and had found the whole thing enigmatic. Julie had cried for two weeks, but as was the case with Tony, she hadn't been able to bring herself to pick up the phone and call him. Tony was trying to tell himself that he was having a great life, free and single and playing for the Red Sox, but there was always that feeling that something was missing, some indefinable ingredient that had created a void that nothing seemed able to fill. He didn't date any particular girl for any length of time. For as much fun as it appeared, it was unfulfilling and empty. It had come to feel like an endless succession of unrelated, meaningless events that appeared fun on the surface. But despite his friends all thinking he was having the greatest life anyone could have, they had no idea how often he felt vacant and wanting...

- Chapter Twenty-One -

Tony had always felt that people were ultimately the ones who controlled their own destiny. That included mentally and emotionally, not just physically. That being the case he had made up his mind to take his mental and emotional state into his own hands by going to a restaurant he and Julie had always liked, the Preston Beach Hotel and Restaurant. There were good, albeit sometimes painful memories connected to it, but his overall feeling toward the Preston was one of endearment and conviviality.

As he pulled the Corvette into the parking lot, the valet, a hip looking nineteen year old, stepped up to the car and opened his door for him. For a brief moment Tony allowed himself the luxury of admitting that being in the big leagues was exhilarating in more ways than one. Having people cater to him, going out of their way to make him feel like someone special, was great. Who wouldn't change places with him if they could? All they had to do was earn it just like he had.

He got out of the car and tossed the valet the keys. "Keep it warm for me. Okay?"

"Yeah, sure. Whatever you say."

Tony detected a note of contempt, but let it slide.

The Valet watched Tony saunter off, then turned and took a long look at the Corvette. Then he looked at the keys, swinging them back and forth as if pondering something. At nineteen, his decision wasn't long in coming.

Watching Tony walk up the steps and into the restaurant, he uttered, "You want me to keep it warm, pal? No problem, I'll warm it for ya..."

Inside, Tony welcomed the soft glow and ambience of the hotel restaurant's foyer. It was known to be a nice place, and was welcoming to its well heeled clientele. Nodding to himself, he approached the Maitre Di.

"You keep a table reserved for Tony Conigliaro, right?"

Appearing mildly puzzled the Maitre Di checked the list on his podium. Shaking he is head, he replied, "I'm sorry, Sir. We don't."

Tony grimaced. Shaking his head, he reached into his pocket and withdrew a twenty-dollar bill, discreetly passed it the Maitre Di, and countered, "You sure about that?"

The Maitre Di appeared to have a sudden recollection as he casually pocked the bill. "My apology sir. It seems we do."

"Great. And one more thing..." Producing another twenty, he passed it to the Maitre Di. "Wait for about ten minutes, then page Mr. Tony Conigliaro of the Boston Red Sox to the front desk. Make sure you mention the Red Sox. Okay?"

"Consider it done, sir."

****

Flashing lights, a tow truck, police cruisers, an ambulance and multiple fire apparatus crowded the side of the highway. Traffic was stopped, and both lanes were completely closed off. The two police officers inspecting the twisted, mangled mess that had once been a car were at a loss for words. Officer Robby Bateman had been on the force for twelve years and had seen his share of car wrecks. Paul Murdoch was a ten year veteran, and could only shake his head in disbelief.

"Can't even tell what make it was. Corvette, maybe," Bateman was saying. "As for the body inside it..."

Seeming to appraise the horrific condition of the car's remains, Murdoch commented, "Had to be doing over a hundred. If someone asked me to describe it, the best I could do is that used to be a little blue something."

The tow truck driver, a short, swarthy, grizzled man who looked like a long-time veteran of vehicle recoveries, joined them. "Sorry guys, gonna have to use a torch. Not even the jaws of life will work on this one."

Murdoch nodded his understanding. "How long you figure?"

"Depends. Never saw one this bad before."

Bateman shrugged his acquiescence. "Do the best you can." He stepped closer to the wreck for a better look. As he did, he paused and pointed at the back of it. "Oh, shit. You got to be kidding, what a shame."

Murdoch looked at the car, but couldn't pinpoint what Bateman was getting at. "What do you mean?"

Bateman stooped down. Pointing to the license plate, he said, "TC-25, that's Tony C's plate."

"Tony *Conigliaro?* From the Red Sox?"

"Yep. I was there when the Governor presented it to him on the State House steps. Gave the hometown kid his own special license plate."

Murdoch was incredulous. "You telling me-"

"Who else could it be?"

"This is going to be tough, better call it in."

An hour later at the Swampscot Police Headquarters the on-duty desk sergeant removed the sheet from the printer, and shook his head. He'd been on the force for nearly twenty years and, despite all he'd experienced, couldn't understand how or why some things happened. He'd known who Tony was, and as a Red Sox fan he'd looked forward to watching him play for 'the Sox'. Now, at the threshold of attaining what had to have been the fruition of a dream, he was suddenly snatched away by one inexplicable act that had probably happened on impulse.

Handing the printout to the shift supervisor, he said, "This is going to be tough. That kid and his family had to be sitting on top of the world, and now this."

The shift supervisor nodded his concurrence. "They ID the body yet?"

"Not yet, they're still trying to cut it out of the car."

Officer Robert Bateman, who had retrieved the plate, handed it over the desk sergeant. "Might as well take this, too."

Murdoch, who along with Bateman, had been relieved at the scene to file their report, asked, "Mind if we go, too?"

"Sure. Let's go."

****

At the Preston Beach Hotel and Restaurant, Tony was having the time of his life. Signing autographs for the stream of patrons who had lined up after he had been 'paged', he was preparing to sign his last autograph of the night.

As he stood up, he handed an autographed baseball to a ten year old boy. "Wow, thanks Tony. This is so cool!"

"Good, because it's cool for me, too. I can't figure out how everyone knew I was here, but hey, it's been a great time."

He winked at Maitre Di, signed another ball and handed it to him. "Good job, we had fun."

"Thanks, Tony. It didn't hurt the restaurant, either."

Outside, Tony walked down the front steps, and looked around. A concerned frown passed across his face and his pulse began to rise. No Valet. He looked further. No Corvette. His pulse rose again. Now thoroughly concerned, he began scouring the lot, searching for his car.

****

It was one of those family nights at the Conigliaro home where everyone stayed in to watch television. This particular night was devoted to game shows, which is where they were all gathered when the doorbell rang. Theresa looked quizzically at Sal, and then went to door.

Upon opening it, the first thing she saw was three Swampscot Police Officers, appearing solemn and regretful. The second thing she saw was the TC-25 license plate in Officer Murdoch's hand. The third thing she did was tense...and then shriek.

"No! *No!!* You wouldn't come here looking like that if this was good. My God! Salvatore!! *Sal-va-tore!!"*

Alarmed, Sal rushed to her side, and seeing the plate, he glazed over in shock. In the background, Richie, sensed something terrible had happened, and unable to define it, began to cry.

As for Billy, he could only stare as he waited for some unimaginable impending doom to reveal itself.

Barely able to breathe, Sal asked, "Are you saying my son... my Tony... Are you *sure*?"

It was Bateman who stepped forward. "We haven't made a positive identification yet, but we will within the next few hours. Even so, we have reason to believe it's Tony."

"But you haven't actually *seen* him?"

Murdoch nodded slowly. "They're trying to do the identification as we speak. We're here because we ran the plate number and the vehicle identification, and we know it's Tony's car."

Beyond bereaved, Theresa began to sob as she spoke. "God, please don't do this to us! Please! Don't take our Tony, don't let it be him!"

Himself deeply moved, Bateman tried to remain calm. "Mr. Conigliaro, do you know where Tony might have gone tonight?"

His voice barely above a whisper, Sal answered, "He said something about going to the Preston Beach Hotel..."

Bateman looked at Murdock, nodded, at which time Murdoch took his leave. Continuing, Bateman asked, "Have you heard from him since?"

Sal nodded, sadly. No, he had not.

Murdoch returned. "I just called the hotel. Tony was there, but he left and there's no sign of his car."

The phone rang. Sal and Theresa exchanged glances mixed with a surreal combination of hopeful anticipation and despair. Almost afraid to answer it, he took the call.

"Hello..."

What he heard next was beyond comprehension, and almost tore the heart of his chest. "Dad, it's me. I don't want to be a pain in the ass, but my car's been—"

"Choo? *CHOO!!*" Over his shoulder, he yelled, "It's him! It's Tony, he's alive!" Then, back into the phone, he added, "Don't worry about it, tonight you can be a pain in the ass all ya want!"

"Dad, what's going on? You okay?"

"Never mind that! Where are you?"

"At the Preston. Someone stole--"

"Stay there! Just stay there! I'll be right over!" He slammed down the phone and turned to his family and the police officers. "I feel bad for whoever's in that care, but our Tony's comin' home!"

Filled with emotions he could barely contain, Sal pulled into the Preston Beach Hotel parking lot. Seeing Tony perched on the porch, he sped to the foot of the steps, jumped out of the car and bolted for Tony. Seeing him as such confused Tony, especially when Sal lunged at him, pulled him close, and hugged him voraciously.

Barely able to breathe, he asked, "Dad, I don't get it. What's going on?"

"What's going on? We thought you were dead!"

"Why? I've been here all night."

"I know, I know. Come with me and we'll talk about it on the way home. Your mother and brothers are waiting for you." Again, he pulled Tony close, hugging him fiercely. "I don't know who you gave your keys to, but don't you ever give your keys to anyone again. Ever! If anything happened to you, your mother and I would *die!*"

- Chapter Twenty-Two -

His 1965 season had been better, and 1966 had been better still, although his batting average at the end of May was an emaciated .206. He'd avoided serious injury, had ultimately batted .265, had collected another twenty-eight home runs with ninety-three runs batted in, and was named the Red Sox Most Valuable Player. And at twenty years and nine months old, he was the youngest player ever to win a batting title.

However good his personal performance may have been, it hadn't kept the Red Sox from finishing ninth for the second year in a row, which had resulted in Billy Herman being fired.

The dating scene had continued to be good to him. When he wasn't chasing the ladies, the ladies were chasing him. As the era of hippies, free love and 'peace, love, dove' descended on America, none of them seemed interested in marriage, just good times. Besides, there was still the memory of someone special from times past that lingered within him, and though not prominent, it remained.

Late in the year, however, after Herman was gone, the Red Sox had announced their choice for the man who would now manage the team. It was Dick Williams, his counterpart with whom he'd traded fastballs at each other's head during spring training two years earlier. They had a natural dislike for each other almost from the day they'd met.

Upon hearing the news, Tony smiled in irony. 1967 hadn't even arrived yet, and it had already begun looming as an interesting year.

****

Julie, now a full-fledged stewardess with Eastern Air Lines, had eventually been assigned to New York. Not that she was complaining; New York was a marvelous city in many ways. It came with its own personality, and to the shock and dismay of some, so did its people. 'New Yorkers' they were called. And she had decided that she liked it. It was exciting, it was busy, it never slept, and it provided the opportunity to meet lots of interesting people, some who lived there, and some who didn't.

She was with her friend Margaret, another stewardess, at Mister Laff's, a nightclub in the old tradition. Located on First Avenue between 64th and 65th streets, it was a well-appointed, sizeable place with brick walls adorned with sports memorabilia, a large dining area, and a large well-stocked bar. Best of all, it was a safe place and it was right around the corner from her apartment. The owner, Phil Linz, was a retired ball player and friend of hers who had played for the Yankees. As a result Mister Laff's had become a major hangout for athletes from both in and out of town. Their common interest in the game, along with mutual acquaintances in baseball had made them quick and close friends. He also kept a protective eye on her to make sure she was doing all right.

"How you doing, kiddo?" he asked as he entered.

"Good," she said. "It's eleven o'clock, Wish I could show up for work at eleven o'clock."

"You want to buy the place, you can have it," he said, laughing as he gave her a hug.

"You kidding? I could never run a place like this, it's not my thing." She noticed two men as they entered. They appeared vaguely familiar, especially the taller one. The place wasn't crowded, so it seemed natural that they should go straight to the bar. As they got closer she realized why both of them looked familiar. One was Roger Maris, the home run hitting machine from the Yankees, who had broken Babe Ruth's single year home run record several years earlier. The other one seemed familiar too, but she couldn't quite place him.

He noticed her glancing at him, and saw the curiosity etched on her face. And that was all he needed to approach her. "No sense looking at me long distance when you can do it up close," he said, grinning broadly. "My name's Ken. What's yours?"

"I'm Julie," she answered, taking his outstretched hand. "I saw you looking at me, so I thought I'd come over and save you from yourself," he continued.

"I didn't know I needed saving," she said.

"Spend any time around him and you will," said Maris, joining them. "Hi, I'm Roger." He seemed as pleasant as Ken, though perhaps a bit more reserved.

"Pleasure to meet you," Julie said. "Say hi to my friend Margaret." To Margaret, she said, "This is Roger Maris, from the Yankees, and this is his friend Ken."

Margaret shook hands with Ken without ever taking her eyes off Maris. Obviously star struck, but skeptical, she said, "You're not really Roger Maris, are you?"

"Sure, I am. Why wouldn't I be?" He was amused, not offended. Most people said hi, then asked for an autograph.

Quite serious, she said, "Are you sure you're Roger Maris?"

"I hope so, that's what they been telling me all my life. I'd hate to find out they're wrong after all these years. What would my family say?"

"That's right," interjected Ken. "Hell, they'd have to go and put someone else's name in all those record books."

Margaret was still unconvinced. "Can you prove it?" she asked. "Show me your driver's license."

Had he not been amused he might have been suspicious. But this girl was benign; she wasn't looking to hurt anyone, she just didn't understand that celebrity athletes could also be real people away from the game.

He took out his license and showed it to her. "See?"

She stared at the license, then back at him, and her jaw dropped. "You're him! You're really him!"

Julie turned to Ken, her interest renewed. "You never told me who you are."

"Ken Harrelson, I play for the Kansas City Athletics. Pleasure to meet you."

- <u>Spring, 1967</u> -

Spring training was to be held at Winter Haven, Florida, and it was the first time the Red Sox had trained there. With spring training had come the first wakeup call under Dick Williams, their new manager. A man known for his brashness, his crew cut, and not caring if people liked what he said, he had assembled everyone who would, or might, be with the team in the locker room.

"Most of you know who I am," Williams began, looking at each of them as he spoke. "I played a lot of years in this league, as well as in the National. I put up with a lot of crap from people whose shoes I would like to have buried somewhere - with them still in 'em. But that was then and this is now, and I'm the one who's going to be calling the shots around here. They're paying me to do that, and I intend to."

He began slowly pacing as a disquieting pall fell over the clubhouse. This wasn't the normal fare that most of them had been reared on, especially those who had been with the Red Sox for any length of time. This had an edge to it, and the tone in Williams' voice made it clear he meant every word of it.

"For those of you who have spent time on this team, playing for the Red Sox has been a paid vacation. You've shown up, gone through the motions, and had a paycheck waiting for you at the end of the week. Maintain that attitude on my watch, you won't even be with the team by the end of the week. They only gave me a one-year contract, so I made a commitment to the people who run this organization, including the man who owns it. More important, I've made that same commitment to myself. You're going to hustle, you're going to play every game at one hundred and ten percent, and you're going to run the bases at full tilt, even if you know you're going to be out. You're going to give your absolute best every minute you're on the field; if you get tired I'll get someone else to replace you.

"Unlike the last seven years, this year's team is going to win more games that it loses. That may seem like a novel idea to anyone who's been here a while, but nowhere is it written that a team, *any* team, and especially *my* team, has to field a loser. So get used to it. A lot of changes are just over the horizon and the end result will be a better team than any of you have ever played on. And one more thing: from now on," and he looked directly at Tony, Mike Ryan and Tony Horton, "anyone who blows curfew is going to cough up a quick five hundred bucks. That's the way it is."

George Scott, who Tony had known and chummed with in Wellsville, glanced over at him as if to say, I think he's talking about you, bro. Tony scowled at him, even though the two of them had become close friends, something that had been instantaneous. George had referred to Tony as being 'color blind', meaning that if someone was okay in his book, and it was because they were okay. Period. It had nothing to do with color, ethnic background, or anything else. That point had been proven one evening in Ocala, Florida, during the Instructional League. Sal and Teresa had come to visit, and Tony had invited several of the ball players to join him for one of Teresa's special home cooked feasts. Among the invited had been two black players, George Scott and pitcher Earl Wilson. The Deep South being what it was, they had been barred from entering the hotel by people at the front desk, despite the Civil Rights Law having already been passed. Tony had been passing by, saw what was happening, and had made a point of telling the players and the desk clerk that he wanted George and Earl to join them. Moments later, Sal had gotten wind of it and had also jumped into the developing fray. It had taken a little doing, but he and Tony had finally convinced the hotel, under threat of copious amounts of unwanted public attention, to let them enter, which the hotel had ultimately done. After that, George had sworn by Tony, and they'd become close. Therefore, when Tony scowled at him, George took the look as Tony's unspoken statement that storm clouds were brewing with Williams. There was a new sheriff in town, he was the boss, and was playing for keeps.

"Some of you have had charmed lives," Williams continued. "I haven't." He looked at Tony, and his voice began to rise. "I spent five years in the minors, and wasn't coddled by anyone." He stabbed another look at Tony. "I don't believe in instant stardom. I let history decide who was and who wasn't a star. What I do believe in is a no-nonsense work ethic. Anyone who doesn't like that can turn in your uniform and go home. There are forty of you here, our roster only has room for twenty-five, and we can only put nine men on the field at a time. Do the math." He started to walk toward his office, then paused, and added, "Oh yeah, one more thing. Any of you who think you've got some special kind of 'in' with Mister Yawkey, and that you can wield it over me, can forget it. I was hired to manage this team, not him. You have a problem with me, you work it out with me. And remember what I said: this year we're going to win more games than we lose. The odds makers in Las Vegas have made us a one-hundred-to-one long shot to win the pennant this year. That's what they think of us. Well, I have news for them. This game's going to start being fun again, we're going to field a winner, and the only way we're going to accomplish that is by acting like grown-ups, professionals, and working our asses off. Have a nice day."

The battle lines had been drawn.

After Williams left, Tony began thinking out loud. "What the hell's his problem?" he asked, to no one in particular. He, George Scott, Carl Yastrzemski, and Rico Petrocelli, with whom Tony had also become close, were talking in the locker room after practice.

"I was that guy's roommate for a couple months, and was on the team with him, and I don't understand how all of a sudden he's running the show."

"He must have something they like," Rico said, "or he wouldn't be here."

"What I don't like is every time he made a threat of some kind he looked right at me. I don't mind taking a little heat, but I don't want to start out with two strikes against me, either."

"Give him a chance, see what happens," Yaz said. "If it gets out of hand call the guy aside, see what's on his mind. After what I saw today, I doubt he'll be bashful about telling you what it is."

****

The next wakeup came not long after Dick Williams' opening day proclamation. It had become an accepted practice for Ted Williams to join the club during spring training every year to help instruct players on hitting and playing the outfield, and Dick

Williams had invited Ted to join them again, thus maintaining the tradition. Tony had been looking forward to it during the entire off-season.

He and Ted Williams, and several other young players, some of them pitchers, were gathered together, and Williams was giving them tips on batting, reading the rotation on the ball, and telling the pitchers how best to set up batters with particular pitches. In the midst of his teaching session, Dick Williams had joined them.

"Ted, do us a favor," he began. "I want you to stick with the outfielders and leave the pitchers alone. I got something else I want them to do."

"Hey, we were just starting to—" Tony began. A sharp look, and Williams' finger shot out, abruptly ended Tony's protest.

"Who's running this team?" Williams asked.

"Well, you are," Tony answered, feeling his emotional blood pressure starting to rise. "I was just—"

"Enough!" Williams interrupted. Turning back to Ted Williams, he continued. "Like I said, I have something else I want the pitchers to do."

"Oh? And what's that?" Ted asked, mildly irritated.

Turning to the pitchers, Williams said, "You guys go over to that volleyball court, choose sides, and start playing. The rest of you stay here with Ted."

"Volleyball?" Ted asked, incredulously. "What the hell's volleyball got to do with baseball?"

"Nothing," Dick answered. "But right now they're standing around listening to you talk about something they don't need to learn. I'll arrange for all the pitching instruction they need. In the meantime, I want them over there, playing volleyball and working up a sweat so they can lose some weight and get in shape. That ain't going to happen with them standing around listening to you." And with that, he walked off. There had been no apologies, no explanations, nothing.

Three days later Ted Williams had left camp without saying goodbye to Dick Williams, and the latter had treated it like business as usual. He'd dismissed Williams' departure with the same dispassion that he'd have dismissed a free agent who'd shown up at spring training without an invitation.

The winner of their power struggle hadn't been lost on Tony, nor had his growing resentment against Dick Williams.

Tony sensed this was going to be very different kind of year.

- Chapter Twenty-Three -

By the time the season began, a lot of changes had occurred under Williams'
regime. The dress code no longer was 'wear whatever you want, it's okay'. *It wasn't
okay.* They made good money; they could wear good clothes. No exceptions. Suits and
ties and sport coats were the new uniforms when they were traveling, as well as at home.
Haircuts were still in vogue; long hair was not, even though American pop culture had
made it fashionable. Defiance, disrespect and insolence were out, so was whining and
tufted cushions; from now on they would be well-behaved, well-spoken professional
athletes and gentlemen. America might be going down the tubes with its drug culture,
acid rock, hippies, demonstrations, and race riots, but the Red Sox were going to be a
bright spot on Boston's landscape. Be it the new disciplines or not, something had
changed the team from the inside out. They had begun to win, and they felt good about
themselves; and they felt good about baseball because it had become fun again. They
were beginning to get the respect and recognition that came with success. Little by little,
Williams' regimens were beginning to pay off. There was another payoff, too. What had
been an average crowd of ten thousand had now become loud, boisterous, enthusiastic
crowds of twenty-five thousand or more. They paid attention to the game, knew the
names and statistics of the players, hung on every play and every pitch, had favorite
players they thought belonged on the All Star Team, and experienced the joys and

sufferings of winning and losing with a team they cared about. And the franchise was making money again, lots of it. The team had a total payroll of under a million dollars, and Tom Yawkey was having the most fun he'd had since Boston had gone to the 1946 World Series.

This, however, brought with it a new thorn in the side of Dick Williams. When Yawkey had first bought the team in 1933 he was a young man who had been a pretty fair athlete in his own right. He'd even been known to practice with his players on a fairly regular basis. But this was a Dick Williams team, and he didn't like it when Yawkey came to the locker room to schmooze with his players. In Williams' eye that kind of camaraderie could undermine his own authority, and he needed all of it he could get. He'd already angered some of his players; the only way to keep them in line was by winning, and that required a bullwhip. Owner or not, he wasn't about to let Yawkey take the whip out of his hand. Nor had Williams forgotten that Yawkey hadn't been fully convinced he was the right man to manage the team. Even Tony had heard those rumors, and would like to have exploited them. But what could he say, they were 'winning more games than they lost', and they were making money and having fun. They had begun to believe in themselves and their invincibility; players and fans alike were delirious. There was a party going on in Boston, and the Red Sox were throwing it.

A trip back to the Army to fulfill his Reserve duty dragged Tony away from the team in early June. Though he was happy to be away from Williams, he hated leaving the team at a time when it had been great to be a Boston Red Sox player. He and Carl Yastrzemski were engaged in an ongoing struggle to assert themselves as team leader and top producer, and it was the buzz of Boston's sports world. He wished he could have put off his Reserve obligation until after the season, thereby keeping their momentum alive. But the army would not allow it; the Viet Nam War was raging – and getting worse – filling America's living rooms every evening with half-hour updates on death tolls and carnage. They'd made it clear that being Tony Conigliaro or not, being a pro baseball player or not, going off to Reserve duty was not a matter of choice.

After a three-week absence, he had returned early in July, and had paid the price for his downtime by promptly going into a slump. For all his homerun hitting ability, slumps were his nemeses, and he'd never made it through an entire season without one.

"Hang in," Rico said. "These things go away. Just fight through it. You've been here before, and you know what it takes."

"Hey, taking three weeks off dulled my edge. They expect you to just walk off the field, and come back pretending like you were never gone. At least with my slumps, when I come out of them, I come out stronger than before. All I need is a little time, and I'll be okay."

A television reporter listening nearby signaled to his film crew to start shooting, and approached Tony, who was standing beside his locker. "Not such a good game today, Tony? How soon do you expect to be back to normal?"

Tony looked at him, and lowered his head. Pinching a small crop of his hair, he pointed and said, "You see those little gray hairs starting to grow in with all the black ones? Those are what I call my 0-for-4's. Every time I go 0-for-4 at the plate, I get a new gray hair. If I don't get back on track pretty soon I'm going to look too old to play, and they'll have to wheel me off the field."

The reporter laughed, then continued. "So it's just a matter of getting your timing back?"

"That and my hand speed," Tony answered. "If I'm going to be remembered as a great player some day, I'm going to have to measure up to it."

"Like Ted Williams, maybe? Wouldn't it be great to be almost as good as him some day?"

Tony paused for a moment, frowning as he considered the question. "I don't know," he began slowly. "Ted was a great ball player, but I want to be even better."

The reporter looked at him blankly, not knowing what to make of the remark. Lost in his thoughts, Tony walked away. The interview was over.

****

Once again, he had fought his way through it, his skills returned, and by the end of the month his batting average was back over .300, with eleven home runs and forty-three runs batted in. Then came the best news of all; Hank Bauer, who was to manage the American League All Stars, called to inform him he had just been named as one of the starting outfielders for this year's team. He was thrilled, and so were his parents, his brothers, and especially the one whose efforts were paying off beyond his wildest dreams: Uncle Vinnie. No one was thrilled more than Uncle Vinnie.

His Reserve duty behind him, and his slump over, he'd worked back into his groove. He was now part of the party, and was sitting on top of his world. Who could ask for anything more...

****

July rolled into August, and the party continued, on and off the field. The girls in the stands, many of them teenagers, shrieked wildly whenever he did *anything*. It didn't matter if it was a hit, a catch, a throw or an error. They loved him, and he loved the attention.

Between innings on one particular evening, he had taken his place in right field, and had just finished his warm-up throws with Reggie Smith. One of his adoring fans, a fourteen year-old girl named Donna Heath, from Plymouth, Massachusetts, was among his fondest admirers. From her front seat in the right field grandstands, she yelled, "Tony, I love you! How old are you?"

"That's a pretty personal question. Sure you want to know?"

"Of course," she persisted, delighted that he would even take time to acknowledge her. "I need to know, or I'll— I'll just *die!*"

"You tell me first," he said, deciding to have some fun with her.

"*Me?*" she asked. "How old am *I?*" She was incredulous. She turned to Carol Montanari, her teenage girlfriend who had come with her, and said, "You don't— you think he really wants—"

"Who cares? Answer him!" she said, awestruck. "Tony Conigliaro is talking to us!"

"I'm fourteen," Donna yelled. She leaned over the railing in an attempt to hand him a program she'd bought from a vendor outside the park. "Could you sign this for me?" she yelled.

He quickly looked toward the home plate area, making sure play wasn't about to resume. He had time. He began to trot in their direction.

Tony Conigliaro... Trotting in their direction?

He took the picture and pen she held in her hand. "Oh my God! *Oh my God!!*" she screamed, *"He's signing it!!"*

"Fourteen, huh?" he said, smoothly. "Fourteen's pretty cool. If *I* was fourteen, I'd think you were pretty cute, and I'd want to get your name. What is it, by the way?"

"It's Donna," she answered, trying to maintain her composure. She never dreamed he'd actually come talk to a fourteen-year old kid, but here he was.

He scribbled something on the picture, and handed it back to her. Glancing toward home plate again, he winked at her. "I better go." He then trotted back to his position.

"What does it say?" Carol asked, beside herself with curiosity. "Let me see!" Donna held it, and read aloud, "To my friend Donna, the coolest fourteen-year-old kid I ever met. Best of luck, Tony C." She turned to her girlfriend. *"Oh my God!!"*

"But he didn't tell you how old he is."

"Who cares?" she fired back. "He signed my picture. Not only that, he said I was cool, and he called me his friend! What else matters?"

- Chapter Twenty-Four -

August 18, 1967

Boston's 'Fenway Faithful', thirty-one thousand of them, had gathered to watch their beloved Red Sox, who were now in a bitterly contested pennant race. No one was more aware of that than Tony's parents and his Uncle Vinnie, who had come to the game at Tony's urging. He loved knowing they were there in the stands watching him. It gave him extra incentive. He was also glad Richie was with them.

"Tell you what," Vinnie said. "Your kid has a chance to make a real name for himself in this game some day."

"Some day?" Sal asked. "What's the matter with what he's doing right now? This team's climbing down the throat of their first trip to the World Series in twenty-one years. That ain't chopped liver."

"You know what I mean. I'm talking about Tony making it into the Hall some day. Nine trips to the All Star game, six hundred fifty home runs, maybe even a shot at a triple crown, stuff like that."

"He does something like that, I'll buy you a brand new car, Vinnie."

"He does that, you can buy me one first," Teresa chimed in. "I carried that boy for nine months, nursed him, fed him, changed his diapers, and washed a couple thousand of his dirty uniforms." Turning to Vinnie, she added, "You never did those things for him."

"Hey, I played ball with him from morning to night more times than I can count. Took him to games, showed him how to hit, how to throw, all of it. And I got to admit—" He paused as he choked up, then, "Got to admit, I loved every minute of it and would give everything I got to do it all over again. God, how I love that kid."

She patted his knee. "I know. You were like a second father to him and we've always been grateful for that." Turning to Sal, she added, "Start working overtime, Sal. You're going to be buying two cars."

"What about me?" asked Richie. "What do I get?"

"How about a snow shovel and a lawn mower?"

"You kidding me? Forget about it."

Down on the field, Tony was trying to determine how best to get his second hit. He'd hit a single the first time up, and would like nothing better than to arc one of Jack Hamilton's notorious fastballs over the fence in left field and down onto the Mass Turnpike. One of Hamilton's fastballs... now there was an interesting thought. Jack Hamilton was Los Angeles Angels' six-foot, two hundred pound flamethrower. It was rumored that he threw 'spitters' - moistened baseballs that took unusual flight patterns when thrown as curve balls. Not that Hamilton was unique; a lot of pitchers were rumored to do it. He also wondered if Hamilton's arm had stiffened during the delay, if maybe it would affect his control.

As he waited in the on-deck circle he pondered the lazy haze lingering over the outfield. He wasn't certain if it would interfere with his ability to see the ball clearly. Earlier, a disgruntled fan had tossed a smoke canister from the left field grandstands, which had caused a ten-minute game delay in the middle of the fourth inning. Grounds keepers had finally extinguished the device and removed it. He wondered why people did mindless things like that.

He watched as Reggie Smith lined to center field for the second out of the inning. Rising, he drew a deep breath and walked toward home plate. Standing in, he paused to better grip his bat. He and Hamilton gazed at each other. He was painfully aware of the slump he was in. But he'd been through this before; it was part of the game, and he'd made a lifestyle out of comebacks.

He stepped into the batters box and glanced toward the pitcher's mound. Hamilton regarded him without moving. Tony responded the way he always did; he grit his teeth, and edged even closer to the plate. The batters box was his office; it's where he went to work.

He subtly glanced toward the Red Sox dugout. Many of his teammates were lined up along the top step, watching him. Carl Yastrzemski, his chief competitor for the team's role of Alpha male, seemed unusually attentive; the others appeared mildly apprehensive.

Jack Hamilton, himself not one to take a backward step, got the sign from Rogers, and stood erect. With the bases empty, he had no one to concentrate on but Tony. Gripping the ball, he went into his stretch and began his delivery. His right arm came over the top with the velocity of a sledgehammer bearing down on an anvil. He released his pitch, and an instant later the ball streaked toward home plate at ninety miles an hour...

Tony watched as it sailed toward him. Normally, he would jerk his head back just enough on close pitches to let them buzz right past him. Realizing this would be an inside fastball, he made to lean back enough to let it pass. But this ball did something different; as he leaned back the ball seemed to follow him. Leaning back a little further, he expected the ball to pass before him, but instead it maintained its pursuit. When it was about four feet away he realized it was going to hit him, and that it was going to hurt because Hamilton threw so hard. He jerked his head backward and tried to turn away, knocking his batting helmet off his head, and exposing it to the pitch. He heard a whistling sound as the oncoming ball pushed aside the air in front of it. Suddenly, he was frightened. As he threw his hands up in front of his face, he saw the ball follow him back just before it hit him flush in the left side of his face. It struck with such force that he thought it would go in one side of his head, and out the other. His eyes slammed shut, his legs gave way, and he crumpled to the ground, conscious but in excruciating pain. A ball that normally sailed off into space had hit him so squarely that it dropped straight down onto home plate and limply rolled a few feet before coming to rest.

Up in the stands his family held their breath, frozen with quiet desperation. Tony was down, and he wasn't moving; he had yet to even sit up. They felt powerless to do anything, feeling as if they were watching from a million miles away. The anguish was too much. Sal pulled Teresa close to him, and hugged her.

"Dad, is he going to be all right?" Richie asked.

"I don't know." Clutching Teresa even closer, "I'm going down there. Vinnie, stay here and keep an eye on everyone." He got up and made his way toward the aisle.

Down below, Dick Williams stared with grave concern as Tony lay motionless in the dirt. Here was this superb human specimen, this young home run hitting machine and local hero, dropped by a pitch that came with its one-of-a-kind signature sound, one he'd never forget. He left the dugout, and raced toward Tony, who was lying motionless at the plate.

Tony's throat had begun to swell. *Suppose this thing closes up,* he wondered. *If it does, I won't be able to breathe. God, please keep me alive...* He knew that if God wanted to take him, He could. But he didn't want to die right there in the dirt, especially with his family watching.

His mouth began filling with fluids. At first he feared it was blood, but it was viscous and didn't taste quite like blood. It had to be fluid coming from somewhere inside his head mixed with blood.

Out on the mound, Jack Hamilton watched in shock. He had not intended for the pitch to hit him. It was a fastball that got away from him. He waited to see if Tony would get up, hoping against hope that he would. But he'd heard the *thwop* when it struck Tony, and prayed it wouldn't be as bad as it sounded.

Rico Petrocelli was the first to reach him. "Just stay still, Tony. You'll be all right..."

The crowd sat in stunned silence, unable to comprehend what had happened. They were waiting for him to get up, to walk off the field and go to the hospital for routine medical help. He'd be back in a day or so, and the pennant race would return to normal. But it wasn't happening; he simply lay there.

Surrounded by members of both teams, Tony groaned as trainer Buddy LeRoux rolled him over and placed him onto a stretcher. "Still with us, Tony? Say something."

"Can't see," Tony moaned. "Head aches... throat's clogging..."

This wasn't encouraging, and LeRoux nodded for his assistants to hurry. Once secured, they carried him off the field and into the clubhouse. A slight applause went up, but most people were too stunned to react. No one, including Tony, had shown up at the park expecting this to happen.

Up in the stands, Vinnie, Teresa, Richie and Billy could only sit there, watching in silent anguish.

- Chapter Twenty-Five -

Inside the clubhouse they laid him out on one of the trainer's tables, and Buddy LeRoux placed an ice bag against the side of his head. "Buddy, this pain...is killing me," Tony said, barely above a whisper. "You have to...give me...something..."

"I can't," LeRoux said, stepping aside to allow team physician Tom Tierney to gain access to him. Any medication Tony got would be Tierney's responsibility. He had arrived almost the same time they had. He, too, had heard the sound and knew right away that it was serious. He'd also been a close friend of the Conigliaro family for years. Knowing he was there made Tony feel better, but when he didn't say anything and began ministering to him right away, he got worried. Acting more like a doctor than as a friend intimated that the injury was serious, and Tony became concerned about it all over again.

"I've already called for an ambulance, Tony," Tierney said, continuing his duties. "In the meantime, I'm going to check your vital signs, reflexes and a few other things. Just relax and be still for now."

****

Back out on the field the game was underway again. The stillness in the air was inconsistent with the rollicking, fun-like atmosphere to which the crowd had become accustomed. The air had grown heavy and dense, and a pall hung over the stadium. As Hamilton completed his warm-up and play was about to resume, he glanced toward the Red Sox dugout, wishing he could tell them how sorry he was. But what he saw was hardly comforting. Several players were perched on the top step glaring out at him. Carl Yastrzemski was perhaps the most imposing, silently regarding him, a bat in his hand being waved at him like a baton.

Hamilton resolved to find Tony after the game, to see how he was doing, and to tell him how he felt. He needed Tony to know. There had been no one on base, with two outs in a scoreless game. No pitcher throws at batters under those conditions. Surely they'd understand; but he doubted anyone on the team wanted to hear it.

****

He had no idea what was happening to him, or why, and his feeling of helplessness began melting into despair. The room was deathly quiet. Not even sounds from the game outside could be heard. Had it not been for the occasional scraping of baseball spikes on the floor he'd have thought something was wrong with his hearing, too. But a couple of his teammates had come in from outside to check on him, and had squeezed his hand without saying anything. Their presence had been comforting.

Something within him sensed his father's presence. He hadn't said anything, but Tony knew; he could feel it. Which in fact he was. Sal was making it easy on the medical staff by staying off to the side, allowing everyone to do their job, unimpeded. Tony was aware of the special calm that his father possessed, especially in times of extreme duress. It wouldn't be until later that he learned Billy and Richie had also come by, though Richie had retreated to a distant corner of the clubhouse to sob, so that Tony wouldn't hear him.

He heard the sound of the arriving ambulance. Thank God, he thought. Now maybe they'd give him something to kill the pain. He'd gotten to where he felt like crying himself, just to relieve some of it. Unfortunately, it wasn't that kind of pain.

He didn't want to scream or cry in front of anyone, but it was hard to simply lie there, holding it back. For the moment, all thoughts of his baseball career, or if he'd ever play again, were banished. He just wanted to live, and realized in those moments just how precious life was. For now, getting rid of the infernal, unrelenting pain was all that mattered.

As they wheeled him out of the clubhouse toward the ambulance, a lot of people were hanging around wanting to know how he was doing. He could hear them yelling to him, "Hang in there, Tony. You'll be back in no time." He'd wished he could appreciate it, but all that crowded his mind was the constant throbbing.

****

The ride to the hospital had felt more like a pilgrimage, even though it was only fifteen minutes from Fenway. Between the driver speeding and the siren, it had been an endurance run. Every time they sped around a corner or put the brakes on he felt as if his head would split open. Fortunately, his father and Dr. Tierney were there with him, keeping him company.

Once they had arrived at Sancta Maria Hospital, across the river in Cambridge, he was sure they'd give him something for the pain. But they hadn't. The first order of business was getting him to an examination room where one of the neurosurgeons looked at him, and took X-Rays. Their greatest concern was that he might be hemorrhaging internally. Fortunately he wasn't, but every time they moved him his head throbbed horribly. The pain had become so intense that even if he had his vision it would have hurt too much to open his eyes. He'd never sustained an injury like this one.

Finally, they had taken him upstairs to one of the rooms. By now all he wanted was to sleep, but the pain was at its worst, refusing to relent. Fluid had begun seeping out of the corner of his mouth onto his pillow. When his parents and brothers were finally allowed to come into the room they hadn't liked what they saw. The pillow was changed, the ooze wiped away, but little else could be done for him. His mother hadn't said much, contenting herself simply by sitting there, quietly holding his hand, her eyes filled with tears. He knew the ordeal was hurting her badly, and he refused to make it worse by telling her how much the pain in his head was hurting him. He silently asked God to please not let them get sick over what had happened to him.

They had stayed a short while, not saying much. They had come to be there with him, without trying to say or do anything. When they were gone it occurred to him that he might never see them again. He was blind, and didn't know if his vision would ever return. There were no guarantees. Death was constantly on his mind, and he felt he indeed had a good chance of dying. None of the test results were in, and no one could calculate the extent of the damage. He hoped the doctors would give him something to put him to sleep for the night. They had finally administered codeine, but couldn't give him anything else until they knew how badly he'd been hurt. Therefore, lying alone in the dark, unable to sleep with a multitude of pressing concerns, a dark, empty feeling crept over him. He wanted someone around to hold onto, but no one was there.

He'd never felt so alone in his life.

****

During the night he managed to sleep in short spurts, fifteen to twenty minutes at a time. If the pain didn't wake him up, the nurse coming to check on him did. They took his blood pressure every fifteen minutes, a sign that disturbed him. Healthy people with a good prognosis didn't get blood pressure checks at fifteen-minute intervals. She told him on one occasion that he'd be just fine, but had then taken his blood pressure, and rushed off to get the doctor. Never before had he ever felt that close to God. He'd once heard that there were no atheists on battlefields. Now he understood why. He'd never been very religious. Going to church on Sunday was something he did because he'd been raised to do it, not because of any deep personal convictions. But for the moment, he wasn't thinking of baseball; he was begging God to let him live.

The next conscious realization had come when he felt someone holding his hand the next morning. Still not being able to open his eyes, all he could do was moan, "Who is it?"

"It's me, Tony," came the familiar, patriarchal voice, "Tom Yawkey."

He couldn't believe it, but then again he could. Tom had always been good to him. He'd always known he could go to Tom with just about anything, even now, in the Williams 'we'll win more games than we'll lose' era. Busy as Yawkey was, he'd taken time to come by and visit with him, sitting there holding his hand, telling him not to worry. It was then that he realized he wasn't playing for Dick Williams; he was playing for Tom Yawkey. Well, not just Yawkey; his family, the fans and his friends mattered, too. He considered Yawkey the best owner in baseball, and the best friend a ball player could have.

"We don't know how this will turn out," Yawkey said. "I hope everything will be okay. We'll get you all the medical help you need, that's for sure. And if the time ever comes when you need somewhere to work, you'll always have a home here with us."

Tony was comforted by Yawkey's words, but resisted them. He still had the intention of playing again, if at all possible. He felt a little better that morning, better enough to already have begun speculating on how soon he might be able to rejoin the team. For the past seven years, sixth place was the best they had finished; the previous year they had finished ninth for the second year in a row. This year, however, they were in a dogfight for the American League pennant, and possibly a trip to the World Series. This wasn't the time to be sidelined; not in what some people were beginning to call the year of 'The Impossible Dream'.

- Chapter Twenty-Six -

He lay in bed, thinking about the beaning. What else was there to do? The big question running though his mind was the same one that had been running though it ever since he'd been hit: had Jack Hamilton done it on purpose? He'd been in a slump, and most pitchers didn't want to wake a hitter who was slumping. Had he been hot at the time, it might have been different. More and more he'd decided to give Hamilton the benefit of the doubt, even though he was known to have plunked players on several occasions. Hamilton had even tried to see him the next day, but hadn't been allowed to enter. That, combined with there being no good reason to throw at him was enough to absolve him. In the end only one person knew if Jack Hamilton had hit him deliberately, and that was Hamilton himself. A couple of days later, Los Angeles had moved on to the next leg of their East coast trip and he'd left town.

****

His vision had begun to return; not great, and not with both eyes; but he could see. And for that he was the happiest guy in the world. The sight in his right eye was fuzzy, but he could make things out. And the things he could make out were encouraging almost to the point of bringing him to tears. Flowers, dozens of them; and mail by the sack. Just being able to see them raised his spirits. The headaches had eased. The left eye that had been hit was still blown up and closed tight, and though looking out of his right eye was akin to nighttime, at least he could see. He still couldn't tell if the weather was sunlit or cloudy, but at least he could see it. Not only that, the pain had subsided greatly. A blur entered the room, and he tried to focus on who it was.

"Good morning, Tony. How do you feel?"

He knew the voice, and was relieved to hear it. "Hi Dr. Tierney. I'm feeling better, thanks."

"That's because we've been able to start giving you pain medication," Tierney explained. "A couple of the clerks in our mail room kept track of your mail for you." he said, "And you've received over thirteen thousand letters from all over the world. Telegrams started rolling in the night you were hit. You've received religious articles from people of just about every denomination, and a lot of prayers are being said for you. You're a popular guy."

"Maybe that's why I feel God pulled me through. Maybe some day I can repay Him and all those people who prayed for me."

"The best way to do that for now is to rest up and get well," Tierney said. "You're a lucky guy. We were really worried about you the first twenty-four hours or so. Had the pitch been two inches higher you would have been dead. Now that you're doing better, I'll give you the facts.

"You've suffered a linear fracture of the left cheekbone, and a dislocated jaw. You took the brunt of the pitch high up near your temple, and the tremendous concussion is what caused your eyes to slam shut." He paused for a moment, and Tony sensed they were now getting to the part that he wouldn't like.

"As both your doctor and your friend, I'm going to be completely honest with you. Even after your eye opens, it will be weeks before we can examine the damage that's been done inside. What does that mean? It means I can't even begin to tell you what's happened inside your eye or your head. The best I can do is speculate; and I would rather not do that. The other thing is that we have no idea when you'll be able to play again, if ever. I wish I had better news."

He appreciated Tierney's honesty, but not his prognosis. "But this is still August. We've got six weeks before the season ends. I'll be back before then, right?"

"I can't say what's going to happen, Tony. All I can tell you is how things stand right now."

"Doc, we're in a pennant race. I don't want to listen to it on the radio. Doing that would make me crazy. I want to jump back in and do my part. I mean, we're looking at maybe going to the World Series this year."

This was the part of Tierney's profession that he'd wished was someone else's responsibility. Not that he couldn't handle it; it was just something he found difficult from an emotional standpoint. Occasionally, things happened that altered people's lives, and some of those people were friends. Others were people to whom his heart went out. In this case, it was both. "Have you tried to watch television, Tony?"

"Yes," Tony answered, quietly.

"And what happened?"

"I have to keep looking away."

"Why?"

"Because the light's too bright, and I can't see it clearly anyhow."

"That's my point," Tierney continued. "Imagine what it would be like out there on the field, looking up into the lights to catch a fly ball, or standing at home plate, trying to pick up a ball coming at you at ninety miles an hour. What's worse is that it doesn't matter if it's nightlight or sunlight, the result would be the same. You'd be at the mercy of your condition, and would be putting yourself at risk. I simply can't clear you; it would be impossible. It will be at least four to six weeks, and even then I can't say for sure."

"No way, that's crazy! I'll be back in the lineup in ten days, just as soon as the eye opens. I'll be able to come back and play, you'll see."

"I think it's time we do something you haven't done yet," Tierney said. Hoping to delay this, his voice was weighted with quiet resignation. "It's time for you to come face to face with your condition."

He picked up a hand held mirror, and looked at Tony. Tony found this sobering. It had never occurred to him to actually look at himself. Until now, coming back had been an issue of desire, not reality. The prospect of doing so was frightening. "Is it that bad?" he asked.

Tierney held the mirror up in front of him, and he took his first look at what had actually happened to him. Blurred vision or not, he saw the reality of his condition, and it devastated him. His left eye was black and purple, and was about the size of a handball. When he leaned close, he could actually make out the imprint of the stitches where the ball had hit him. The pattern, though days old, was distinct and unmistakable. He also saw that his face had become drawn and pale, and emaciated. Nor had he shaved since the night he'd been hit. All together, it sickened him.

"I look like I'm starving," he said. "What the hell happened to me?" This was disheartening beyond anything he could have imagined.

"Because of your dislocated jaw," Tierney continued, "we've not been able to give you solid food. And because you can't chew we've been forced to feed you through a straw. And I have to be honest; it's going to be like that for quite a while. You're a long way from returning to your old self. For now you'll just have to be patient."

****

Time dragged in the hospital. By the end of the first week the vision in his right eye had returned to almost normal and his left eye had opened slightly. Even so, he still felt as if he were in a dark room most of the time. Being cooped up was beginning to irritate him, and he was growing restless. He continually wondered how long it would take before his sight returned to normal. He'd just found out that the Red Sox had put him on the twenty-one day disabled list, which meant he'd not be eligible to play for at least three weeks. That meant he'd be out until September 9th, which was half of the rest of the season. It occurred to him that coming back before the end of the season was in serious jeopardy. Moreover, the Red Sox would have to replace him while he was out. Rumor had several names in the mix, and the team would have to act quickly. It didn't feel right, having someone else play a position that he'd been playing for the past four years, and which he felt belonged to him. He didn't resent it on a personal level; it bothered him because it reinforced the gravity of his dilemma, and how little there was he could do about it.

He'd heard that Ken Harrelson might be taking his place in right field. The move in itself was smart; Harrelson could hit, and he was adequate for the position. What bothered him most was that the Red Sox were in the midst of a pennant chase, in this, the most exciting season they'd had in two decades. He felt cheated and angry at not being a part of it. His grievances, and whom he liked or didn't like, seemed light years away. Everyone was part of the same team, all in it together, and it should have been a great experience. The team had youth and spirit and desire, and it was great to be a part of that. It had been a joy going to work every day; he even enjoyed having the writers around because they'd been machine-gunning him with questions about the Sox' pennant chances and how he might contribute. Every game was big, and the players were too excited to be tired.

He wanted to get back to all that, but every time he asked Tierney when his eye would clear up he would always tell him the same thing. "It takes time, Tony. Right now, I really don't know."

- Chapter Twenty-Seven -

Home in her apartment, Julie answered on the second ring. "Hello," she said, curious as to who would call after eleven o'clock at night. For her this was late, and very few phone calls of a happy nature came late at night.

"Hello, yourself," came the voice on the other end of the line.

"Kenny?" she answered, surprised to hear his voice this late. He knew better. After their initial meeting in New York, he'd wanted to date her, but she hadn't been up for it. If for no other reason it wasn't practical; they lived too far apart. And now, after being reassigned to Boston, it was even farther. Nevertheless, they had maintained their friendship since first meeting at Mister Laff's. "Is everything all right?"

"It's better than all right," he said. She could hear the excitement in his voice. "I've just been traded to the Red Sox. I'm their new right fielder."

"You're taking Tony's place?" she asked, stunned.

"Yep, they just picked me up from Kansas City. I was given my outright release after getting into a beef with Charlie Finley, the team owner. Just got the word tonight, I'm coming to Boston. I'll call you once I'm settled in."

****

When all he could do was lie in bed and think, he did exactly that. And something had begun creeping into his mind, gnawing at him. Many of the players, Rico, Mike Ryan, George Scott, Yaz and others had come to visit him. Some had sent flowers; others had called. But there was one person who had been conspicuously absent, and that had been manager Dick Williams. They'd never been on the best of terms, and had banged heads on many occasions. Their problems had begun in 1964, when he'd been a rookie trying to break into the club, and Williams had been a veteran trying to hang on to his job. He hadn't liked the way Williams had talked behind Pesky's back, saying how differently he'd have done things if he'd been running the club. Hell, they'd even swapped bean-balls. But this was different; this felt personal. Tony had done his job well. He played ball and didn't cause more problems than anyone else. He was cocky perhaps, but he had made sure he contributed his share to the team effort, and had given them everything he had. Now that he'd been hit in the face and had almost lost his life, he felt the least Williams could do was acknowledge what had happened. But he hadn't. Now time was running out, and so was the season.

****

He hadn't wanted to make a dramatic exit when he left the hospital. He'd asked them to please not notify anyone of the exact day and time. They did their best, but there were four photographers waiting outside when the time had come. Sal helped him to the car, partly because Tony's legs had become weak from lack of exercise; partly because he'd lost much of his strength, and his eyes were so sensitive to light that the sun literally blinded him. He needed someone to guide him.

Fortunately, Tom Yawkey had kept his word and the Red Sox had paid all his medical bills. That had cemented his belief that he was playing for the greatest owner and organization in all of baseball. They had always shown that they cared about him, the only departure from that being perhaps when they'd gone back and forth during contract negotiations, and that had been nothing more than business.

Just before he'd left, Dr. Francis Gregory, a smallish, kindly man who was the hospital's resident ophthalmologist, had stopped in to see him. "I'm going to run some tests before you leave, my boy, and we'll see how you're coming along." Later when he'd returned, he'd given Tony the news. "You've got 20/80 vision, which isn't too bad considering how recently you've been hit. If it's all right with you, I'd like to run some more tests before you go home."

"I've got to get away from here," Tony said. "This place is driving me crazy. I want some time away for awhile, then I'll come back."

"Okay my boy, no harm done, I suppose. When you return call me, and we'll schedule an appointment."

He'd then thanked the doctor, grabbed his things, and with his parents guiding him, had headed for the door.

****

Donna Heath, the teenage girl who had magically secured Tony's autograph at Fenway earlier that year, stared out the window, her eyes glazing over. It was seventh period, the end of a long school day, and a long week. She barely heard the voice of Mr. Robinson, her History teacher as he droned through his lesson. What did he know about life's *really* important things, she asked herself. He couldn't even wear the same color socks to school. Today it was a green sock and a blue one. She bet he had another pair just like them at home. Didn't his mother teach him about dressing in the dark?

The dark: how ironic. Her musings had begun when her mind drifted back to the day their school band had taken that field trip to Fenway Park. She and Carol Montanari had bought programs. Not that they'd needed them; they knew the lineups forward and backward. By now Carol had fallen head-over-heels in love with Mike Ryan, just as she had with Tony. And it wasn't long before Carol had gotten caught up in the frenzy, just like everyone else in Boston. Carol had put together a scrapbook on Mike similar to the one she had on Tony. Each contained volumes on both players; news clippings, photos and memorabilia. They had cut out articles on all the games. And whereas Carol loved Mike and she loved Tony, there would be no disputes over who would get which player. Though she was only fourteen, Tony was only eight years older than her, and she hoped he'd wait for her to grow up. Then she and Tony and Carol and Mike could have a double wedding. How cool! All Mike and Tony had to do was discover them, and then decide who they would invite to the wedding. It was great to dream, and to have heroes; it was great for young girls to fantasize and be in love.

At the game they had gotten seats close to Tony. Twice they had a gaggle of girls, all of whom were deeply in love with Tony – though not as deeply as she was, of course-- count to three, and yell, *"Tony, we love you!!"* He'd looked over at them, waved and shook his head. She'd clutched the program to her chest, as if to say '*Be still, my heart!*' Indeed, that was the day she'd fallen in love with Anthony Richard Conigliaro, just before they'd stolen that special moment when he'd autographed her program. She'd had it framed, where it now hung in reverence right over her bed.

The summer had gone on, game after game. The Red Sox were going to do it, she just knew. And then she'd heard it while listening to the game that night on her little transistor radio. Tony had been hit in the head by a pitch, and was seriously hurt. She'd gone out the next day and bought newspapers from all the surrounding towns. Her knight had been struck down, and she had to know the truth about his injury. Exactly how bad was it? Would he ever play again? Then she'd seen the pictures of his swollen, blackened face. She worried so much about him, especially now that it appeared the Red Sox might make it to the World Series. But it wouldn't be the same without him, and word was that his injuries were more serious than first believed; they didn't know when he'd return. Her heart was breaking for him. Later, she'd seen a picture of him alone in the locker room, his head in his hands. God only knew what he must be going through. He'd been such a large part of the team's success, and she wanted so much for him to know that he was still her hero.

- Chapter Twenty-Eight -

Shortly after his release from the hospital, he had quietly spent the next twelve days at Grossinger's, a year-round resort in New York's Catskill Mountains. He'd chosen it because it was far removed from the crush of inquiries he'd been getting since his release from the hospital, especially those from the press. Grossinger's was also known for its younger crowd, especially the girls. The food was great and he'd taken advantage of it to gain back the weight he'd lost in the hospital. But food and girls weren't his top priority at the moment, although he wouldn't have minded having Julie to talk to. It had always been something he'd loved about their relationship; he'd been able to talk to her about anything, completely open and at ease. Now his only concern was getting well again. Initially, he'd sensed his sight was getting better, but when he'd sit alone outside, testing the vision in his left eye, he realized his progress was almost negligible. It was frustrating, especially as the team continued to play great baseball and was winning some really exciting games, many of which they'd pulled out late, or in extra innings. Boston was on fire with their Red Sox, the games were sellouts, and fans and players alike were embracing it.

One night he'd tried to break the monotony by going to a nightclub, but soon had to leave because of a terrible headache brought on by all the smoke and bright lights. His eyes were still too sensitive, and he knew he wasn't ready to play. He'd forced himself not to dwell on it because every time he did his eyes would well up. He wondered if tears might help his condition. If so, he had plenty that he'd been holding in reserve. The entire experience was heartbreaking, and trying not to feel sorry for himself had required constant effort. He began to wonder if it would ever end.

He was two weeks out of the hospital after his return from New York, and had only one week left on the Disabled List. But he was soon forced to admit that his eye really hadn't improved, which gave him all the incentive he'd needed to call Dr. Gregory. Now, as he sat in Gregory's office preparing to take a basic eye test, he hoped the little doc could give him an estimated return date to start playing again.

"All right, my boy," he said, "let's see what we've got here. I want you to cover your right eye and start reading from the chart with your left."

Tony covered his eye with a small piece of cardboard, and began reading. "Well, the top line is an 'E'. And the second line is...the second line is..." After a long pause he slowly removed the paper from over his left eye, exhaled slowly, and stared down at the floor. Very softly, he said, "I don't know what the second line is because it's too blurry."

Dr. Gregory wasn't encouraged by Tony's inability to read the chart. He sat down on a stool directly in front of him and began examining him with several instruments. When he had finished, he sat back on the stool and took a deep breath. "This is not so good, my boy. Your eye has grown worse since the last time I saw you. I think we should go see my friend Charlie Regan at Retina Associates. He's equipped to do things I can't do here. The problem is in your retina, and I want him to see it."

Tony suddenly felt weak all over. His throat felt stuck and he didn't know if he could even talk. What was happening to his dream? Where had it gone? Deep down inside he knew there were problems before he'd even arrived at Gregory's office. He'd kept telling himself that it was still too soon to expect much in the way of improvement. It was to be expected. Surely it would clear up in time. But instead Gregory was telling him things had gotten worse.

"What does all this mean?" he asked. "Will it get better?"

"I can't tell you that right now," Gregory said. "I think you might have a bleb on your eye, or to be more precise, on your macula. That's where you get all your direct, central vision. When the ball hit your cheekbone the bone gave way. The macula is the weakest part of your eye, and I'm beginning to suspect that you have a bleb on it that's causing all your trouble."

"What's a 'bleb'?" Tony asked.

"That's slang for cyst. Call it a blister if you like. It's normal after an injury like yours. But I can't tell you any more until we've had a closer look."

The next day he met Dr. Gregory in downtown Boston at Retina Associates. They were a group of eye doctors who worked out of the Massachusetts Eye and Ear Clinic, one of the most renowned medical institutions of its kind in the country. If there was any good news to be found, it was learning that Dr. Regan was also one of the leading ophthalmologists in America. That, however, was of little comfort being passed from doctor to doctor, and none of them could tell him if he'd ever play again. He was trying not to fear the worst. He wanted to remain optimistic and remain calm, telling himself that everything would be okay despite the growing evidence that it wasn't. Staying with the team had become more difficult than making it.

When the introductions were done, Dr. Regan, a middle aged, distinguished looking man, motioned him to a special chair, and said, "Let's get on with it, shall we? I'm going to ask you to put your head back and I'll give you a local anesthetic so I can do some tests. Part of what I'm going to do is test for glaucoma, which sometimes occurs from injuries like yours." As the anesthesia was administered, Tony tried not to squirm. Having been in a multitude of doctor's offices over the years, he'd never grown comfortable in them.

Regan began his testing after the eye was numbed. Within a few minutes, he announced, "Ah, I see it now."

"See what?" Tony asked.

"The edema," he said, without looking up. "That's the swelling that resulted from the impact of the ball. It's formed by fluid, and it's a fairly common occurrence in this type of injury. I'll do a few more tests, and then we'll discuss what I find."

When it was over he sat with Dr. Regan. "You have a blind spot which was caused by the formation of a cyst. This is a byproduct of the swelling. The blind spot is on the macula, which is in the center of the retina. The macula is extremely small, and the cyst is on top of it. As small as it is, the macula is the source of your vision. It allows you to read small print and the like. Of greater interest to you, however, it allows you to see baseballs coming at you at high speed. In your case the blind spot has impaired your depth perception, and your vision is only 20/100. In layman's terms, you're almost blind in your left eye."

Tony didn't need to be an eye specialist to know that his condition was serious. "So what you're telling me is that I can't play ball." He suddenly felt empty inside and needed to be away from that place, as if getting away would somehow improve his vision. But he knew better. "Will I *ever* be able to see well enough to play again?" He was almost afraid to hear the answer.

"I don't know," Regan said. "It's possible that your eye may still be undergoing changes. It's only been four weeks since you were hit; it may still be healing. It's something we'll have to watch for a while. I'd like for you to come back next week."

Tony closed his eyes, and silently nodded in the affirmative. For the first time since it had happened he began to fear his season might already be over.

****

Tony stopped by his parents' and found Richie inside, wearing his baseball glove. Richie had begun showing even more potential than either Tony or Billy, who by now was in the Red Sox minor league system. Richie would be graduating from high school the following year, and speculation had it that he too, would likely end up in the pro's.

"Feel like going outside to try some things with me?" Tony asked.

"Are you kidding? Sure!" Though both of them were older now, Tony still held a place of high honor in Richie's life. Tony was still the star in his sky.

Outside, it was Tony's intention to find out – safely – how well he could see a thrown ball. Their yard was sizeable, so they'd be able to put some distance between them; it would also allow them to put some steam on the ball without Tony risking injury.

Right away he noticed his vision was no longer the same as it had been. Unless he concentrated hard on the ball with his right eye, he would catch it on the heel of his glove. He glanced at Richie, and saw him watching very closely. He wasn't saying anything, but Tony knew what he was thinking. How bad is it? Is there a problem?

Would he be able to play again? Other than the doctors, Tony hadn't said much about his condition to anyone, even his family. But one thing had remained unchanged: Richie was still the one he could be himself with and not worry about personas, or expectations. His mother had said that when Tony wasn't home, Richie was hard to find; when he was, one had only to look for Tony and there was Richie, too.

"Hey," Tony said, "let me try pitching a couple." In high school Tony had been a pitcher, and a good one. For a long time he'd harbored the notion that he might make it as a big league pitcher. He could throw, and unlike most other pitchers he could hit. It had already occurred to him that he might make it back as pitcher if he couldn't come back as an outfielder. Either way, he was determined to beat this thing and make it back onto the team.

Richie got a catcher's mitt, and they began practicing. Once again, Tony noticed the difference. He could still fire the ball for a strike, but when Richie tossed it back he had trouble following it. He dropped the ball a couple of times, trying to look nonchalant, and wondered if Richie knew there was a problem. After a dozen pitches, Tony decided to experiment with his other area of concern: hitting.

"Let's try some pepper," he said, picking up a bat. Richie pitched to him, and Tony would softly hit it back. Or try to. He was able to get his bat on the ball most of the time, but on several occasions he missed. For the average person this might not have been a big deal; for Tony, it was. He'd never missed hitting a ball playing pepper in his life. He'd missed it now, and he knew why.

"Okay, that's enough." He found it extremely discouraging. His vision simply wasn't up to it, and if things didn't start looking up pretty soon, it was beginning to look like he could kiss this season good-bye, World Series, or not.

- Chapter Twenty-Nine -

Although his apartment was within walking distance of the ballpark, he'd been staying away from it. He couldn't stand the thought of being there without being able to play. But it had been over a month now, and he felt it was time to reconcile the situation. It wasn't a case of being afraid or ashamed; it was a case of being able to cope.

When he walked in, everything had looked the same. The guys were in the locker room, preparing for batting practice prior to that night's game. At first they paused for the slightest instant, then all of a sudden they were all over him, welcoming him back. He found it both warm and uplifting. Yaz, Reggie Smith, George Scott, Mike Ryan.

"Hey, kid," said Rico, "You look great. How are you?"

"How you doing, roomie?" asked Mike Ryan. "Come down to give the troops a pep talk?" It was good to see them. They'd sent flowers and cards; they'd called and shown they cared. He hadn't been forgotten. Mike Ryan, having been barred from visiting him like everyone else, had climbed the hospital's fire escape and snuck in anyway. "Got a couple of babes and a case of beer in the car," he'd said. All Tony had been able to do was groan, crack the faintest of smiles, and meekly give him the finger. But even in torment, Ryan had made him smile. He was great.

"*TC!*" said George Scott, embracing him. "Gimme five, man!" They slapped palms, and broke into wide grins.

Then Tony's gaze went deadpan. Dick Williams began walking toward him from the far end of the locker room. "How do you feel?" he asked, sticking out his hand to shake. Tony's hand went out as a reflex action more than anything else. He did it because he felt obligated. He'd been raised that way.

"I'm okay," he said. But the thought that crossed his mind was, *'Where the hell were you? Why couldn't you come to the hospital at least once?'* He might have been busy with a million other things, but he could have taken time to come see him. Or written him. Or called. Tony didn't think that was expecting too much. After all, he was one of their big guns and he'd been hit on the head during a game. He could have died. Seeing Williams was proving to be the hardest part of going there so far; he reminded himself he was there to see the guys.

Ken Harrelson walked over to him. "Sorry about the eye, Tony. Hope it gets better. The team misses you."

"Yeah, me too. Just keep doing a good job, we need to win the pennant and prove all those Vegas guys wrong."

As Harrelson walked off, Tony watched everyone prepare for the day's activities. As a Red Sox player, he'd begun to feel inadequate, like an outsider. This had been home for four years; now he felt like he didn't belong. He couldn't contribute, he couldn't help them in their pennant drive; he was just a visitor. He felt all knotted up inside, and if he didn't get out of there in a hurry he felt like his insides would burst.

"Hey guys," he said, "it's great to see you. I've got a headache that comes and goes, and it feels like it's coming back. I can't stay for the game, but I'll watch you tonight on television."

He walked back to his apartment on Commonwealth Avenue. He didn't watch the game; he didn't even turn on the television. He stared at the wall, listening to the sounds of Kenmore Square ten stories below, wondering where to go from there. When it seemed he could take it no longer, he walked out onto the balcony that overlooked Kenmore Square. Down below, the streets were bustling with cars and foot traffic as people made their way to the park. He surveyed what had once been to him the most beautiful view on earth. A half-dozen clubs, Fenway Park, and the conjunction of four major thoroughfares assured there would always be an endless supply of bright lights and activity. The traffic, though heavy at times, was far enough below so as to be almost silent when the balcony's sliding door was closed. On the other hand, there was always something happening ten floors down. The pulse of Kenmore Square's endless nightlife being what it was, assured that. Being a well-known fixture with the Red Sox hadn't hurt, either.

Now all that had changed. His once cherished view of Fenway Park, its brilliant light stanchions, the roar of the crowds, and the view of his 'office' in right field had lost their luster, and were now a source of pain and frustration. Ken Harrelson had taken his place in right field during this, the greatest year in franchise history. He had been a force in that quest until Hamilton's pitch had tailed in on him and changed everything. Now all he could do was watch and long for what might have been. Moreover, not only had Harrelson taken his place in the Red Sox lineup, Tony had recently found out he had also moved in with Julie. As much as he tried telling himself that it didn't bother him, it really did. There was something just too ironic about it. It was more than natural coincidence. As painful as it had been when he'd broken off his relationship with her, he also realized she would become a free agent in the dating scene, therefore available to anyone she pleased. But Ken Harrelson, his replacement on the Red Sox? It ate at him like a festering sore. He and Julie had remained in touch with each other since their breakup three years earlier. They had even gotten together in New York a few times. He had also stayed close to her family. Even though he had no immediate plans to resume their relationship it seemed odd that his mind would wander back to her from time to time, second-guessing the prudence of his decision. He also wondered why he'd never had a long-term, meaningful relationship with anyone since then. Going out with lots of great looking women was all well and good, but it had never given him the wholeness and fulfillment that being in love and committed to someone had given him when he'd been with Julie. Of one thing he was certain: he'd have plenty of time to ponder such things now. He went back inside the apartment, slammed the balcony door and shut out the world to which he no longer felt connected.

****

A week later he went to his appointment with Dr. Regan. They ran him through series of tests, only to find that nothing had changed. His vision was still the same. When they were done, they sat down in Regan's office.

"The blind spot is still there, Tony. Nothing has changed since last week. At the same time it hasn't gotten any worse, either. You still have a good deal of swelling in there, and your distance vision is so poor it would be dangerous for you to play ball any more this year."

The next day the Red Sox announced that he was done for the year.

****

Donna Heath had been keeping close track of Tony's recovery, and then had heard the news: Tony's injuries would not allow him to return for the rest of the year. This had been hard to take. She wanted so much to see him out there in right field again, to sit near him in the grandstands, to call out and wave to him, to have him wave back at her. And now this... Would they let him get visits from teenagers? After all, he'd given her his autograph.

She wrote to the Swampscott Chamber of Commerce, requesting Tony's address. She simply had to let him know how sorry she was for what had happened, and how much she cared. She was sure a lot of other people would be writing to him, wishing him well, and hoped that maybe he'd read her letter some time and write back to her. When his address had arrived, she'd sent the letter off to him, and had even included a picture of herself, asking him if he remembered her, and the day he'd signed her program. She might hear back from him, she might not. All she really wanted was for him to know how much she cared. He'd been the focal point of her fantasy, the hero who wasn't in a movie, a book, a dream or a scam. He was the one she had seen and talked to, and it was Tony who had brought all of this to life with one simple act of kindness. He'd taken a moment to acknowledge a young and seemingly insignificant teenage stranger. He'd made her feel like a princess, and for that he'd have her undying love and loyalty.

But for now all she could do was stare out the window, and agonize. Her gladiator had been struck down, her champion had fallen; her heart was breaking, and her eyes were beginning to fill with tears...

- Chapter Thirty -

Tony stood outside on the balcony of his apartment, staring down at right field. He was situated so as to be able to see the corner of the playing field that had once been his: right field. Now Ken Harrelson was there, doing all the things he'd dreamed of doing, and couldn't because of a spontaneous fluke that had come out of nowhere. Fluke or not, it had changed his life, his present and his future. He no longer saw the game, or his part in it, as he had before. Things were different now; the dream was tarnished, perhaps mortally wounded. All he could do was watch it happen, unable to do anything about it. He was a spectator, just like the fans in the stands. He refused to feel sorry for himself, but could hardly ignore the reality of what had happened. A friend of his had once said that ten percent of life was what happened to him; the other ninety percent was how he handled it. And there on the balcony he committed that he'd handle it; if not this year, then next.

Somehow, he'd make it back.

Even though he wasn't going to play for the rest of the season he went to the ballpark whenever the team was on the road. Never when they were home, though. Doctors or no doctors, he just had to keep trying. And it always was the same; Keith Rosenfeld, the team's batboy, would throw soft, slow pitches and he'd tap them to the infield. Sometimes he'd get so disgusted he'd quit early, then jog around the outfield, telling himself that at least he was keeping his legs and cardiovascular in good condition. But his mind raced with angst. Would he ever be able to see well enough to play again? It had begun giving him that same 'driven' feeling he'd had as a boy. It was something he had to do. And encouragement hadn't totally abandoned him. When the season was down to its final few days he'd launched a couple of Keith's pitches up into the screen. For whatever reason, he'd begun to see the ball again. Granted, it was against Keith and not professional pitching, but he was seeing the ball. It gave him hope.

The team returned home the next day for its final two games of the season against the Minnesota Twins, one of the teams they were locked in mortal combat with. Once they were back he made a point of staying away from the batting cage. He'd leisurely shag fly balls in the outfield, trying to give the impression that he was staying in shape. In reality, he was staying away from the writers. Whenever they'd question him on his medical condition he'd tell them the eye was steadily improving, though he'd not be back for the remainder of the season. Even if there was more to tell them he had vowed not to. His previous experiences with the press had taught him a few things, and he wasn't anxious to give them anything they could take out of context. He didn't want management looking too closely, either.

Then he got some great news. General Manager Dick O'Connell had called him aside and told him he'd just received special permission from the Baseball Commissioner to sit on the bench for the last game of the season. He wanted to be a part of it, especially after they'd beaten the Twins the previous day on a Carl Yastrzemski homer, and were now tied with Minnesota for first place. The Tigers were still in it, but they were facing a double header with the Angels. This all came after Chicago had knocked itself out of playoff contention by dropping a doubleheader to Kansas City.

The last game of the year he'd sat on the bench and cheered until he was hoarse. The Twins had taken a 2-0 lead and it had stayed that way for five innings. Meanwhile the Tigers had taken an early lead in their first game with LA. Tension ran high at Fenway, and the crowd was hanging on every pitch. The place almost went ballistic when Boston scored five runs in the sixth. It was at that moment he just knew they'd do it. The Twins scored another run later on, but Jim Lonborg, who had already won twenty-one games for them, was looking strong and had finished the game, handing them the final win that would possibly get them to the World Series. Those who had been there said the celebrations, jubilance, sheer joy and exhilaration was like nothing they had seen since John F. Kennedy had been voted president. Some declared it was on a par with the 1946 World Series; others since the end of World War II.

By the time Boston had won their game, Detroit had taken the first game of their doubleheader and now needed to win the second game to knock Boston out. In the clubhouse as in all of New England, players and fans were glued to their radios and televisions, waiting to see what happened between Detroit and LA. If Detroit won...

But they didn't. Los Angeles took the second game of the doubleheader and the Red Sox were going to the World Series. The Red Sox had grabbed the brass ring, and Boston's Impossible Dream was in the books.

****

The thrill of winning the American league pennant was the capstone on Boston's pyramid of dreams, but it soon turned bittersweet for Tony. What normally would have been the chance of lifetime, of stepping into the ultimate pressure cooker would now be a spectator event for him. He couldn't play; he could only watch. Though once again given permission to dress for the game he could only force himself to be enthusiastic. He was happy for the fans, the team, and management, but his personal sense of loss was unbearable. Several times he wanted to go back to the locker room, change, and leave the park midway through the game. The ultimate dream had become the ultimate disappointment. At one point he even thought he saw Julie in the stands where the players' seats are reserved. Try as he might, being there was insufferable. Ken Harrelson batted only .077, and his alternate Jose Tartabull, hadn't done much better. When the Red Sox had finally gone down to defeat in seven games he watched Carl Yastrzemski during a post-game interview.

"Do you think it might have gone better if you'd have had Tony Conigliaro's bat in the lineup?" the announcer asked him.

"If he'd have been available," Yaz said, "we'd have won it."

Moments later, George Scott had said the same thing. "Ain't no doubt in my mind, they'd be poppin' corks over here, not over there."

Later on Tony had heard that Bob Gibson, who had won games one, four, and seven was asked the same question and had said, "I don't know how the Series would have turned out, but it wouldn't have changed games one, four or seven." Angered upon hearing that, he hoped that if he did make it back, he'd get a chance to face Gibson. He'd hit against him in spring training, and if he got to hit against him again, he'd make him eat his words.

****

The off-season had been another succession of disappointments. The doctors offered nothing encouraging; people constantly reminded him of his eye injury simply by asking about it. He managed to stay in great physical condition, training as if there was no eye injury. But there always came a point where all the conditioning in the world couldn't overcome the uncertainty of whether or not he could play again. In time he began functioning on blind faith and little more.

Then he was invited to go to Viet Nam to visit the troops with Pete Rose, Joe DiMaggio, Jerry Coleman, and Bob Fishel of the Yankees' front office. He'd accepted, and it turned into one of the most humbling, spiritual learning experiences of his life. They'd landed in Saigon and stayed in Viet Nam for two weeks. He also had discovered there was no such thing as a soft, gradual landing. Whenever they landed he was certain they were going to crash, but they hadn't. He had asked why it was necessary to put everyone through an ordeal like that and was told it was necessary to minimize getting shot down by enemy fire. Suddenly the war on television became the war outside the window, and he quickly developed a greater appreciation for the sacrifices people were making by being there.

They traveled to different bases and hospitals doing what they could to raise peoples' spirits. In doing so, Tony had gotten to see many of the places he'd heard about in the news, and they were different than what he'd perceived. These were real people, suffering real hardships, losing real family members and living with the real and constant threat of death. As bad as his beaning had been, this was much worse. Something could drop down from the sky, burst from the bushes or explode beneath his feet at any given moment. He himself would only be there for a couple of weeks; those who lived there had to endure that ordeal day in and day out. This was their life. It brought back memories of the best friend he'd had during his entire childhood: Freddie Atkinson. He'd loved Freddie, and they'd been inseparable. In 1964 Freddie had joined the military and shipped off to Viet Nam. As they were saying goodbye he'd had the unsettling feeling that they were saying goodbye for the last time. Then Freddie had become one of the first casualties in Viet Nam, and when Tony heard about it he had ached so badly that he'd curled up on the floor in physical pain. Until then nothing in his life had hurt like that. Now, actually being there, he realized what Freddie had sacrificed by putting himself in harm's way for something he believed in. The thought of Freddie's passing still brought tears to his eyes.

He was also amazed by all the troops who knew who he was and had heard about him being hit. Most amazing of all, however, were the people who had lost arms and legs, whose bodies had been maimed and ripped apart by mines, shrapnel and mortar fire, yet were more interested in how his eye was healing than in their own wounds. It had really put things into proper perspective for him.

****

The trip had been a success, and one of the first things he'd done upon returning had been to check with the doctors. After being subjected to the usual tests, the news this time was different.

"It seems the inner wall on the macula has broken," Dr. Regan began. "So as not to confuse you, it doesn't mean that the eye has grown worse. In fact I can see no further deterioration and the eye seems to have stabilized. Your vision has improved to 20/50, same as last time, but the fact that the outer wall of the cyst is holding is a sign that things have grown no worse. We may have reached a turning point."

Tony asked the only question that mattered to him. "Does it mean I can play?"

"You'll have to find that out for yourself. Your eye still isn't normal, but it has stabilized and doesn't appear it will degenerate. I can't tell if you'll have more difficulty catching the ball or hitting it. Go out and play pepper, play catch, and see how it goes. You won't know until you try it. Even then *you'll* be the only one who can tell whether you're ready or not."

"You know I'm going to try it," he said. "I have to."

He left Regan's office and went out to the street. There had never been a time when he'd been afraid to close his right eye to see what the left eye could see. When he looked out of the left eye things looked fuzzy; when he looked slightly to the side of objects, he could see them. Tests or no tests, bleb or no bleb, he'd keep on trying. He had to, because without the dream there was little left in life for him to hold onto.

- Chapter Thirty-One -

<u>Two Months Later</u>

Christmas brought with it one of the coldest, most bitter winters in recent memory. But even in the dead of winter baseball was still his passion. As far as he was concerned, there were only two seasons; the seasons you trained and played, and the seasons you trained and trained.

Down in his basement, he tried to not let the frigid air bother him. Then he heard footsteps at the top of the staircase. "Tony?" came the tentative voice. "Tony, you down there?"

"Sure, come on down." He paused to watch his brother, Richie, fourteen now, make his way down to the cellar. He often wondered who was more the other's hero, he as Richie's, or Richie as his. He knew Richie worshipped the ground he walked on, and he relished having that type of relationship with him. He saw how some of the other kids treated their younger brothers, and he couldn't understand why they did it. Anything from calling them 'squirt' to making them chase around doing menial errands for them; or beating them up and abusing them in front of their friends, so as to make themselves look like big shots. That had never happened between himself and Richie, and never would. The closest he'd come to it had been the time he had mistakenly thought Richie had stolen ten dollars from him, and had punched him over it. Having later found the money he'd misplaced, and having realized the injustice he'd inflicted on him, he had wanted to cut off the hand he'd hit him with. After calling him aside and apologizing, he swore to himself that would never happen again. Besides, how could he play baseball with only one hand?

"Are you crazy, or what?" Richie asked, taking a seat several steps from the bottom of the stairs.

"No, why?" Tony asked, amused.

"It's December, and it's freezing down here."

"Hey," Tony reminded him, "there's no off-season for trying to make a comeback at something you want to do for the rest of your life. People who are out there taking the winter off? While they're having good times in the snow, I'm down here in the cellar, working hard to get ready for next year even though it's still months away. Know why? Self-confidence, that's why. I always try to remember how hard I've trained every time I step to the plate. And after what happened to me, I need to do everything I can to have my body ready if my eye makes it back.

"But what if it doesn't happen? What if you work real hard and don't make it?"

"I won't allow myself to think about not making it. It's one of the mental disciplines I use on myself. Being a professional baseball player isn't as much a dream as something I know I'm going to try again some day. It's no longer a passion; it's an absolute. A week after I got those two homers off Danny Murphy he got drafted right out of high school and into the pros by the Chicago Cubs. They gave him a bonus check for a hundred thousand dollars. Me? I just want to play again, and if the chance comes I want to be prepared.

Richie always tried to envision what it must feel like to be his older brother. He wondered what it felt like to hit home runs, to have people cheering for him, to drive a car, to be strong, and to be so in love with baseball as to be willing to do all the crazy things he did to become better at it than anyone else. Maybe some day he could be like that.

"So why don't you practice someplace warm? How come you have to do it down here? It's freezing!"

Tony loved his brother's curiosity. It made him think about why he did the things he did, and kept them fresh in his mind. "Practicing down here in the cold does more than just sharpen my baseball skills; it conditions my mental toughness. The cold makes me hunker down. Got be tough between the ears, not just in the body. While I'm concentrating on developing my physical skills, I have to focus on not letting the cold air, the sting of a cold bat, sweating in freezing conditions, the ache I feel when my muscles scream, and the possibility that my eye will never be the same again get to me. I don't allow myself to think about how much time I have left down here before I'm done, or the time I already spent down here before I can go back upstairs where it's warm. I can't afford to listen to the negative part of me tell me I might be doing all this for nothing. I have to overcome the fear, the pain and the temptation to quit, and that takes discipline. Some day people are going to pay to watch me play again, and these are the dues I have to pay for that. This is what happens away from the cheering crowds, our family, the reporters, the scouts and all the other stuff that comes with fighting for something you want. Those people don't get to see this part, but you can bet your ass I'll never forget it. "Now hand me that lead bat." Richie came down the rest of the stairs and retrieved the item that had become Tony's constant companion for the past twelve years.

Richie watched with fascination, wondering if Tony knew how cool it was to be watching him. Knowing him, he probably did. He watched as Tony began his routine for the third time that day. He started swinging the bat, slowly at first. But as his body and muscles warmed to the task he began swinging with more authority. Always mindful of his technique, something that had been ingrained in him by his Uncle Vinnie, he now added force to the mix. See the invisible ball – determine it was in the strike zone – make the hardest contact possible.

He settled into his rhythm; work harder, pause, then harder still. Maintain the rhythm, and then crank it up. Let his muscles begin first to warm, then to burn. Ten, twenty, forty, fifty, seventy, ninety, and finally one hundred times. This would be the third time that day. Now there were only two hundred swings left. Later on he'd practice flicking the bat with his lead arm a hundred times to improve his bat speed. More screaming muscles. More agony. More bat speed. Harder hit balls. More four-hundred-fifty-foot home runs.

He took a break and drank deeply from a plastic water bottle. "Know what this is?" he asked Richie, perched on the bottom step. "This is a combination of fruit juices, spring water, and special minerals. I take it because I have to replace the things my body burns off as I work out. That way I don't get tired so easy. It helps with stamina. Got to have stamina if you're going to compete against the best."

Taking a deep breath, he eyed the item that would bring the next round of calculated torment. An eighteen-inch length of wood connected to two ten-pound weights suspended by a five-foot length of rope. He pictured it in his mind, preparing himself for the excruciation that was sure to follow. He extended his arms before him as Richie watched intently, mystified by these unusual things he was witnessing. No wonder Tony's home runs had gone out of sight.

Tony then began the torturous process of wringing the eighteen inch length of wood, which would then wind the rope around it, pulling the two ten-pound weights up to shoulder level. He would then slowly reverse the process, feeling the muscles in his forearms contract and burn as the weights made their slow, agonized journey back toward the floor.

"This is to make my hands and wrists and forearms real strong. It helps me get the bat around quicker, and it helps me hit the ball harder. And it makes it almost impossible for them to strike me out as long as I swing at pitches that are in the strike zone. This is what makes great hitters great, and it's going to happen again some day." He continued on until he'd completed the set of repetitions, then put the tortuous device back on the floor.

"See what I mean? Look at that." He made a fist and his forearms leaped up like corded steel, his hands looking like vice grips. "That's from doing all this stuff again and again while everyone else is taking the winter off."

Richie looked at him and, almost frightened by his brother's compulsion that he asked the only question that seemed to make sense. "Please don't get mad, Tony, but are you nuts?"

Tony breathed deeply. "No, I just need to do this."

"How long you going to do it?"

"I'm going to do it until I'm back in Fenway Park, and people are paying to watch me play baseball again. I just wish there were things I could do like this that would make my eye get better."

He took a final sip from the bottle, breathed deeply, then reached for the eighteen inch length of wood...

- Chapter Thirty-Two -

The Season Of '68

When spring training finally rolled around, it had an ethereal feel to it. He'd asked the Red Sox for the chance to begin practicing with them and – with medical clearance – he'd been given the chance. In some ways he felt ready, in others he didn't. This was a challenge of a different type. He'd always felt confident in himself and his physical abilities, but privately the shadow of doubt hung over him. He fought off the feeling of inadequacy, not allowing himself to give in to it. His teammates had been welcoming and gracious, and it was comforting to see their response to his return.

Even Dick Williams did his part. Calling him aside, he said, "You're on your own this spring. Train at your own pace. You can do anything you want; I won't push you. When you feel ready to play let me know. If there are pitchers who are going to give you trouble we'll just keep you out of the lineup. Everything's up to you this spring." Tony was surprised that was all he'd said; maybe it was the closest thing to an acknowledgement he was capable of. Maybe that's the most he should have expected. Some people were like that. Still, it rankled. He would like to have some sort of acknowledgment beyond being told he could return at his own pace.

Even so, it had been difficult. He constantly felt as though there were a hundred sets of eyes on him. His father and Vinnie joined him, and every time he got a hit they expounded on how good he looked. He knew they meant well, but the pressure was getting oppressive. His family, the press, and his teammates were watching his every move. He was living under a microscope, when all he really wanted was some privacy to work things out on his own.

Dick Williams was watching him in the batting cage one day as he lined a shot over the fence for a home run. Later, Tony had heard him tell several writers, "He's doing all right. I have a hunch he's going to have a big year."

Then it came time to face live pitching. First it was teammate Dick Ellsworth, and then Bill Landis. Ellsworth had done little more than try to get the ball over the plate so Tony had a reasonable chance to make contact. There had been none of the trademark big league steam and brush-back pitches that separated them from the minors. No one wanted to take the chance of him not being able to get out of the way of a scorching inside fastball. After only five pitches he had sent one over the fence. Landis, a lefty, had served up something a bit more challenging and he'd sent one of them outside the park, too. It felt great watching the ball fade from view.

Although he could see the ball, it still wasn't the same as before. He couldn't pick it up as he once had, and really had to concentrate on it from the instant it left the pitcher's hand. It would blur up as it got closer, and he would have to swing at it just before he lost sight of it. It almost felt like guess work. His progress was slow, and his reservations were many.

One day he'd been sitting in front of his locker when several sports writers joined him and began asking questions. One of them had asked, "Tony, what would you do if you thought someone was deliberately throwing at you?"

The answer had leaped from his mouth impulsively. "I'd go out to the mound with a bat and bang him in the head with it!" When the quote had reached the paper it wasn't the same as he'd made it. It had read, "If any pitcher tries to brush me back with an inside pitch I'm going to go out to the mound and break my bat over his head." The rearrangement of the quote had angered him; moreover, it had set up a situation that occurred in their first exhibition game.

He'd told Williams that he felt ready, and Williams had put him in the lineup. They were playing the White Sox that day and their ace Tommy John was on the mound. His first pitch put Tony flat on his back in the dirt, and he was sure the pitch would have hit him in the head if he hadn't gotten out of the way in time. He promised to never forget John for that, nor would he forget the writer who had misquoted him. Later in that same game he'd been plunked in the ribs by pitcher Don McMahon. That was how he'd spent his first day back in baseball. Fortunately, they were the only two pitchers who tried to knock him down for the remainder of spring training.

****

His problems weren't over just because no one else had thrown at him, and he knew it. He still had to play well, and to make it back to peak form. He was out having dinner one night with close friend and teammate Rico Petrocelli, and he was in bright spirits.

"I think I'm going to make it back," he began. "I think my skills are almost there, my swing is almost back to what it was. I think I can do it."

"I know," Rico said. "And I think you're right. You're looking good. You'll hit one out and you'll be feeling like your old self again."

Tony had believed it, even though he still wasn't seeing the ball as well as before. But after two weeks in spring training he felt ready to start the season.

His problem, however, was that during the remaining two weeks before the season began he sensed his damaged eye had begun to decline. He started against the Cardinals in St. Petersburg, and had a really bad game, which had included striking out twice. He was no longer seeing the ball by the time it reached home plate. In the ninth inning he had hit a double and was pulled in favor of a pinch runner. People had cheered. He would have felt much better had he not known it was a lucky hit. He had guessed the approximate location of the ball when he hit it. It had been by accident. If it had been an inside pitch meant to brush him back from the plate it could have killed him because he never saw it. As time went on, other pitchers around the league were making him look bad. Most of the time their pitches were strikes, but he was missing the ball by more than a foot; he was often swinging late on the ball. It was frustrating not being able to make contact. Williams was giving him a lot of extra batting practice and all it did was further expose the problem. The crowning blow came against Jim Bouton of the Yankees, when he had struck out four times.

The next day he simply couldn't take it any more. After a sleepless night of restless anguish, he tried to buy some time and called in.

Trainer Buddy LeRoux answered. "Buddy, it's me, Tony. Is Williams there? I can't make it in today. I got a sore throat that's killing me." He'd listened to LeRoux pass the message to Williams, and had heard Williams' comment.

"Tell him if he stayed out of nightclubs he'd be a pretty good ballplayer."

"Put him on the phone, Buddy!" came his enraged response. "I'm so sick of this with him!" To Tony, this was the epitome of indifference on Williams' part. He hadn't come to the hospital, hadn't written or called, and now he was blaming a non-existent nightlife for his failure to perform. It re-opened their unhappy history, and this time he wasn't going to stand for it.

"Tell him I don't want to speak with him," came Williams' directive to LeRoux. "Tell him we made it without him last year and we'll do it again this year."

"Put him on the phone!" Tony screamed. "Put him on, or I'll come down there and pound him!"

LeRoux remained cool. He had suddenly found himself in the middle of something he wanted no part of, and loathed to make it worse. "Stay where you are, I'm coming over."

LeRoux's words hadn't even registered. Tony slammed the phone down, showered and began getting dressed. He was going to the ballpark and he was going to straighten Williams out once and for all...for *a lot of things*. As he was about to walk out the door, there came a knock.

He opened it and was surprised to see Buddy LeRoux. "Calm down," he said, easing him back into the room. "If you go over there right now you'll only make things worse." Then, holding out a bottle, he said, "Here, take some of this. It'll do your throat good."

"Buddy, it's not my throat. Don't you understand? I can't see!"

He paused for a moment, appearing to deliberate. Finally, he said, "I have to let them know about this."

"I know," Tony said, surrendering to the inevitable. "I think it should be Dick O'Connell."

"You're right," he said, sadly. "I'll take care of it."

The next day he headed back to Boston after their exhibition game with the Braves, during which he had struck out his last time up. It was a grim period. He had hoped that seven months off and lots of rest would heal his vision, and that he could resume his career. After the game Yaz noticed something was awry.

"What is it? What's wrong?"

Knowing he was about to head back home, Tony could hardly talk. "It's no good, Carl. My eye... I'm going back to Boston to have it checked." Yaz had shaken his head; there was nothing he could say. Tears had begun streaming down Tony's cheeks, and to no one in particular, he said, "It's over, my whole career is gone. I don't need the doctors to tell me what I already know."

****

Back home the doctors did their tests, and the results confirmed what Tony already knew. He'd overheard Dr. Tierney tell his father, "We're sorry, Sal. He can't see well enough to play, he's all done."

His father had called Dick O'Connell, and it had been a long ride home. He'd spent the rest of the day in his room, gathering himself and his resolve. Somehow he'd continue, but he'd need time alone. Later that day, family attorney and friend Joseph Tauro had come by and helped him draft his farewell address to professional baseball, the fans and to the team. Two days later it was in all the papers.

"There are those that tell me I've had a tough break, and I guess I have. But despite it all, I'm still a lucky guy. I've had an opportunity to realize my lifetime ambition to be a big league ballplayer, and to play with the greatest bunch of guys in the world.

Most important, I've been blessed with a wonderful family and great friends who have stuck with me during good days and bad. This is one of the bad days, and I can't begin to explain how much it means to have the prayers and good wishes of so many good people.

This is what is important to me, and I want all these friends to know that I'm not going to quit and that somehow, some way, there will be good days again."

Soon the whole country knew he was through. The phone rang constantly, but his mother told everyone that he was in no condition to talk to anyone. He stayed in his room, ate in silence and watched television.

The first weekend had been miserable. He watched television and saw sports reports from spring training, showing old clips of him playing. They showed his first at bat on Opening Day, with its magical, one-pitch home run. They showed him making several circus catches in right field, they showed him being congratulated at home plate by his teammates after hitting game winning home runs, they showed highlights of the 1967 season. And, without fail, they repeatedly showed the tape of the night he'd been hit.

His father sat in quiet anguish, his mother wept, and all he could do was dream of what might have been.

It was going to be a long, hot summer.

- Chapter Thirty-Three -

After a few weeks of licking his wounds he began to sift through the things in life that were still available to him. He could work out, which he did; he could spend time down on Cape Cod, which he did; and he could spend time with his family, which he did. He also began dating and easing back into the club scene. Though clubs were fun, he had to ration the number of times he went there so it wouldn't lose its affect. They were a great place to meet single women, to relax, and to enjoy the company of his friends. Earlier in the night he had been out 'vulturing' with several of them. 'Vulturing' was the term they jokingly used in reference to prowling for ladies.

Ultimately, they had found their way to *Lucifer's*, one of the clubs directly below his apartment. The ranks of his fair weather friends and hangers-on had thinned out dramatically since his retirement, which had been both enlightening and disappointing. It saddened him to see how many of them had been there just for the ride. In the end he decided it was better to know than not, and he'd gotten over it. At least the friends he had now were real.

As was the plan, they had met three lovely young women, one of whom had taken a particular interest in him, and with whom he had spent a lot of time dancing. Earlier, there had been plenty of room and a friendly, uncongested atmosphere. But as the night progressed, the place had become crowded and smoky, and was also getting loud and tedious.

Leaning closer to Paula Hines, the woman he'd been dancing with, he said, "I don't know about you, but the smoke in here is starting to bother me. How about if we grab the others and go somewhere else?"

She smiled and winked. "That's fine with me. Let me ask my friends what they want to do."

Five minutes later he tipped the doorman on his way out. The man nodded, pocketed the tip, and looked up into the night, motioning upward with his thumb. "The usual?"

"I think so," Tony answered, with a knowing smile. Living upstairs from Boston's hottest nightclub complex had a lot of advantages.

He breathed deeply as they stepped out into the fresh night air. Cool and crisp, and lacking the stuffiness of the crowded club was a relief. "This is more like it."

"Where do you feel like going?" Paula asked.

Tony looked up at the night sky. "How about up there?" he asked.

"Up where?"

"Up there," he repeated.

One of the women, an attractive brunette with an hourglass figure asked "What's up there?" She looked as though she wouldn't have minded being with him herself.

"It's called The Jungle in Apartment 10-D," he answered.

"What's so special about that?" Paula asked, now becoming amused. "Tell me there's something special there."

"There will be as soon as we get there," he said, draping his arm around her. "Actually, it's where I live. Guy's got to have a place close to where he works. That way I can walk."

"What if it rains?" asked the third woman, a shapely blonde who was almost six feet tall.

"Hey, if it rains I don't go to work, that's all."

"Where do you work?" she asked.

"Over there," he said, nodding toward Fenway Park without being specific.

"Wish I had a job like that," she said, locking arms with Jimmy, the man who had now become her date. They fell in stride behind Tony and Paula.

"Come on, I think you'll like it."

Five minutes later they walked into the apartment.

"Wow!" said Paula. "It's like a museum." And in a manner of speaking, it was. Tony and his roommate, Anthony Athanas, the son of one of Boston's foremost restaurateurs, had gone on an African safari to get away from the madness of inquiring reporters, city life, and the desire to simply get away. While there they had bagged several prized game which, after the meat had been eaten, had been stuffed as trophies and shipped back to Boston. Now those trophies were mounted on the walls, as were numerous other artifacts and souvenirs. Shields and spears, hanging beads, headdresses, mats and blankets were everywhere, giving the place a very pronounced African look. Tony had loved the trip, and never regretted it.

"Know where the rest of those animals are?" he asked.

"No, where?" asked the tall blond.

"Their asses are all sticking out of the wall in my roommate's bedroom, right over his bed." Everyone laughed. "Every once in a while he has to change his pillow case."

"Got anything to drink?" the brunette asked.

"I think so," Tony said, going behind a wet bar and pulling out a tray of bottled liquor. He then opened the freezer and pulled out a couple trays of ice. Next he opened the refrigerator and produced a couple six packs of beer. He wasn't a drinker, and never really had been, something for which he'd been grateful. Alcohol could affect some people easier than others, and he preferred not to find out if he was one of those people.

"This ought to be enough to get us started," he said, reaching for a supply of cups and coasters. "Jimmy, turn on the stereo, get the music going. We'll make a night of it."

****

Downstairs at *Lucifer's*, Eddie Barberra, a young man of about thirty entered the club and started looking around as if searching from someone. After several fruitless minutes he went back to the doorman. "Hey, you didn't see three real nice looking girls in here tonight, did you? A couple of blondes, and a great looking brunette? One of the blondes is about six feet tall; looks like some kind of Amazon chick; the others look like a couple of centerfolds. I was supposed to meet them, but got hung up."

The man was a little on the hard side, but didn't seem overly imposing. He was well dressed, hip, and looked like he came from deep inside the music scene, maybe a promoter or record exec. His long wiry frame was adorned with leather, a conch belt, silver studded cowboy boots, and long hair that was in a ponytail and well kept. The doorman took everything into account and decided the guy was probably all right.

"They're upstairs," he said, motioning with his thumb.

"Upstairs? Upstairs where?"

"At Tony C's place."

"Tony C? From the Red Sox?"

"That's him."

"Man, they were supposed to wait until I got here. Where is it?"

"Tenth floor, apartment D."

The man reached in his shirt pocket and pulled out a hundred dollar bill. "This is yours, my man. Not just for the info, but to keep it off the record. Cool?"

"Yeah, sure," the doorman said, suddenly wondering if he'd made a mistake by giving out Tony's information. He paused for a moment, and then shrugged. He got his hundred bucks; if there was a problem. If there was a problem it was Tony's, not his. Let him work it out.

****

Upstairs, things were just hitting their stride when the doorbell rang. Jimmy looked at Tony, and frowned. "You expecting somebody?"

"Not really, unless the music's too loud," Tony answered. "But hey, might as well find out. Maybe some more people who want to join in."

Tony opened the door and was instantly backed into the room by Eddie Barberra. The thing that made it easy for Barberra to back Tony up was the gun he was holding.

Barberra scanned the room, then walked straight to Paula and snatched her up off the couch. "You're not his," he said. "You're mine, and I'm getting sick of this bullshit with you. Got that?"

She appeared shaken and looked panicky. "Tony, I don't know what this is about," she said. "I really don't; you have to believe me."

"He seems to know what it's about," Tony said, leveling a piercing gaze at Barberra. "What do you want, coming up here like this?"

"What do I want? I'll tell you what I want!" He strode over to Tony with the gun still in his hand. Holding it up beside Tony's head, he said, "Stay away from my old lady. And to make sure you understand how serious I am about that, I want to show you how dead you'll be if you don't."

Without warning, he fired two shots into the ceiling. In the confines of the apartment it sounded like canon fire. The explosions were deafening and Tony recoiled from them reflexively.

"Get the message, punk? You better, because if I come here again it won't be for a talk." Turning to Paula, he said, "Grab your stuff, you're coming with me."

She fearfully gathered her things and together they left. When they were gone, Tony and the others could only look at each other in bewilderment. "Who was that guy?" he asked. He'd never seen him before, and was barely more than a casual acquaintance of Paula's.

"I don't know him personally, but I know who he is," Jimmy said. "His name's Eddie Barberra, he manages rock bands. He thinks he's a major player in Boston."

"Think he's serious about coming back?" Tony asked. "This isn't exactly how I planned my night."

He pointed toward the two bullet holes in the ceiling. "Kind of looks that way, doesn't it? One thing's for sure, he's not afraid to pull the trigger."

"Write his name on a piece of paper for me. I don't need guys like him coming around here, firing guns and making threats every time I date some girl."

- Chapter Thirty-Four -

The people closest to Tony were his family. The next closest were almost family. One of those people was Jerry Maffeo. They had first met at Sonny's, a club in the Kenmore Square Complex. Jerry had grown up on the streets; he knew a few people, and he knew his way around. His life had taken him from being a dance instructor to becoming a pretty solid amateur middleweight boxer. His outward appearance gave him the look of someone who was rough around the edges and didn't apologize for it; or, as he put it, "Harvard? *Me?* Forget about it!"

Jerry had almost ten years on Tony, and it didn't matter to either of them. What Tony liked about him was his honesty and loyalty. Jerry was not a man who needed a watch to tell someone what time it was. One need not be a psychologist, a psychic or a detective to figure out what was on Jerry's mind. He spoke his piece, and wore it on his sleeve. Yet, there was no more trustworthy or dedicated friend than Jerry. He could also do something else that mattered a great deal to Tony: he could make him laugh, which was something he needed now more than ever. So when Tony entered the Sugar Shack, a soul and R&B Boston nightclub and Jerry's place of employment, it was natural the two should embrace.

"How you doing, pal?" Jerry asked, taking a quick glance at his eye. "Not yet, huh?"

"No, and maybe not for a while," Tony answered.

"Sorry to hear that. But if there's anyone who can make it back, it's you. I got faith in you."

"Thanks, Jerry. I appreciate that." He paused, and looked around for a moment. He appeared restless.

"What's going on?" Jerry asked, reading his body language. "You got that thing about you, like there's something up. What is it?"

"I don't know," Tony said, hesitantly.

"Hey, we need to have a talk or what?"

Tony nodded. "Yeah, we do."

They went to one of the back offices. The sound of the music was now little more than a thumping in the background, allowing them to think. More important, it allowed them to talk privately. "Tony, we been close for a long time, and I think I know you pretty well. I don't see you like this very often. Your eye bothering you or what?"

"My eye is always bothering me. But this is something else."

"So tell me what I can do to help."

Tony handed him a piece of paper. Jerry looked at it, read the name. "This guy causing you grief?"

"He came over to my apartment earlier tonight. He was upset because I was with a girl he likes, and he wants me to stop seeing her."

"You like this girl?"

"She's a nice person, but she's just a friend. This guy says she's his girlfriend, and he doesn't want me seeing her any more, or he'll come after me with a gun."

"He what?"

"That's what he said." Tony appeared perplexed more than anything. "I was at my place, hanging out with a few friends. We were playing music, dancing, having a couple of drinks. That's all. Next thing I know this guy shows up with a gun, and threatens me. Then he blew a couple of holes in the ceiling of my apartment. He did it right in front of everyone. Jerry, I haven't gone up against a thing like this before. I'm an athlete, not a gunfighter."

"Don't worry about it, you won't be going up against it again." He looked at the slip of paper. "Look, I've heard of this guy and know a little bit about him." He reflected for a moment as if they'd met before.

"Tell you what," he continued. "I think we can straighten this out without any problems. But I'm going to need you to come back here tomorrow night around ten o'clock. We'll take care of it then. Okay?"

"Sure. And I appreciate it."

"Forget about it, that's what friends are for."

They embraced and Tony left. All he needed was for word to get out that people were in his apartment shooting guns. He'd never make it back on the team.

****

Ken Harrelson and Julie had spent a quiet night watching television. Between her flight schedule, which took her all over the country, and his public appearances, taped interviews and game schedule since being traded to Cleveland, it was nice to have some down time to themselves. The Red Sox, having nothing near the year they had enjoyed the previous season, were grinding through a season that wouldn't get them into any post-season play. He himself was having a great year, but it would be for his personal stats, not for a shot at going back to the World Series.

They had known each other for three years now, and had been together for almost a year. Both knew Tony was aware of their relationship, and were also well aware of its irony. Ken had taken over his position in right field when he'd been injured; now he was in a relationship with Julie, his high school sweetheart. Not that he'd approved of it entirely; but he realized he had no claim to her, and was all right with that. He just felt she might have, as he put it, 'made a better choice'. For her part, she was content.

"I love playing ball," he said, "but there are times when I'd rather be home. The American League schedule is not a respecter of people. Not even me."

"Neither are flight schedules," she said. "But every now and then we get a night like tonight..." The phone rang, cutting her off. She looked at him in exasperation; he nodded begrudgingly that she should pick it up.

"Never know who it might be," he said.

"Hello?" She listened briefly, then her face clouded, and her eyes grew distant. A moment later, she passed him the phone. "It's for you, it's Jack Hamilton."

Ken took the phone from her. "Hey, Jack, how you doing? Ready to kick their ass tomorrow?" He paused for a moment, listening. Then, "You sure you want to do that?" Julie watched as he listened again. Then in closing, Ken said, "Okay, we'll do it tomorrow night after the game."

After he'd hung up the phone, Julie asked, "Is that the same Jack Hamilton I'm thinking of?"

"Yes," Ken answered.

"What does he want?

He quietly regarded her for a moment, then, "He wants me to set up a meeting between him and Tony."

****

The next night Tony was escorted down to the Sugar Shack's basement. Even though he felt secure with Jerry, there was something in the air that made him tense. He knew Jerry had friends who traveled in certain circles, and that was fine. His relationship with Jerry was about friendship, nothing else. Whatever he did on his own time was his business. All he knew was that Jerry had always been there as a friend, someone who could make him laugh until he cried. Tony had also grown up down the street from a well-known family, the Angiulo's, who received their share of scrutiny from the State and Federal Organized Crime Task Force. Jason Angiulo had been a close friend during childhood, and still was. He'd spent time with him off and on for years. Society might have had questions about what went on in the lives of these people, but Tony didn't. His involvement with them was camaraderie, nothing else. But tonight he felt something was different.

When he was led into a small room near the wine cellar, he made instant eye contact with the man who had shot the holes in his ceiling the previous night, and his intuitions were validated. It wasn't just seeing him that did it; it was seeing him strapped to a chair with duct tape. When Tony entered he thought the man would throw up.

Jerry was in the company of two large, imposing men who had stationed themselves off to one side like silent sentinels, and who likely did their talking with things other than their mouth. The man who led him there now took up a position near the door – after he closed it. Tony didn't need to be a scientist to know there was trouble brewing.

Jerry turned to Tony. "This the guy?" he asked.

Tony didn't like the tone in Jerry's voice. It sounded menacing without sounding menacing. "Yeah, that's him."

Jerry turned to Barberra. "You remember him, right? You went to his home last night and shot holes in his ceiling while you were trying to act like some kind of tough guy. How tough you feeling right now, pal?"

"Hey, I—"

"Shut up!" Turning to Tony, he said, "Go ahead, give him a slap. Let him know he made a mistake."

Things were taking a turn for the worse, and he felt powerless to stop them. Not now that they were all here. "Jerry, I don't want to give anyone a slap. I just want to make sure he doesn't come around my place any more."

"You don't want to give him a slap? You sure?"

"Of course I'm sure."

"Hey, no problem. *I'll* give him one." *Whack!* Jerry's hand came around like a ball bat, catching Barberra flush on the cheek with his palm. Barberra's head snapped to the side, his eyes watered and a huge red welt immediately formed on his face in the shape of a hand. To his credit Barberra didn't say anything, nor did he scream. He acted with the decorum of someone who knew the rules, and was committed to saving his self-respect. Even so, Maffeo didn't seem moved.

Jerry dropped to one knee beside Barberra. Barely above a whisper, he said, "You see this kid? You stay far, far away from him. Understand? We found you once; we can find you again."

Turning to Tony, he asked, "You sure? Not even a little slap?"

"Jerry, that's not what I came for."

"I hear ya. Go ahead, you can leave. I think our friend here is smart enough to know the score after this. If he isn't, we'll be getting together again."

"Thanks."

As he went upstairs and made his way through the crowd, he spotted two familiar faces at the front door. The sight of them stopped him in his tracks. Ken Harrelson and Jack Hamilton were engaged in conversation with the doorman. It was as unlikely a combination as he would have ever expected.

"We're looking for Jerry Maffeo," Harrelson was saying. "Is he around?"

"He's here, but he's busy," said the two hundred fifty pound African American doorman. "You can wait, or you can leave a message."

"I guess I'll—" seeing Tony making his way toward the door, their eyes met simultaneously. To the doorman, he said, "There's a friend of mine. Mind if I see him for a minute?"

The doorman nodded, and motioned for Harrelson to enter. "Hey, Tony, what's going on? How are you?"

"I'm okay," Tony said, gazing past Harrelson at Hamilton. "That's Jack Hamilton, right? What're you doing with him?"

"We got both got traded to Cleveland during the off-season. We're in town, and he figured maybe I'd be able to set up a meet between you and him. That's why we're here. He wants to talk to you, Tony. He still feels bad about what happened. We're here for the weekend, and all he wants to do is tell you how sorry he is for what happened."

A million things ran through Tony's mind as he stood there, looking out at Jack Hamilton. After thinking it over, and having relived that night a thousand times, he knew he'd been beaned by mistake. Anyone he'd ever spoken to about Jack Hamilton had said the same thing: no way in the world would he ever do it on purpose, especially under the conditions that existed that night. Nevertheless, it had changed his life and everything in it. He could forgive Hamilton, but he wasn't ready to sit down and discuss it with him, either.

"Let me tell you something," Tony began, trying to maintain his composure. Having the guy who was now living with his ex-girlfriend bring him to the guy who had changed his life in an instant to sit and talk wasn't something he relished. This on top of what had just taken place downstairs in the basement.

"That guy rearranged my life and every dream I ever had. And yeah, I know he didn't do it on purpose, but it still affected me the way it has. I can't expect either of you to understand what it's like walking around inside my skin, and that's okay. But sitting with you guys? I can't do it; not yet anyhow. Tell him you mentioned it to me, but I haven't reached that place where I'm willing to sit with him. Tell him I don't blame him, and I don't hate him. It's just going to take a lot more ticks on the clock before I'm ready. That's the way it has to be for now."

"Hey, it's your call, I just thought I'd ask."

Tony looked at Ken Harrelson and paused. He wasn't a bad guy, and everything he'd done was what the Red Sox had asked of him. As for the rest...

"How's Julie?" he asked.

"She's doing okay, still flying for Eastern."

"Tell her I said hello."

"Will do." They shook hands, and parted company.

- Chapter Thirty-Five -

- <u>Winter, 1968</u> -

His problem with Barberra had been solved, but there were others that remained. He, like so many other athletes who had achieved notoriety, had been paid for endorsements. These often generated income approaching the player's salary. For Tony, one of those endorsements had come from Macgregor Golf Clubs. He'd been flattered when they asked him; it was one of the many trappings that came with success, and further proved that he'd arrived. But the opposite had occurred when, after he'd foregone the 1968 season due to his injuries, Macgregor had called and told him to send back the golf bag. Now it became a stamp further confirming that his career was over, and that he'd been relegated to the status of 'average Joe'.

There had been another painful experience, which had burned him. He and Jerry Maffeo were walking through a park in Swampscott, when they came across a group of twelve and thirteen-year-old kids playing ball. He'd paused, intent on having some fun with them.

"Hey, pitch a couple to me," he said.

One of them, a twelve year old, said, "But you're Tony C. How can I pitch to you?"

"It's okay, don't worry about it."

The kid struck him out on three pitches. The kid had been thrilled, and Tony appeared to make light of it. The reality was he hadn't been able to see the ball as he should have. This further fueled his desperation. How could this be happening?

A few weeks later there had come an unexpected development. After going through yet one more battery of tests, Dr. Regan called him into his office. Tony sat across from him, holding his breath, hoping against hope. Until now, Regan had forbidden him to even jog for fear of him detaching his retina. Even so, Tony had refused to give up.

"So, what does it say?" he asked.

Regan put down the folder, and looked at him. "Well," he said, "it seems there's been a change."

"Meaning?" Tony asked. There were times when he liked drama; there times when he didn't. This was one of the latter. What hung in the balance was drama enough.

"The sight in your left eye has improved from 20/300 to 20/100."

"Why? How come?"

"I can't really say. But what I *can* tell you is this: you haven't developed a detachment from the retina, and it doesn't appear that you will. It's healing. In fact an entire healing process seems to be in the making, which is why your vision has improved."

Tony hung on Regan's every word. And then Regan said the words he thought he might never hear again.

"I see no reason why you can't begin working out again. There are no guarantees you'll make it, of course. But you're free to give it your best shot. Good luck."

The exhilaration Tony felt leaving Regan's office was akin to how he'd felt the day he had negotiated his new contract with Mike Higgins.

****

The next morning he went down to the beach and began to jog. As he did, he began formulating a plan of how best to accomplish his comeback. He'd always been a good pitcher; so that's where he'd begin. He'd train relentlessly and give himself no quarter, not compromising *anything*. He'd been given a second bite out of the apple and wasn't about to let it slip away. Whatever it took, he'd do it.

Another encouraging thing was him not being swept under the carpet by his fans, which was often the case when stars dropped out of the limelight. Despite having missed the entire '68 season, the mail sacks from well-wishers continued to flow in. His presence in the lineup might have been gone, but his presence in the hearts and minds of his fans and well-wishers was not. His was becoming 'the name that wouldn't fade'.

Nor had he been forgotten in other quarters. Tom Yawkey, after receiving the medical report, had invited him in for a talk.

"Congratulations, Tony," he said, extending his hand. "I think it's absolutely marvelous that there's a possible light at the end of the tunnel."

"You're right, Mr. Yawkey, it's great news." Then laughing, he added, "The better news is that the light at the end of the tunnel isn't a train coming at me."

"Tell me, what have you been doing so far?"

"I'm working myself back into playing condition, and I thought I'd try my hand at pitching. I used to be pretty good at it. That may be the best place for me."

"Possibly," Yawkey said. "I say that, believing you're still one of the best hitters this team's ever had."

"Thank you, Sir. I appreciate that."

"As you know I used to be a pretty fair hitter."
Tony's smile was genuine. "That's what I'm told. A feared man, as they say."

"I'm still pretty good with a bat. What say we go outside and I'll hit you a few. You can pitch to me."

"My brother Billy came with me. Mind if he joins us?"

"Not at all. As you know he's in our farm system, aspiring to play outfield for us. That being the case, we'll let him play outfield while we practice."

Outside they did the drill for nearly an hour. Tony pitched, Yawkey hit, Billy played outfield. It had been pleasant, but it had also been a learning experience. After a few minutes Tony began to get the yearning for his old haunt, right field. If pitching were the only way he could come back he'd settle for it. Not much in the way of hitting was required of pitchers. But pitchers often were pulled from the lineup in favor of pinch hitters, and they weren't given much time to practice their hitting skills. He on the other hand had the inherent craving to stand in at the plate, swing at baseballs, and launch them off the left field wall, or over the screen.

At the end of the workout, Yawkey called Tony and Billy to join him at home plate. He'd worked up a healthy sweat, and had drilled several long balls. "You go ahead and develop your pitching skills, Tony. But I also want you to devote an equal amount of time to hitting. Okay?"

"Yes, sir."

"I'd like you to attend the Winter Instructional League. Come spring time, I'll see you in camp."

When he was gone, Billy looked at Tony and shook his head. "Sounds like he still wants you to be a hitter."

"How can I say no to a guy who owns the team and took time to come out here and play with us? I'll do whatever he wants."

- Chapter Thirty-Six -
The Season of '69

Tony and Billy, who had made his presence felt within the organization, and had been invited to spring training, had decided to drive to Winter Haven a few days early to get some relaxation at Doral Country Club. The plan was to loosen up, get some sun, and settle in. Even so, the heat was on and Tony knew it. Just before they had left he had talked with his father, who he still viewed as his mentor and confidant.

"Dad, when I get to Winter Haven I'm going to act just like any other guy there. It'll be a tough comeback, if I make it back at all. I'm not going to fool around. I'll be in bed early every night, I'll eat steaks every day and I'll bear down. I'll work harder than I ever have before."

"I know you will, Choo," Sal had said, hugging him. "Just stay focused. Your Uncle Vinnie and I will be down to see you in a couple of weeks. I know everything's going to be all right."

He'd been waiting for this day since August 19, 1967, the day after he'd been hit. Now he was on the threshold.

He and Billy arrived the first day of camp, and everyone was glad to see him. It was like an old fashioned reunion in the clubhouse. The guys swarmed around him, wished him luck and told him how good he looked. Even Dick Williams seemed glad he was there. One of the first things Tony did was ask Williams to allow him to have his own room so he could concentrate on getting back into baseball. Everything he'd told his father had been gospel; he'd meant every word of it.

Williams had agreed to go along with him. "Look," he said. "You're on your own again. You can play in the regular games whenever you want, just let me know."

"I appreciate that," he said. "But it's important that you and everyone else know that other than rooming alone, I want to be treated the same as everyone else. There's nothing like playing under game conditions, and I want to play in exhibition games right from the beginning."

"If that's what you want, you'll have it," Williams said. Tony had stood there for a moment, sort of expecting more to be said, but after a brief, awkward silence Williams looked up at him from his desk, and asked, "Is there something else you want?"

Tony wanted to scream, *You bet your ass there is*, but he thought better of it. Rather than say anything, he simply said, "No, I guess not," and left.

Camp gradually turned into the regimen that he'd always known. Long days of batting practice, intra-squad games, and then exhibition season. He found himself under the same scrutiny that he had in '68, and with it came all the same pressure. But this time was different; this time he could see the ball.

It took a while, but as he endured numerous strikeouts and weak hitting, his keen eye for making good contact and picking up the rotation of the ball gradually came back. Even so, there remained one problem; he'd always been a power hitter, and it was what he'd been known for. Despite making solid contact, however, he had yet to hit one out, and there was only a week left to spring training. Sometimes it seemed life was nothing but a series of endless challenges. And then he realized that some of those challenges were self-induced, which was how he'd discovered what was wrong. He'd been standing farther back from the plate and had switched to a longer, heavier bat to compensate for it. He'd abandoned the formula that had made him the feared hitter he'd once been. What he'd really done was try to fix something that wasn't broke.

On March 27th, he defied both the odds and nature by hitting a monstrous shot over the left field wall against the Cincinnati Reds. The wind had been blowing in with a vengeance, and no one had hit one out all day, not even during batting practice. When he'd come to bat, however, he'd been determined and prepared. And when he got his pitch he'd hammered it.

As he ran down the first base line he watched it, screaming, "Get out of here! *Get the hell out of here!*" And it did. It was his first home run since August 9th, 1967, and he found it almost as big a thrill as the day he'd bought his Corvette. When he got back to the dugout his teammates had surrounded him and congratulated him. He was back, and it felt like he'd just won the World Series.

He accepted their accolades, thanked God, and said, "Looks like I'll be seeing you guys in Fenway Park."

****

As the beaning had changed his life, so had rejoining the team. Even though it was still exhibition season, life was great. For the first time in two years he actually felt relaxed. He was able to sleep again, and his personality changed. He laughed a lot more. On April 2nd he hit another home run against the Minnesota Twins, then two more against Houston. By the time exhibition season was over he had played in twenty-three of the twenty-six scheduled games, had batted .243, collected four home runs, and eleven runs batted in. Far surpassing all that, however, was his belief that Dick Williams had been right; he'd told the press that Tony C would be in right field Opening Day. Not only that, but his brother Billy had made the team and would be there with him.

****

For the Red Sox, the 1969 season opened in Baltimore, and was one of the most challenging days of his life. He'd eaten breakfast with Billy and writer John Devaney, from *Sport Magazine*, who was following his progress along the comeback trail.

"Doesn't look like you're eating much for a guy who's about to jump back into the big time," Devaney said.

"I want to leave a lot of room so the butterflies in my stomach won't bump into each other," he said. They'd all laughed, but he'd meant it.

Later on in the locker room, as everyone was making final preparations to go out onto the field, he was unpacking a brand new glove that he'd not yet broken in.

George Scott had asked him, "New glove, huh? Where's the old one?"

The question had rocked him, and an unanticipated flood of feelings had come surging to the surface. In a voice more emotional than he'd intended, he said, "I gave all my gloves away last spring. I didn't think I'd need them any more."

He went outside to warm up. As he was jogging around the outfield, he heard a voice yell, "Tony! *Tony!!*" He looked up and saw a face he remembered. It was the face of Donna Heath, the teenage girl he'd met two years earlier at Fenway Park. She was couple of years older now, but there was no mistaking her. He remembered every person who had ever asked for his autograph, and he remembered signing her program back in 1967. This was something else he had come to miss: the fans. They were the life's blood of baseball, and they were part of *his* life's blood, too.

He paused for a moment, and walked to her. "Hey you, I remember you. What are you doing here?"

With a sideways wave of her hand, she said, "Me and my friends drove down to see you play on Opening Day. Look what we brought for you." Beaming, she unfurled a large banner that read, *'Welcome back, Tony C!'*

The very sight of it overwhelmed him. Where else could he get love like this but from people who wanted nothing more than for him to play again? Looking up at her, he said, "You still carry that pen around with you?"

"Yep, sure do," she said, digging into her bag. He took the pen and stepped closer to the banner, which was now draped over the railing. On it he printed, *'Thanks for welcoming me back. You're the greatest! – Love, Tony C'.*

As he handed the pen back, they heard a loud whistle. Turning toward the infield they saw one of the umpires walking toward them. Using hand motions he indicated that the banner would have to be removed.

Tony found it irritating. "That wouldn't have hurt anyone," he said. "That wouldn't have hurt anyone at all." Looking up at Donna, he winked and smiled. "Thanks for coming. People like you will never know how much you mean to me." With that he trotted away. When Donna read the 'Love, Tony C' she almost fainted.

His first game back was an exercise in courage and faith. Suddenly the batting cage came down, the ground crew swept the infield, and they played the Star Spangled Banner. He was back in the dugout and in the starting lineup, watching as the batters ahead of him took their turn at the plate. With each batter his intensity level heightened. This wasn't sandlot, it wasn't the minors, and it wasn't spring training; this was the pros, and it had his undivided attention. He watched Reggie Smith lead off with a walk, then felt the excitement grow as Mike Andrews followed with a single, followed immediately by Carl Yastrzemski's double that scored Reggie.

Now it was his turn. As he left the on-deck circle there came a small ripple of applause that soon built into a roar as he stepped into the batters box. It was more than exhilarating; it was overpowering. To hear so many people cheering for him on his first day back – in the other team's park – was something he'd never forget. He was back in the big leagues and the dream was alive again.

His first at bat wasn't all that he'd have wanted; he struck out, but the encouraging part was the realization that he'd have to adjust his thinking about crowding the plate. Pitches that previously appeared as balls outside the strike zone were now strikes.

Later on, when Boston took the field, there had been a high fly ball to the outfield. It should have been Reggie Smith's play, but he'd lost it in the sun. This had forced Tony to make a run for it and he'd caught it mid stride. Just feeling the ball slap into his glove precisely as he'd gauged it was reassuring, and it rid him of the last of his butterflies. His eyes were serving him well, and faith in his depth perception was growing.

His next at bat had been another out, but he'd made another adjustment at the plate that he believed would make him harder to get out. And his belief was justified. Next time he'd gotten a single, for his first big league hit since he'd been beaned. The Orioles tied the game in the eighth inning, and had sent it into extra innings. This was his territory, his kind of situation, especially now that he had found his groove. Carl Yastrzemski led off the tenth by reaching on an error, which brought Tony up to the plate. He'd played a cat and mouse game with pitcher Pete Richert, and had almost been called out on strikes. He'd felt the umpire's hesitation before calling the pitch a ball, and breathed a sigh of relief. These were the times he lived for. Though slightly tense, he began coaching himself through the situation. Settle down; be quick but not jumpy. Then he got the pitch he'd been waiting for. Richert served up a fastball that he hit about as hard as any ball he'd ever hit, and sent over the left field wall for a home run, scoring Yaz ahead of him.

I did it! He thought as he ran the bases. As he rounded second he was grinning like a little boy, and third base coach Eddie Popowski was jumping up and down, yelling, "Hey Tony! Hey Tony!" For his part, all he could do was yell, "Oh Pop! Oh Pop!" When he crossed home plate George Scott was standing there, waiting for him. As they slapped hands, Tony said, "What do you think of that, Boomer? How about that!"

Everyone in the dugout was yelling and screaming, and reaching for him. His brother Billy, Reggie, Rico, Yaz, all of them were pounding his back and grabbing him by the shoulders. Even Dick Williams came over and kissed him on the cheek. Tony would loved to have bitten Williams on the neck in return.

Frank Robinson came up in the bottom of the tenth and tied the score with a home run, driving the game deeper into extra innings. In the twelfth Tony led off and drew a walk on six pitches. It was important that he got on base to advance the team's cause; but even more important to him was that he was seeing the ball well enough again to distinguish between good and bad pitches. That would allow him to advance the team's cause over an entire season, which was proven a little while later. Boston had loaded the bases, now putting him on third. Dalton Jones came to the plate, hit a long fly to deep centerfield, which had allowed him to score the winning run.

Back in the clubhouse his teammates surrounded him in droves. "Way to go, C!" and "Hey, just like old times!" Red Sox commentator Ned Martin had requested an on-air, post game interview; even the writers had been all over him. He had a checkered history with some of them, but decided to celebrate the moment and let the past rest with the past.

At the end of their media session one of them asked, "Do you feel you're all the way back now?"

His answer had gotten a laugh from them, but it had been poignantly true. "I hope so, because I went a hell of a long time between my 104th and 105th home run."

And for now, it was great to be back.

- Chapter Thirty-Seven -

When he'd hit that home run on Opening Day in Baltimore, the cheering of the crowd, the backslapping of his teammates, helping to win the game, and the pure joy he felt in is heart should have been the whole story. He was back in the big leagues; he had hit a home run, and was where he'd been before Hamilton's pitch had cut him down. Everyone believed it. But that was where the secret lay; he was far from back, but he was the only one that knew it. He had fostered the illusion by telling writers his vision was fully recovered and he could see as well as he ever had. The eye tests he'd undergone had confirmed it. The doctors and Retina Associates had gone so far as to release a statement saying that his vision was now 20/20-1, meaning that he could read the entire twenty-line chart with the exception of one letter. Technically, that was so; in reality, it wasn't. The reality was that if he looked out at the mound and straight at the pitcher he couldn't see the ball or the hand that was holding it. But if he looked approximately a foot of the left of whatever he wanted to see his peripheral vision would pick up both the hand and the ball. What he'd done opening day and beyond had been almost entirely with his right eye, not his left. Even in Regan's office he could only see the 'E' on the top of the chart by staring directly at it; everything else had required that he look to the side so his peripheral vision could read the remainder of the chart. All this he kept to himself. But the other secret he'd kept was the knowledge that if indeed he ever made it back into pro ball it would be with one eye, not two. Better to try and come back like that than reveal the facts and create unnecessary doubts. He felt he owed himself the opportunity of playing again, no matter what the risk. The last thing he'd ever have wanted was to go into a slump and have them say, "Well there it is. He's gone blind in the eye and can't see." What fair chance might he have gotten after that?

****

The most challenging moment of his year had come in Cleveland. During 1967, '68 and '69 he'd not paid much attention to who was playing where, other than the players who were with the Red Sox. Therefore, in an extra innings game against the Indians he unexpectedly came face to face with the worst night of his life.

It was the thirteenth inning, and the Indians brought in a new relief pitcher. That pitcher was Jack Hamilton. As Tony stepped in against him a million thoughts and memories ran through his mind. But one was noticeably absent; he had no desire to run. He'd step in against him, no matter what. He didn't hate Hamilton, nor did he feel he'd been deliberately hit by him. This was something he had to do; he'd never look at himself as a man if he didn't face him. His teeth grinding with desire and his heart pounding, he now faced the man whose fastball had nearly killed him.

As he dug in he told himself he'd stand even closer to the plate than usual. It was imperative he prove to both of them that he wasn't afraid. There was a runner on base, and when he looked down the third base line to Eddie Popowski for the sign, he was told to bunt. He wanted to scream at 'Pop', but didn't. He laid down the bunt and advanced the runner.

He came up again a couple of innings later, and Hamilton was still in there. He'd never wanted to get a hit against anyone as much as did then, and never for such a personal reason. With no one on base there was no bunt sign, and he was free to swing away, which he did. He leaned over the plate, waited for the pitch he wanted, and pounded the ball as hard as he could. It was a long line drive, which was caught by Lee Maye for an out. It didn't have to be a home run; it didn't even have to be a hit. He'd faced the challenge, had stood against his demons, and had beaten them down.

After the game the writers had swarmed all over him, asking him what it felt like to face Hamilton again. Tony had chosen to play it close to the vest. "He's just another pitcher to me," he said. "Did I feel funny standing in against him? Maybe for a minute, but then it passed." He wanted the incident to die a quiet death. It had to, or they'd never leave it be. He wanted to forget the beaning, but hadn't been sure he'd forgiven Hamilton for it. But now he'd faced him and stood in against him like he would any other pitcher. He hadn't gotten a hit, but that was almost incidental. He'd faced him. Period.

****

It seemed most of his family tree had been waiting for him at Boston's Logan International Airport. And it wasn't just for Tony; Billy C was a full-fledged member of the Red Sox, and they were there as much for him as they were for Tony. Tony had always felt badly that circumstance forced Billy to follow behind him. It set up a natural inclination for people to compare them, and to always note his accomplishments compared to Billy's. He'd always felt that Billy was every bit as deserving of his own notoriety as he was himself. They were brothers, but they had their own lives, both on and off the field. Tony's by nature had been high profile, and it shouldn't have cast a shadow on Billy's. It was one of the reasons he'd been so happy that Billy had made the team. He'd done it on his own merit, no one else's.

After that everyone had piled into vehicles and gone back to the house in Swampscott. It was a time for reunion and celebration, and Teresa had been anxious to do her part. She was a world-class cook as far as they were concerned, and she'd prepared a spread that would have been worthy of The White House. But this was the Conigliaro House, so it had to be even better. And it was.

The next day Tony and Billy went to Fenway Park for the Red Sox Opening Day. Tony wanted to make a low profile entrance because so many fans would ask the inevitable questions about his eye, and how it felt to be back in a Red Sox uniform again. He loved them all, but this was his first day back at Fenway. This was not an average day and he felt tense. That's not to say their day passed without any humor. Upon entering the clubhouse, George Scott had taken note of something that may or may not have happened by chance. He looked at the lockers, and said, "Look at that, Billy Conigliaro, Tony

Conigliaro, Rico Petrocelli...and me. Ain't it nice the way they put all us Italians together?" Tony had laughed until he felt like his ribs would crack.

When he went outside, however, the tenseness came back. He went down the stairs into the darkened hallway, and finally into the dugout itself. He stopped as he entered, looked up, and saw the bright, crisp blue skies over Fenway. As he reached the top step of the dugout, he did his ritualistic 'tossing of the glove' out onto the field. Now he felt back more than ever.

No one had arrived yet. It was the same as it had been when he'd come to the park alone and had Keith pitch to him. He knew what day it was. He knew it all the way to the pit of his stomach, which was quivering like Jell-o. He ran to the outfield to jog for a while, trying to calm himself. This shouldn't have been necessary, considering he hadn't slept the previous night. The real problem was trying to convince himself that even though he had a long way to go, it was all right. The anxiety led him to believe he might not live until game time.

He retraced his steps to the dugout to retrieve his glove. He glanced at the stands and saw that the crowd was beginning to trickle in. As he reached for his glove one of the attendants came over to him. Pointing, he said, "Your grandfather is here."

Tony looked where the attendant was pointing and sure enough, there was Grandpa Albert, his mother's father, meekly waving in his direction. He was eighty-two, and had come to see him play.

Tony ran up into the stands to see him. "You came! You have no idea how much this means to me!"

"You just go out there and have the best day you can," his grandfather said. "You go be the best *Tony* you can be." Tony kissed him and went back to the clubhouse, feeling higher than a kite.

He wanted to rest up and collect himself before the game, so he decided against batting practice in favor of some quiet time in the locker room. How much of this had really happened, and how much of it had been a dream? It was too big to contemplate, and too late to ponder. This was Opening Day; he was there, wearing a Red Sox uniform.

****

The stands were buzzing when he returned to the dugout. Red Sox color commentator Ken Coleman was at the plate holding a microphone. After introducing the day's opposition, the Baltimore Orioles, he began to introduce the Red Sox. He started with the managers, Dick Williams, Eddie Popowski, Bobby Doerr, and Darrell Johnson. Next he introduced the players, beginning with Mike Andrews. He went through the lineup. As Tony listened the knot in his stomach and the emotional upheaval inside him became almost unbearable. All that he'd worked through, all that he'd endured, all that he'd dreamed and fought for all his life, before and after the beaning, were about to happen again. When Coleman got to number twenty-four, pitcher Juan Pizzaro, another loud cheer had gone up.

And then came the moment. "And now, playing right field, number twenty-five—"Coleman never got to say Tony's name over the PA. As Tony ran from the dugout and onto the field a thunderous roar went up from the crowd. It was deafening. He was grinning and shivering at the same time. As he took his place beside Pizzaro, the cheers from these people he loved so much sounded like the most beautiful symphony he'd ever heard. He waved, but they wouldn't stop; he took off his cap and tipped it to them, and they didn't stop; he slowly turned in a circle, and faced them all, and it still didn't stop. It didn't stop for over two full minutes, and left him feeling like he'd gone to heaven without having to die.

This was a huge game, and it was important that he give the best account of himself that he could. His first at bat resulted in a pop fly to right field. His second at bat had been a scorching shot to shortstop Mark Belanger. He'd made it to second, but had gotten Carl Yastrsemski caught in a rundown that resulted in an out. The third at bat was the kind he dreamed about. The bases were loaded, the game was tied, and it was his turn to come to the plate. He hungered for these moments. The first pitch from Mike Adamson had buzzed high and inside just beneath his chin. The crowd had sent out a collective gasp. They, like him, still remembered August 18, 1967. The next two pitches missed, but the one after that was a soft ground ball down the third base line that he'd beat out for a hit, and had scored what proved to be the game-winning run. Indeed, the dream was alive and well again.

And best of all, he was back.

- Chapter Thirty-Eight -

The relief he'd experienced at the end of 1969 didn't carry over into spring training of 1970. He got off to a slow start, and went on to have a lackluster preseason. The zeal, the inspiration, the desire to excel that had once driven him to achieve greater things was missing. He couldn't put his finger on the underlying cause, nor did he feel it was permanent, but it was an ongoing distraction.

Early in the regular season he hadn't done much better, having slumped to the extent that he was again taken out of the cleanup position by Eddie Kasko and dropped to sixth in the batting order. But he didn't let it get to him; he was convinced he was simply waiting to happen. He was seeing the ball, making good contact, but not so as to set the league – or his career – on fire. Then, as had been the case so many times, sudden thunder had struck and he'd gone on a tear, hitting home runs and driving in base runners prolifically, and at critical times. His rivalry with Carl Yastrzemski had resumed, not in a malicious or hateful way, but in an effort to re-establish himself as one of the team's leaders. He'd never aspired to mediocrity, and couldn't stomach the thought of living in obscurity.

The season had gone on with he and Carl going back and forth at the top of the team's offensive statistics. It was good for the fans, the team, and the game. Most of all, it was good for him. Even at age twenty-five, he still craved recognition for his accomplishments. This, he felt, would never go away, nor did he want it to. It was part of what drove him.

There were times when these things came from unexpected sources, some of them humorous. One day he'd been granted a freebie homerun by one of the umpires when he'd hit a long foul ball that one of the other umpires had mistakenly called fair. Tony had laughed when it happened, but he hadn't volunteered to give it back to them, either. Besides, who was he to turn down a blind umpire's gift?

If there was a more serious incident that year, it involved Cleveland Indian pitcher Fred Lasher. Lasher had dropped him with a high inside pitch that would have beaned him, had he not gotten out of its way. Tony interpreted that as a personal challenge. He'd remained cool, had gotten up, dusted himself off and promptly hit a home run. A jawing contest had begun between them in the newspapers, which writers loved more than just about anything. These things sold papers and got writers and players extra attention. Threats had passed back and forth, and the table had been set. The next time they met, Lasher hit him, and the benches emptied with both Lasher and Tony at the heart of it. It would have been interesting enough had it ended there, but it had taken yet another twist. Tony got tossed, and Lasher was allowed to remain in the game. Ironically, his brother Billy had replaced him in right field. On Billy's first at bat against Lasher, he'd driven a Lasher fastball high into the upper deck for a home run. Final score: Conigliaro's two, Lasher's zero.

The season continued, but the Red Sox were in no danger of winning the pennant. With nothing to distract them, the team's flaws and personality clashes were brought out in bold relief. Tony, ever seeking greater heights, had begun feeling that Carl Yastrzemski and several other players were getting preferential treatment, and had begun speaking openly about it. So had brother Billy. The tension had returned, and the camps were reestablished. It was no secret that Tom Yawkey worshipped the ground Yaz walked on, and they were very close. He'd even made Yaz a gift of the turf that had been removed from Fenway's outfield for use in his yard at home. But what was he supposed to do? Have no opinion on anything because another player was close the man who signed everyone's check?

Club unity had begun to disintegrate, and once again it became something Tony found uninspiring. Guys that used to be friendly, outgoing and supportive of one another were back to treating each other like strangers. Subtly, the atmosphere of camaraderie had evaporated, and the clubhouse had gone back to one of tense silence. Any conversation between members of opposing camps was forced and strained. It was neither healthy, nor happy, and it reeked of 1968 all over again.

With strife and turmoil from within, it didn't surprise him that the team finished the season well off the pace. Much of August and all of September had been little more than going through the motions. That wasn't to say it had been a lost cause for him. He had won the American League batting title with thirty-six home runs, and had driven in one hundred and sixteen runs, which was good enough to finish second in that category. He had nearly taken two-thirds of the Triple Crown, and that wasn't too shabby. Best of all perhaps was the simple joy of getting to play again. Great seasons and great performances were to be commended, but for him the consummate joy of getting to play the game at all was what mattered most. In 1970 he'd done that, and done it well.

****

Tony walked down the gangway into the terminal, feeling the autumn chill. Boston's Logan International Airport was open and spacious, and naturally lent itself to windy conditions. It became even more pronounced during times of higher than average humidity. He'd expected his father to be there waiting for him, but not wearing the expression he had. Something had happened, and it didn't bode well if the look on his father's face was any indication. Fortunately, the season was over. Boston had finished well behind the league lead, but that wasn't his fault. His personal numbers had been good, despite the team's overall performance. It was time to relax until next year. Short of a family emergency, whatever was bothering his father surely couldn't be that bad. Besides, after all he'd been through, nothing much surprised him any more.

"Hi, Choo," his father said, hugging him. "Good trip?"

"Yeah, it went fine. How about you? You look like something's on your mind."

"Yeah, I suppose it is," Sal answered. He seemed disconsolate, as if he'd heard one shoe drop and was now waiting for the other one.

"So what is it?" Tony asked. "Did something happen to Mom, or Billy or Richie?"

"No, they're okay. If it was something like that, I'd have called."

"So what's the problem?"

"The Red Sox made some trades today."

Curious, Tony asked, "Oh yeah? Who'd they get?"

"Ken Tatum, Jarvis Tatum and Doug Griffin."

"Huh," Tony said. "Who'd they give up?"

"Gerry Moses, Ray Jarvis, and..."

"And who, dad?" The look in his father's eye said it all. "You're not saying...you're not saying they traded me? I mean, how could they do that? I'm a home town guy, and I just had a great year. Tom Yawkey promised me himself that I'd always have a home here as long as he owned the team."

"I don't know what to say, Choo. They just announced it and I wanted you to hear it from me first."

He paused for a moment, then asked, "Who'd they trade me to?"

"The California Angels."

"The *Angels?* That's the team that beaned me! Not only does he trade me, he trades me to the team that almost killed me?"

"It gets worse. Someone leaked it to the press and there's a bunch of them waiting for you in the lobby." As he and Sal walked through the terminal, they were surrounded by reporters, eager to get Tony's reaction to the trade. He'd been known for making his share of quotable one-liners in the past; who knew what he might say under these conditions?

Uncharacteristic of his usually compliant nature, he and Sal made their way to the exit and went straight to their car. There would be no sound bites that night.

****

His initial reaction had been to consider retirement. They couldn't force him to go anywhere if he retired; but that wouldn't be in keeping with his character. When the time came to retire it wouldn't be so that he could run away. When retirement came, he'd walk away on his own terms. He tried to find out whose idea it was to trade him so he could get their reasoning for it. But every time he inquired, no one seemed sure how it had come about. This had frustrated him immensely, because he felt there had been an agenda at work. Had it been because of his eye? Was it the discord on the team? Was it his on-again / off-again clashes with Carl Yastrzemski? Why now? What was the point? Certainly the players they got in return weren't sufficient reason.

The longer he thought about it, the more inflamed the wound became. Neither Kasko, Sullivan, O'Connell, nor Yawkey would pinpoint the culprit behind the decision. Yawkey had promised him this wouldn't happen, and now that it had he felt betrayed, even humiliated. He'd just finished his best year ever, and it hadn't mattered to them. They had declared openly in front of the whole nation that they didn't need him any more. It wouldn't be the same playing anywhere else.

As time went by, however, he began to look at it from another angle. Maybe going to the West Coast would give him a completely fresh start. New people, new management, new team; even the landscape would look different. There was one thing of which he was certain; he'd be a forty-five minute ride from one of his favorite places: Hollywood. He'd thought about it more than once. Some day he'd have to do something after baseball, and a film career might be the answer. Even Merv Griffin had suggested he consider it.

He'd given a brief, sanitized statement to the press, saying that the trade had left him feeling confused, which had been a monstrous understatement. He'd been devastated. Boston was supposed to be home; he was supposed to finish his career there. Right after he'd given his statement he'd left town and remained incommunicado. He'd learned from all the other times he'd drawn public attention that they were never satisfied; someone with a new question and a new angle would always want more answers.

This time they could wait.

- Chapter Thirty-Nine -

The Season Of '71

One of the players who had been part of the trade was Red Sox catcher, Jerry Moses, who had been one of Tony's closest friends on the team. Like Tony, he'd come to the Red Sox straight out of high school and had gone to Wellsville. They had later become roommates at Scottsdale, when Billy Herman had been the team's manager. Being only a year younger than Tony, it had been natural that they socialized together. They had often joked how their thinking had been altered by the combination of baseball and girls. At night when they went out, they would talk about baseball; at practice the next day they would talk about what they'd done the night before. Though not overly cocky himself, Moses believed that some players needed to be a bit full of themselves in order to pump themselves up. Confidence had a lot to do with success, especially at the professional level.

They had been brought together again on the big team in 1967, two weeks after Tony's beaning. It wasn't until the 1969 season, however, that they actually had gotten to play together. They had become even closer, so it was only natural that Tony would call him when he found out they'd been part of the same deal.

"Have you heard what happened yet?" Tony asked.

"Yeah," Jerry said, toweling himself off at his home in Mississippi. "I been driving for two days, so I didn't hear until I hit town at three o'clock this morning. Sullivan left a message for me to call him. Hell, I figured being traded would be the last thing on his mind. Baseball can be a cold-blooded business, I guess. It's a great game, but a terrible business. I just can't believe they did it with both of us coming off the best year we ever had."

"I don't know what to do," Tony said. "My father says everyone's calling and asking for interviews, but I don't know what to say. I know what I'd *like* to say, but I doubt they'd print it. Then again, maybe they would. I feel like I got stabbed in the back. I still can't believe it."

"Where are you now?" Jerry asked.

"Las Vegas, but don't let on if anyone asks. I need some time to sift through this."

"There's a part of me that would like to tell them how I feel, too," Jerry said. "I was happy there, might even have settled down there. Hell, I still might. I wish there was something we could do, but we're stuck. I'd retire, but I'm too young to do that yet, and I'd like to play long enough to get a pension. I actually have to work a day job during the off-season to make ends meet. I'd love to see the day when we don't have to do that anymore."

"Money's the least of my worries now that this has happened," Tony said. "This was my home town, I gave them the best I had for seven years. I'd love to say I'm pissed about it, but the truth is it makes me ache more than it makes me angry."

"Look at the bright side. They got some great looking women in LA. They still wear hot pants and all kinds of stuff like that."

"Hey, you're a married guy, you can't fool around."

"I'm being a good boy," he said, laughing. "When I got married they put the ring on my finger, not through my eyes. I can look, I just can't touch."

"Phillips is the manager out there, right?" Tony asked.

"Yeah, Lefty Phillips. I've seen him a couple of times. Kinda talks like a gangster, but I guess he can manage."

"At least Hamilton's gone. I don't know how I'd handle having to play with him."

"That might be a two-way street. Anyone I've talked to says he's real sorry about what happened. Playing with you might've been hard for him, too. Going to look for a place to live?"

"Might as well, looks like I'll be playing in LA next year."

****

Tony had settled into his new place, but not his new circumstances. He'd been used to having family and friends and supportive fans all around him in Boston, but LA was proving to be very different. The comfort zone he'd always enjoyed was missing. He and Jerry were still close, but the rest of his teammates were strangers. With one exception: Fred Lasher. Fate had landed him there the same time it had Tony. Fortunately, one of the first things they had done was make their peace. But these were new fans, a new ballpark, different haunts and a completely different part of the country. The scenery was beautiful, but everything else that was dear to him was three thousand miles away. If he could have brought the topography, the climate and the beauty back east, or bring the people from back east out to LA, he'd have loved it. Moreover, the team and the fans had expected great things from the Angels, including a Western Division Championship. The experts had picked them to take it, and he'd been brought there to play a major roll in that. He came in as a high profile player, and was being paid accordingly. Eighty thousand dollars brought lofty expectations, both real and unreal. 1970, which had been his best year, was now becoming a handicap because everyone expected him to improve on it, and lead the Angels to the same glorious heights as the 1967 Red Sox. The absence of family and friends, the expectations, and the unfamiliar climes had turned his transition into a crash course. But he had committed himself to succeeding out there, and was firm in his resolve, if for no other reason than to show Red Sox management they'd made a big mistake in trading him. In the past he couldn't understand players' determination to show the team that traded them how wrong they'd been in doing so; wounded egos needed that kind of medicine. Now he knew what that meant.

As time progressed more subtleties began to surface. Whereas the guys on the Red Sox had seemed like kindred spirits, most of his teammates in Los Angeles hadn't bonded the way they did back in Boston. Maybe he'd been spoiled by the players and good times of the '67 season, many of who were still on the team, but this had a different ambiance. The same overall camaraderie was missing. Try as he might, he couldn't adjust. Then came a succession of injuries. He'd been plagued by them in the past, mostly from getting hit by pitches or chasing down fly balls. But that was nothing to what it had now become. He was missing time out of the lineup, his eye problem had begun to recur, and his numbers were showing it. The game was becoming a struggle again; joy had packed its bags and was threatening to move out of Mudville. But his had been a life of comebacks and overcoming adversity; he wasn't about to give in just yet.

Perhaps the hardest, most emotional part had come when the Angels had gone to Fenway Park for a weekend series. The feeling of being a visitor in what had once been home for seven years was eerie. Being in something other than a Red Sox uniform felt unnatural. The fans had been politely enthusiastic, but nothing like they had been when he'd been a Red Sox player.

And still the injuries continued. He'd been struggling with them all year, and had begun to think maybe they were partly due to the constant stress he was under. Stressed players were more susceptible to injury; muscles, tendons, ligaments and reflexes didn't respond under stress the same as they did when they were relaxed.

Los Angeles' much anticipated Impossible Dream year wasn't happening, which to some extent they were holding him responsible. Fans complained, management didn't like it, and at one point several players had gotten together and set up a 'shrine for the walking wounded' in front of his locker. They had set up a stretcher with his uniform neatly draped over it. Ace bandages and crutches had been part of the package, and so were some feminine napkins smeared with ketchup. Tony and Jerry Moses had entered the locker room together. At first, Jerry thought it was funny, but that quickly faded when he saw Tony's reaction.

"What the hell is this?" he said. "Someone around here questioning my desire? They think I lost my nerve? That I like the way things are going? They think I'm whining? What are they? *Crazy?*" He shook his head. He'd been through more in one lifetime than most people would experience in five, and was doing his best to endure what had become his least enjoyable, and least fulfilling season.

The worst night of all had come on the road. His eye had regressed to it worst since 1968. Bad enough it had never totally come back and everything he'd accomplished since then had been with only one good eye, including winning an American League Batting Title. He'd also won the touted Hutch Award for courage, and had won the Comeback Player Of The Year Award, all with bad eyesight.

His condition was getting worse. His headaches were back; his skills and abilities were slipping away, and it was reflected in his batting. Life was no longer the joyful experience it had once been.

His frustration finally became too much for him to contain one night in Oakland. He wasn't seeing the ball, and had gone 0-6. Called out on strikes for the fourth time he had gone ballistic on the umpire, had thrown his helmet into the air and had hammered it with his bat, for which he'd been immediately ejected from the game. He'd stormed after the umpire for several minutes, went back to the clubhouse, packed his things, and flew home to Boston.

The desire was gone; the fire was out, his career was over.

- Chapter Forty -

After notifying the team of his decision, the next thing he'd done was forfeit the remainder of his salary. At halfway through the season that had come to forty thousand dollars. He felt forfeiting the money was worth it; having to play the rest of the season would have been more than he could stand.

After taking time off to decompress, he began contemplating where to go from there. One place he wouldn't go was baseball. In *any* capacity; enough was enough. If he couldn't play in Boston he wouldn't play at all. Besides, there were no more mountains to climb. It had stopped being fun, his eye had worsened, and the allure of home was too compelling. But he needed something to do. Then both inspiration and opportunity came knocking. He'd always liked the club scene, the women, the music, the excitement, the singing. Therefore, it seemed only natural that he got a club of his own. A piece of property in Nahant, the small Boston suburb where his parents lived, had unexpectedly become available. It came with a small pond, a golf course, and a trailer park. After considerable expense, a lot of sweat equity, and help from friends and family, the renovations had been completed. *Tony C's* was born during the spring of 1972.

The nightclub, plush, hip, colorful and rocking, hit the ground running. With an abundance of lights, music, high energy and excitement, it took on a life of its own and was an overnight success. Not even the liquor license had been a problem. Life was good again, and within months *Tony C's* became an institution. People came from all over. The golf course, a nine-hole affair complete with a pro shop, and not far from the ocean, came into its own at precisely the right time of year. It was convenient yet off the beaten path, and was a twenty-minute ride from Boston. He had a new sense of purpose and a place to call his own. It didn't take him away from home for weeks or months at a time. It was idyllic. He was close to family, friends and Boston. For the first time in a long time he felt like his life was finally his own again. A new dream had been born. The time and effort had been worth it.

****

Julie stared down at the ocean below, pondering its vast expanse as the plane approached Boston's Logan International Airport. This latest trip to Florida had been revealing in more ways than one. She'd been with Ken Harrelson for five years now, and had come to a couple of conclusions. Some things could be fun, but weren't meant to last forever; other things seemed to never fade, but hadn't lasted nearly long enough. She watched as the plane touched down, hearing the squeal of the tires and feeling the jolt as the engines reversed their thrust on their approach to the terminal.

Inside, she picked up her bags, then took a cab home. No sooner had she entered her apartment than she picked up the phone, dialed a number and waited. The voice on the other end was familiar.

"Hello," it said.

"Ken, it's Julie."

"Back home safe and sound?"

"Yes, I just got in."

"Everything okay?"

"Yes...and no," she said.

"That's an interesting answer."

"It's an honest answer, and it's why I'm calling."

"What's going on?"

"I'll put it as simply as I can. I did a lot of thinking on the plane, and I've decided I can't do this."

"Can't do what?"

"Us, I can't be in this relationship. You've been telling me for three years that you're going to get a divorce, and you haven't done it. You're a great guy, but I'm tired of waiting. It's over."

"You're kidding, right?"

"No, I'm quite serious. I can't go on like this."

"Why don't we--?"

"Kenny, it's over. Good luck, I have to go." With that she hung up. It was over.

****

Tony's life had continued to improve. Baseball, though something he'd never forget, and for which he would always be grateful, was no longer the all-consuming, driving force it had once been. He'd settled into his new life, and was enjoying his freedom from the rigors of pro ball. On this particular night he had invited his parents, his brothers, and his Uncle Vinnie and Aunt Phyllis to be his guests for dinner and drinks at *Tony C's.*

"Dad, I can't begin to tell you how good this feels," he said. "Baseball had to end someday, and I couldn't have asked for more than this. I'm really glad you guys could make it."

"I got to be honest," Sal said, "at twenty-seven years old you're doing a whole lot better than I was when I was your age."

"That's because I had a good teacher and a family that loves me. After that all I needed was a break, and I got it. But I couldn't have done it without all of you."

"You make us proud, Tony," Uncle Vinnie said, trying not to choke up. What had happened to Tony had been almost as hard on him as it had on Tony. He'd spent all those years with him, watching him work hard, training to develop into the player much of the world had come to know. Seeing Tony writhing in the dirt beside home plate had nearly killed him, too. But now he had this, and in Vinnie's mind, no one deserved it more.

"Thanks, Uncle, you had a lot to do with that, too."

"Ahh, forget about it. It was nothing."

"Yeah, right," Phyllis chimed in, tapping his shoulder. "All those times you were playing with him when I wanted you home. Ask *me* if it was nothing!"

Everyone laughed, and Vinnie kissed her on the cheek. "She's right, Tony. Make sure you give her credit, too. If she'd have got tough with me over that, we might have been in trouble."

Tony leaned over and hugged her, then turned toward Billy. "Let's make sure we never forget that I wasn't the only one in this family who was a pro ballplayer. And he worked just as hard as I did. Even got a World Series ring. Put up with almost as much crap, too." Raising his glass in a toast, he said, "This is for you, Billy. May all that you accomplished never be forgotten. I love you." Everyone toasted Billy, and took a sip from their glass.

Turning to his mother, Tony said, "Who could have done it without you, ma? Not me, that's for sure. You've always been my best girl, and you still are."

"There's been times when I wished I *was* your only girl, but we know how *that* went!" Again, everyone laughed and toasted. Then, she added, "Richie, I still don't know what you're going to do with your life. They say you could be an even better ballplayer than your brothers, but after what I saw them go through I'm not sure I'd want that for you. There's too much business, and not enough game."

Turning to his family, Tony said, "You guys sit tight, and enjoy yourselves; I'm going to get some air. I'll be back in a little while." He kissed his mother and father, and headed toward the stage.

Just making their way into the club was Julie and one of her girlfriends. Seeing them, Sal waved them over to join them. Their son may not have been her boyfriend any more, but that hadn't made her a stranger. Julie was still close to the Conigliaro's, and Tony was still close to the Markakis'.

Julie and Teresa had remained particularly close. After the breakup Julie had cried without stopping for two weeks. Her mother had become so concerned that she had called Teresa, wondering what to do. Teresa had shaken her head, not knowing what to say to

Tony. She knew he'd gone through his own difficult time, but had seemed firm in his decision not to get married at such an early age.

Seeing her now, Teresa stood and gave her a hug. "Hello, Julie," she said. "You look lovely, as always."

"Thank you," she said, embracing her. "The way the airlines are, I have to exercise and watch everything I eat." She paused, and then asked, "How's he doing? Is he happier now that he's away from baseball?"

"He was at first, but I think playing still crosses his mind from time to time. It's in his blood. Me? I like having him around again."

Julie turned toward Sal, who was silently looking at her. He didn't appear angry; he'd never gotten angry with her. But he did appear somber. "Is everything all right?" she asked. He was usually outgoing and pleasant.

It took him a moment to answer. "Yes, I am," he said. And then he stood up. "There's something I need to say, and I'd like everyone's attention. Please." They looked at him curiously, not because of what he'd said, but because of how he'd said it.

When he had their attention, he continued. "There's something that's been on my mind for a long time, and I think this is when I should say it." Looking at Julie, he said, "I believe it was a terrible mistake, what I did to you and Tony. You were so happy, and I interfered. For that I am extremely sorry. I know now that nothing would ever have interfered with his baseball career because of how passionate he was about it. I also know that you were never a threat to it, and that you always supported him in it completely. I'm sorry for what I did to you, to your life and your happiness, and to his. Please forgive me."

They sat in stunned silence as he took his seat. Julie, who had always considered herself a strong woman, had all she could do not to unleash the tears of a hundred agonized nights when she'd lay in a darkened room, staring at a black ceiling, recalling what might have been. She harbored no bitterness toward this man, whose son had been her shining star. But now that he'd made this brutally honest apology, and had acknowledged the harm he felt he'd done, it welled everything up inside her. The pain, the seeming unending loneliness, the part of her spirit that had been shorn away, the deep disappointment that had left its imprint on her soul all came back in bold relief. At the same time, hearing Sal's apology had lifted a colossal burden she'd been carrying for so long that she'd forgotten she was carrying it. Until now, she hadn't known how much she needed to hear this, and as a result something had left her, leaving in its wake a peace that would take time to comprehend. Even as she wept, and reached for a tissue to wipe the tears streaming down her cheeks, she sensed she had just emerged from a tunnel.

For the moment, the best she could manage was to nod at Sal, and continue wiping away the tears.

****

Things at the club continued to roll along, and from a financial standpoint it was a solid success. But it had begun to have its problems. Heavy traffic to and from, noise, fast cars, loud people and late night chaos had begun wearing out *Tony C's* welcome in Nahant. As its popularity declined in the eyes of the neighbors and town fathers, its popularity declined with Tony, too. It had been a fun ride, but he sensed it was getting on time to move in another direction.

That direction was baseball.

- Chapter Forty-One -

It had taken some maneuvering, but Tony had arranged to become available on the open market. The Angels had put him on the waiver wire, making him available to anyone who wanted him. When there had been no takers they gave him his outright release, allowing him to sign with anyone who wanted him. In his mind it wasn't *who wanted him*, it was *who he wanted*, and who he wanted was the Boston Red Sox. A hat-in-hand call to Sox General Manager Dick O'Connell had gotten him the green light to report to spring training early in 1975.

He took advantage of the Florida warmth and put himself through grueling training sessions. His workouts were inflicted upon himself, and bordered on torture. Endless running, countless hours of batting practice, and overall physical conditioning were meant to do one thing: bring him and the dream back to life. The team had a solid outfield, so that wouldn't be where he'd seek to break in. He was aiming at another niche, something that hadn't been there when he retired: the American League designated hitter position. He wouldn't have to play any of the defensive positions; his sole responsibility was to hit, which had been his trademark. He could do that.

****

By the end of spring training, he was beside himself. His hitting had been marginal, although it had taken a decided upswing over the past week. Even so, he wasn't the same cocky kid he'd once been. There were a lot of good players on the team, and he wasn't sure how management had graded his talents. If the past week meant anything he'd have a shot; if they gauged him on his performance over the entire spring the issue was in doubt.

Manager Darrell Johnson sat near the front of the bus. They were returning from a preseason exhibition game, and the regular season was looming. Tony had had a very productive day that day, and was hoping they'd remember that more than the beginning of his preseason.

Seated near the back, he watched as Johnson got out of his seat and began walking toward him. He had been looking at Tony almost from the moment he'd stood up. Something was coming.

As he reached Tony, Johnson leaned close to him, and asked, "Do you think you can contribute to this team's chances at being successful this year?"

"Darrell, I've staked everything I own on making it back this year. You better believe I can contribute."

"Good, so do I," Johnson said. He stuck out his hand, and said, "Welcome back."

If the bus had a restroom, Tony would have used it.

****

They were the echoes of ancient glories. It was Opening Day, and Fenway Park was filled to capacity. Excitement was in the air, and a buzz was running through the crowd. The Milwaukee Brewers were in town, and with them had come 'Hammering Hank Aaron', Baseball's all-time home run champion. They had had their part of the first inning and came up empty. Now it was Boston's turn to bat. As the introductions were made each player before him had received a cheer from the crowd. Then it came his turn. For months he'd sweated and agonized his way back, and had no idea how the crowd would react. The last time he'd played at Fenway was in a California Angels' uniform;

now he was wearing the only uniform he'd ever really wanted. He was back with the home team; he was back with the Red Sox.

When his name and number were announced the crowd was on their feet, and the ovation had begun. Though he was thirty years old now, he felt as if his clock had suddenly been turned back to 1964, when he was a nineteen year old kid making his first appearance as a major leaguer in Boston. Pins and needles ran through him, and the thrill of playing in front of friends and family and the hometown fans was indescribable. On his first at bat he didn't hit a home run into the screen, but he did get a hit and for now that would be good enough. There would be time enough to get his swing back; right now the most important thing was taking good swings and making contact with the ball. Two days later he got his first home run of the year in Baltimore. He felt like he could make it. Even so, the pressure he felt to perform was constant. At thirty he knew what the stakes were far better than he had at nineteen.

On their roster were two rookies who were highly rated, charismatic and productive. Fred Lynn and Jim Rice had come up through their farm system and had caught everyone's attention. They were nicknamed The Gold Dust Twins, and had captured Boston's heart. Lynn would play in the outfield, and Rice had been tagged first as alternate designated hitter, and had later been given the job full-time as his fearsome power was demonstrated all over the league. Tony's headaches had returned, his injuries had returned, and he spent more and more time on the bench, watching instead of playing. There was no complaint on his part; he knew what was happening. His numbers were indication enough, and the injuries he suffered punctuated his declining physical attributes. However, he was granted one final personal triumph before the end came. He was put in the game against Oakland's Vida Blue, one of the greatest pitchers in the league, who also happened to be the last pitcher he'd faced before his retirement in 1971. Vida Blue and the Oakland A's were in town, and Tony would have his chance at vindication. Though there was a half-full crowd, with no one on base, and no riveting moment to rise to great heights, he stood in against the great Vida Blue. He harbored no ill feeling towards him, he just wanted to do something that must be done while there was still time. Even in May, he already suspected his days were numbered.

And then it happened; a fastball down the middle, the quick swing of his bat, a loud *crack*, and the ball lofted high into the night sky and was lost from view as it sailed over the left field screen, high atop Fenway's infamous Green Monster. It would be the last home run of his career, and it had come in the friendly confines of Fenway Park. It wasn't necessarily how he'd have written the script, but he'd take it and be grateful. Even better, he hadn't needed to hobble around the bases to get it into the record books.

- Chapter Forty-Two -

This time he knew it was over, and he was at peace with it. He'd later been sent to the minors, which had only further served to demonstrate his diminished physical abilities. Nearly four years away from the game had been too long. Not that he'd given up or become bitter; he'd simply seen the writing on the wall and had resigned to the inevitable. It was that time. If there were any regrets it was that he'd never had the chance to make a serious run at the all-time home run record or baseball's Hall Of Fame. But he knew there could be no going back and rewriting his life; it had gone the way in had gone, and that was that. At least he'd been able to do what he'd done, and to fulfill a childhood dream that most people never got to experience.

Numerous offers had come in once the word was officially released. Ultimately, he chose broadcasting. He had initially decided to stay close to home. And when a job at Providence, Rhode Island station WJAR-TV had been offered to him he'd taken it. Within a year he was offered another position in San Francisco, and had then accepted that. This had almost proven to be a disaster. Imperfect technology, his inexperience, a language barrier and a succession of unpredictable events had contributed to a rocky start in the big leagues of professional sports broadcasting. He'd brought his Boston accent with him, and had never studied Spanish. Humbling, indeed. But having always respected the need for training to become good at something, he allowed himself to be schooled formally and had returned to the microphone.

He settled into his new career and environment, making new friends and contacts as he went. Then he had a chance meeting with Satch Hennessey, a close friend, and whose family he had become extremely fond. That bond, and seeing them interact, gave rise to him being stirred in a way he never had before. They had all the same closeness he'd always enjoyed with his own family. But this time he considered family life from the perspective of a father and a husband instead of a son or a brother. This was a different side of family life, and it became something that keenly interested him. The thought of getting married had come to mind back when he'd been with Julie, but that had been as a teenager with little insight into such things. Now, as a grown man in his thirties, he was seeing it from a completely different viewpoint. The prospect of being a father and provider, the head of a household, a parent with responsibilities and loyalty to one woman only, of being accountable in completely new ways was intriguing beyond anything he'd ever contemplated. He still had no desire to settle down yet, but this gave him something to think about. It was a side of life he might face some day. One of the mainstays of him being single meant absolute fidelity to his wife with no exceptions, which was something he strongly believed in. He didn't want to make that commitment to anyone until he was positively certain he could carry it out. It was one thing to be involved in the good life and the dating scene, but the responsibilities of raising a family brought with it ideals and disciplines he had long since come to perceive as necessities. In the meantime, he would watch and learn and participate and remember. And most of all enjoy.

Then tragedy had struck when Kelly, Satch's two-year old daughter, had been diagnosed with leukemia. He'd been close to this child and it had touched him in the deepest regions of his heart. He saw what a father and family goes through when one of them is stricken. It reminded him of what his family must have endured as the result of his beaning. But this time he got to see it from a parent's perspective.

Tragedy had struck again when Shari, Satch's wife, was diagnosed with breast cancer. Again, he'd seen what they had gone through a second time. They had all come together as one, and it had given him the experience of seeing it from a husband's perspective. He saw what it meant to be a parent, a husband and a provider. He saw what being strong was *really* all about. He'd been socializing on such a non-committed basis for so long he had entirely overlooked what it might be like to have a family of his own. Now, after having gotten so close to the Hennessey's, he'd seen family life on a much deeper, more meaningful level, and it had made him begin to wonder.

****

Eventually, things in the San Francisco Bay area had reached a point where they were played out. A health food business had been successful, but not enough to make him want to stay there. Several real estate investments with close friend and confidant, Joyce Huff, had proven very successful, but even that couldn't keep him. A serious relationship had ended, and was one of the last strings attaching him to Marin County. His broadcasting experiences had declined to where he needed greener pastures.
The path leading to those pastures took him to Los Angeles and the world of professional sports agenting.

****

He'd always had a great rapport with other professional athletes, and had been able to communicate with them easily. Their common ground in the ranks of professional sports, his understanding of sports as both a game and a business, their relationship with fans, the competitive nature of the arenas, the vulnerability of the athletes when it came to salary negotiations, and the dictates of the owners they played for were all familiar to him. He spoke the language and understood the trade options that owners had and the susceptibility of players who were at the mercy of longstanding systems set up to give owners all the advantages. The climate in this lopsided situation had begun to change when Curt Flood had challenged the owners under the Anti-Trust laws, having taken it all the way to the U.S. Supreme Court. In doing so, he had uncovered a blight that had kept athletes under management boot heels since the dawn of professional sports. A new breed of representatives had sprung from the ashes of Flood's failed efforts, and slowly the advantages had begun evening out through what had come to be termed as 'free agency', whereas players could shop the marketplace to see if other teams thought more of them than their current employer. In essence, teams would now have to compete with one another for players' services. As a result their salaries had begun to rise. For that to happen, however, they needed someone knowledgeable to represent their interests, and that was where representatives, or sports agents, had come to their aid. As a result both players and agents were beginning to flourish. No more would the teams hold all the aces. The playing field had begun to level.

Tony had met Dennis Gilbert in the Instructional League back during the winter of 1967. They had become fast friends, their common ground being their dedication to the game. They had stayed in touch over the years, and when Tony had decided it was time to move on after San Francisco, he had called Dennis to test the waters in Los Angeles. Dennis, now in insurance, had invited him down and began introducing him around town. One of the people Tony met was Beverly Hills attorney Dale Gribow, with whom Tony lived while he was feeling his way around Los Angeles and the sports market place.

The other person Dennis introduced him to was heavy hitting sports agent Mike Trope, whose clients were among the tops in professional football. In all, his client list would ultimately include no less than nine Heismann Trophy winners. Tony's background lent itself perfectly to something Trope had been contemplating. He wanted to broaden his horizons and branch out into professional baseball, and what better ambassador for that than Tony C? Tony had then done some scouting for Mike, and had even recruited a couple of clients into Trope's ranks. That being done, Tony saw the potential for a career in the field. Yet there was still a gnawing reservation, one that he'd been wrestling with off and on for a while. He was torn between Los Angeles and Boston; home games versus away games. He needed to find out which of these was what he wanted, and the only way to do it was go back to Boston and find out for sure. Then something happened that really stirred the mix: an invitation to audition for the recently vacated position of television color commentator for the Boston Red Sox.

- Chapter Forty-Three -
December, 1981

It was with mixed feelings that Tony got off the plane at Boston's Logan International Airport. For sure, it was good to be back in Boston, visiting for the holidays. He missed his family terribly, and spending the holiday season with them was his favorite pastime. The prospect of a new career was also encouraging. Being a sports agent was something he'd never considered because during his playing years there had been no such thing. Now, however, he was appreciative of its place in America's emerging new sports landscape and understood its need. He only wished it had been available when he was playing; he'd have made a lot more money for his considerable talents.

There was also the prospect of coming back home as a broadcaster for the Red Sox. Ken Harrelson, who had held the job for the past six years, had announced he was heading to Chicago, and the position had become available. He'd called WSBK-TV to test the waters and they had invited him to apply for the position.

Most of his mixed feelings had to do with logistics. The thought of spending more time away from home was not particularly uplifting. He'd had to admit he really wanted to get back to his friendly, familiar home turf of Boston. It had always been home, and it always would be. His roots there were too deep for him to be happy anywhere else. Yet, if it *absolutely had to be,* he'd make as valiant an attempt as possible out west until either he couldn't take it any more or could transfer back home.

On the other hand, there was the possibility of going to work, broadcasting for the Red Sox. They were his team, be it as a player or a commentator. His eyes were certainly good enough for that, and the wealth of expertise and personal experience from which he could draw was immense. WSBK had told him to call and set up an appointment when he got to town, which he was anxious to do. Were he given the choice of one over or the other, the broadcast job in Boston would win hands down.

He walked into the terminal and was met by Sal, Teresa, Billy and Richie. What greater sight was there than to be met by the family he loved more than anyone else in the world. After his experiences in Marin County, and what he had seen Satch Hennessey and his family go through, his view of family life had been reshaped forever.
Teresa was the first to reach him. Hugging him, she said, "Tony, it's so good to see you! Let me look at you." She held him back and looked at him from head to foot. "You seem okay. Very good."

"Of course he's okay," said Sal, grasping Tony by the shoulders. "He's home! What's not okay about that? Great to see you, Choo!" he said, hugging him. "You still feel solid, so I guess you're looking after yourself."

"I have to. I don't feel right if I'm not in shape, and out there the weather let's me do it all year round."

Tony then hugged Billy and Richie. The fact that they were his brothers, and that they were all grown men, made no difference to any of them. They were family and he loved them. He had always felt sorry for families that couldn't express their love each other openly; it was as though they were cheating themselves.

He looked outside at the snow that had begun to fall. "I don't know," he said, shaking his head. "That doesn't look like Los Angeles to me."

"That's *better* than LA," said Richie. "It's *home,* and it's good to have you back!"

****

It was now January of 1982. The holidays had come and gone, and it had been good to visit old friends. Jerry Maffeo, Anthony Athanas, Jerry Moses, Rico Petrocelli, and a host of others had filled his holidays and his life, compensating for the bitter New England cold with all the warmth he could want. He'd even gotten to make the rounds of his old haunts, including several clubs. The ghosts of yesterday may have been gone, but his life was still rich with friends and family.

As fate would have it, his audition for the WSBK color commentator position fell on Thursday, January 7th, his thirty-seventh birthday. Regardless of how the audition went, he made plans to go out afterward with his brother Billy and Anthony Athanas, to celebrate.

The audition had been set up with Ned Martin, the Red Sox play-by-play announcer for all their games. It would consist of taking a game that had been taped, and then deleting the sound. They would then do a running commentary on it as if it were a live broadcast. When it was over, Martin had no doubt that Tony was qualified for the job. His insight was detailed and relevant, and his experience as a former player demonstrated again and again that he had a deep understanding of the game. His broadcast experience in the Bay Area had also been another advantage. His expertise and historical perspective on the Red Sox organization and their players allowed him to pour himself into the task with a zeal that seemed both natural and authoritative. Indeed, he had all the earmarks of someone who knew and loved of what he spoke, who was eloquent and polished, and who had been there and done it. He was also personable and looked good on camera. Martin was impressed.

When they were done, Martin had shaken his hand, chatted with him for a while, and informed him that he'd pass his recommendations along to Joe Dimino, who was the new station manager, and who had been watching from one of the booths. He would make the final decision. Tony thanked them for the opportunity and left. It had been a good day.

****

During Tony's stay on the West Coast, Jerry Maffeo had moved on from The Sugar Shack, to the night manager's position at an upscale nightclub and restaurant in Boston, called Jason's. As he was about to sit down for dinner he saw a familiar face enter the dining area. It was Joe Dimino, from WSBK.

Jerry stood up and motioned Dimino to join him. "Hey Joe, have a seat, we'll break a little bread." Dimino smiled and joined him. They had recently met, and between their common Italian culture and love of Italian food and the Boston sports scene, it was natural that they should become fast friends.

"How you doing?" Maffeo asked.

"I'm doing okay," Dimino said, taking a seat at the table. "Right now the biggest thing on my mind is filling Ken Harrelson's spot in our broadcast booth."

"How's it going so far?" asked Maffeo, motioning to one of the waiters.

"We've narrowed it down to two people," he said, accepting a menu from the waiter.

"Something to drink?" asked the waiter.

"Not right now," Dimino said. "Water will be fine."

"So who are they?" Jerry asked, hoping one of them was Tony. He couldn't tell Joe how to do his job, but he was pulling for Tony. Tony was like family.

"Two former players on the team," Dimino continued. "One of them is Bob Montgomery, who used to catch for Boston. The other is Tony Conigliaro."

"So which way you going?" asked Maffeo, holding he breath.

"I like them both, but I have some reservations about Conigliaro. He's a good looking kid, he's friendly and he knows his baseball. But I'm not sure how many people still remember who he is."

Maffeo dropped his fork. "Joe, you got to promise me you'll never talk like that in public."

Mildly confused, Dimino asked, "What're you talking about?"

"You weren't around here ten years ago."

"So?"

"*So?* Look, I realize you're from down around New Jersey and Philly, but if you're gonna be living up here you have to know the lay of the land. Come with me, I want to show you something."

Maffeo started leading Dimino through the club. He stopped at a table where two couples were seated having dinner. "Excuse me, but do any of you know who Tony C is?"

"You're kidding me, right?" answered one of the men. "Tony C's one of the best ballplayers this city ever had. Everyone knows that."

Jerry looked at one of the women. "You know who Tony C is?"

"What are you, from out of town? He's the most gorgeous ball player I ever saw. If I could have married him, I wouldn't be sitting here with this lug."

Maffeo decided to move on before he broke up their marriage. "Come on, Joe. We're just getting started. Follow me."

They began making their way along the bar. Jerry stopped beside a young man, barely old enough to be there. "Excuse me, but do you know who 'Conig' was?"

"'Conig'? As in Tony Conigliaro, Tony C? Who doesn't know him? I watched him play when I was growing up. That guy hit some of the longest home runs in baseball history."

"Great, thanks."

"Come on, Joe," Jerry said. "School's not out yet."

He dragged Dimino along behind him, and stopped beside a couple of middle-aged women who were sitting further down the bar. "Hello, ladies," Maffeo said. "You didn't happen to see Tony Conigliaro wandering around here tonight, did you?"

They sat upright and their eyes began darting around the room. "Where? Where is he?" one of them asked. "I want to see him. He's the most handsome man in America, and could he ever hit. Where is he? I want to meet him."

A man was passing by at that moment, and Jerry asked, "Tell me something, pal. You ever heard of Tony C?"

"You serious? Who else could've come back from an injury like that and win an American League batting title two years later with a bad eye? And you're asking me who he is? Gimme a break." And he walked off.

Maffeo turned to Dimino. "You want to ask a few more, or you starting to get the picture?"

Raising his hands, he said, "All right, I get it, I get it. Can we eat now? I'm starving."

"Sure. I ought to make you pay for mine too, after the education I just gave you."

****

Later on, Tony, Billy C and Anthony Athanas showed up in the midst of celebrating Tony's birthday. Upon seeing Maffeo, they joined him where he was sitting at a booth with Dimino.

"How you guys doing?" Jerry asked. "Sit down, take a load off." As they sat down, Jerry said, "Tony, say hi to Joe Dimino. Joe, this is Tony C."

Tony's face lit up. "We've already met. Hi Joe. Now that we're away from work, welcome to Boston."

"Hi Tony, good to see you again." He felt Tony's grip, and made note of how well-conditioned he was. "You look like you could still play," he commented.

"If God would give me a new pair of eyes, I might try it," Tony said. "But that's okay, I had a great run for seven years, and I have a lot to be thankful for. Besides, I turned thirty-seven today, and there's not a lot of room for thirty-seven year-old players in the league. For now, I'm happy to keep in shape."

"Happy birthday," Dimino said. "You don't look a day over thirty-six." They all laughed and settled into a night of storytelling and more laughter.

When it got near closing time, Dimino decided he had to go. He'd had a great night. He made a pit-stop to the restroom just prior to leaving, then joined Tony and Billy, who were at the bar, schmoozing with the bartender. Jerry Maffeo was with them.

"Great night tonight," Tony said to Dimino.

"Yes, it was," Dimino said. "Actually, it might even be better than you think."

"Oh? How's that?"

"I've done some thinking and I've seen all I need to know. The job is yours, Tony. You're our new color commentator. Congratulations."

"Hey, that's great!" Maffeo said, delighted at the prospect of Tony coming back home.

"Way to go!" said Billy, happy that the whole family would be together in Boston again. Athenas slapped Tony five.

"Great, Joe," Tony said, shaking Dimino's hand. "This means the world to me, I can't thank you enough."

"I think you'll do a great job for us, Tony."

He paused a moment, then added, "I'm going to ask you to do me a favor."

"Sure, whatever you want," Tony said.

"Let's keep this among us for now until we can make a formal announcement. This is going to be a big deal with the media, and I know you're getting ready to head back out of town again. How long do you think you'll be?"

"I have to go to Atlanta for a business meeting, and then to Puerto Rico and Venezuela for a couple of days to scout some prospects. Then I'm back on the West Coast. I can be back here in three weeks if that's okay."

"Great, that'll give us time to prepare things on our end."

- Chapter Forty-Four -

It had been less than thirty-six hours since his meeting with Joe Dimino, and Tony had been doing a lot of thinking. He knew where his heart lay, and that was in Boston with WSBK. But there were other things to consider. He had to arrange to sell his property in Marin County; Joyce Huff could handle that for him; she'd been a staunch friend and real estate advisor for years. He also had a few other details to iron out in Los Angeles, and these were on his mind as he rode to the airport with Billy that Saturday Morning.

"What are you going to do about the sports agent job?" he asked.

"I don't know," Tony answered. "If I hadn't got the broadcast job, I'd jump right in. Even so, I'd like to find a way to stay with it, but my first responsibility is going to be the broadcasts. Mike Trope and I are supposed to work out the details in Atlanta later today. If he'll let me do it during the off-season, I'll take it. Even then, it would have to be from Boston, not LA. I'm all done living somewhere else while my heart's living here. I'll have to talk to him and see how it goes, I guess."

"Still doing the trip to Puerto Rico and Venezuela?"

"Yeah, I owe them that. I made a commitment, and I'll keep it. What happens after that depends on how our meeting goes in Atlanta."

"I hope it works out." Billy paused for a moment as he let a truck pull in ahead of him. Then, "What's with all these girls that are still calling you? As soon as word got out that you were home the phone began ringing and hasn't stopped." When Tony didn't answer, he asked, "You keeping that a secret, or what?"

Still no answer. He turned toward Tony, and was confronted with an incomprehensible horror. Tony was clutching his chest, his face etched with agony. He appeared unable to breathe; worse, he couldn't talk. Billy wasn't a medical expert, but he knew an apparent heart attack when he saw one. Instinctively, he immediately sought medical help. There were a couple of smaller facilities within driving distance, but they weren't really set up for emergencies. He had been dating a nurse from Massachusetts General Hospital, which is where he decided to go. One glance was all he needed. Wherever he went, it would have to be fast.

Fortunately, he was already on Route 1A and headed for the airport, which was in East Boston. Mass General was in the same direction. The trick now would be getting there in time to save Tony. Another glance, and he saw that his eyes had closed, and that he seemed to be lying in the seat very still. It didn't look good.

Billy weaved in and out of traffic, grateful that it was the weekend. Had this been commuter traffic he'd have little hope of getting him anywhere in time to save him. Tires screeching, he veered his BMW from lane to lane, cutting people off, swerving all the way from the breakdown lane to the passing lane. The toll collector at the entrance to the Sumner Tunnel saw little more than a blur rush past him as Billy blew through the tollbooth.

He continued weaving in and out of traffic, almost hoping he'd be flagged by the police. They could call ahead to the hospital and be ready for him when he arrived. When he finally screeched to a halt near Mass General's Emergency entrance, he jumped from the car and raced inside. Standing in the doorway, he yelled, "Got a heart attack victim in the car, I need help!"

"What's the problem?" asked one of the nurses.

"My brother's outside in the car, and he's having a heart attack. I need help getting him inside!"

There was a flurry of activity and two EMT's went outside with a gurney. Inside one of the nurses called for Dr. Roman DeSanctis, a renowned cardiologist who happened to be in the hospital. When Tony was wheeled in, Billy's heart leaped into his throat when he overheard one of the technicians say he couldn't get a pulse.

Inside the Emergency Room, the cubicle where Tony had been brought was a portrait of frenetic activity. As nurses and technicians arrived and began gathering various machines and other medical paraphernalia, Billy rushed in, saw Tony for the first time since he'd been extricated from the BMW, and was shocked. Despite all activity around the life support equipment, not much else seemed to be moving forward.

"He's not-- He didn't..." Billy stammered.

Mary Jane Crowley, normally the charge nurse for the Intensive Care Unit, had been transferred down to the ER for the day to cover for the nurse who usually held down the position. It wasn't expertise or knowledge that Crowley was lacking; what she needed was for an attending physician to step in, take charge and begin giving orders to the technical staff.

Knowing that someone would quickly be assigned, she wanted to properly prepare the room until the attending physician arrived. "How long did it take you to get him here?" she asked.

Billy glanced at his watch. "I don't know, maybe seven or eight minutes."

"And you've been here five more? That's not good."

That's not what Billy wanted to hear. "What are you saying?"

It was then that the attending physician entered. "I'm Dr. DeSanctis, I'll be treating your brother." To Mary Jane Crowley, he said, "Set up life support." Turning back to Billy, he added, "What she's referring to is oxygen deprivation."

"Oxygen deprivation? What's that mean?"

"When someone suffers a heart attack their lungs can also be affected, and that restricts the flow of oxygen to their bloodstream. That subsequently impedes the flow of oxygen to other parts of the body, including the brain." He subtly motioned several staff members to begin the appropriate procedures.

"How does that affect my brother's condition?" Billy pressed.

"Oxygen deprivation to the brain beyond five minutes begins the deterioration process and damages its ability to function. Tony's blood and oxygen flow may have been impaired for ten or twelve minutes. That can weigh heavily against his chance of survival."

"You're not telling me you're going to let him die without trying to save him?"

"I didn't say that. I said the odds are against him. What I've done is order Tony put on life support. After that we'll let God decide."

Billy was fighting off bereavement as he sat in the waiting room outside. Last night and this morning had been a period of joy and celebration; now it was a life-and-death struggle against time. *Oh God, please don't let this happen,* he thought. How would he ever tell his parents? Telling them about the heart attack would be bad enough. Sal had already undergone bypass surgery four years earlier. This might be more than he could handle. Realizing that, he asked one of the nurses to have a couple of nitroglycerine pills on hand, no matter what the news.

When DeSanctis finally came out to see him, Billy was sitting quietly in the waiting room. The look on DeSanctis' face wasn't encouraging. "How is he?" Billy asked.

"Not very good, I'm afraid. As I said earlier, oxygen deprivation beyond five minutes initiates deterioration, which is directly related to its function. Your brother has gone at least eight to ten minutes beyond that. I have to be honest with you; if he lives, he may not be the same person you've always known."

"But *will he live?*" Billy asked.

"We've done everything we can," DeSanctis said. "His heart had stopped and failed to respond to conventional methods, including electrical stimulation. We tried more extreme methods and we've managed to get it going again. I have to tell you, the next twenty-four hours will probably determine whether he makes it or not."

Relieved that he wouldn't have to tell his parents the worst, he said, "At least he's not dead. I'll be back in a little while. I'm going to tell my family what's happened. And please do me a favor. Don't let word of this get out to anyone. I'm sure you know who my brother is, and I don't want my family to hear about it on the radio before I have the chance to speak with them."

"Understood," DeSanctis said. "I'll inform our staff." He paused for a moment, then said, "Actually, I do know who your brother is, and if there's anyone who can survive this, I believe it's him."

****

It took less than twenty-four hours for Julie to get to the hospital. Though still with the airlines, she made flying back to Boston and being at his bedside her top priority. Unbeknownst to most people, she and Tony had remained close despite no longer dating each other. That indefinable, inexplicable thread that had once made them soul mates still bound them together, even after nearly twenty years. They had had dinner together in San Francisco as recently as the previous year when she and her mother had been out there on vacation. Now, as she was about to see him for the first time since his heart attack, the Charge Nurse in the Cardiac Care Unit tried to prepare Julie and her brothers Alex and Louis before they actually entered Tony's room.

"You have to understand something," she said, in a soft, conciliatory tone. "Tony, for all intents and purposes, should have died yesterday. Were it not for the urging of his brother we might not have continued trying to revive him for as long as we did. It took over two hours before his heart began to beat. In the era before life support machines it would have been impossible. I'm sure you already know that he suffered oxygen deprivation to the brain for twice as long as it takes for deterioration to set in."

"What do you mean by that?" asked Alex. He appeared tentative, and it was obvious hospital settings and extreme medical situations were not his forte. He'd already been told something about Tony's condition and was apprehensive about what waited inside compared to the kid he'd caroused with back in high school and his early days with the Red Sox.

She paused for a moment, then quietly added, "He won't look the way you remember him."

"But he's alive..." Julie said. The comment was more a hopeful statement than a question.

"Technically, yes," replied the nurse. She'd been at this too long to candy coat the reality of what they were about to see.

Julie's younger brother, Louis, was growing more anxious by the moment, and appeared even less able to handle the situation than Alex.

"I think we'd better go in," he said, "The more I listen to this, the more it bothers me. We keep this up I won't want to go in at all."

They were led into Tony's room, which was softly lit. The only sound came from the half-dozen life support machines and various monitoring equipment that were sustaining him. Tony lay in bed, covered with a sheet up to his chest. Myriad tubes, monitors and patches were connected to his arms and head, and an IV was taped to his forearm. The most striking thing, perhaps, was his physical appearance. The loss of oxygen, the effect of the defibrillator paddles, which were designed to restart his heart, had taken their toll on him. Indeed, he wasn't the Tony they remembered. The best Alex and Louis could do was stand in the doorway, staring in shock as Julie slowly approached the bed. No matter how he may have looked at the moment, this was the man who had stolen her heart and her affections for a lifetime. This was the man she'd never forgotten. She placed her hand on his cheek, bent over and lightly kissed his forehead. Was love blind? At the moment that didn't really matter. What mattered was her memory of the man who had captured her soul twenty years earlier. Was it better that he should have been allowed to pass rather than lie here near death with little hope of returning as the doctors had suggested? For now, she'd rather see him the way he was than to part with him forever. If time should later prove her wrong, then so be it. But until then...

"I wish I could be more optimistic," the nurse said, "but I can't. In time the family will have to make a decision that will be difficult to make. Cases like this simply don't make it back."

"He's been surviving things all his life," Julie said. "He'll come back from this, too."

- Chapter Forty-Five -

But it seemed he wouldn't come back. A month later his heart had grown
stronger, but he still lay in a deep coma. The family had gathered around him, relatives
had come from all over; fans and former teammates were sending letters, flowers and
religious articles, and were holding prayer vigils. The stream came and never ended. Julie
had also come by to see him, and to offer comfort to Sal and Teresa. Her brother Alex,
earlier one of Tony's closest friends, had been devastated upon seeing his condition. No
one but close friends and family were actually allowed in to see him. As DeSanctis had
said, he wasn't the person they'd always known. Many of them had found it
heartbreaking, and had burst into tears. And yet, they maintained hope.

The press had descended in droves, and speculation was rampant. Those who
knew Tony were fully aware of how health conscious he was. Alcohol consumption was
minimal; drug consumption was non-existent. Their argument was that if he'd been such
a health fanatic, how could his heart attack be explained, especially at only thirty-seven
years of age.

DeSanctis tried to offer a variety of possibilities why such things happened to
otherwise perfectly healthy people, especially athletes. "It's possible that an arrhythmia
developed, and had silently progressed undetected. He may also have had a heart valve
dysfunction, where it had opened, but was unable to shut. A blood clot might have

developed and blocked his heart from pumping. Until we have a chance to do proper testing – if and when he comes out of the coma – there will be no way of telling for sure." It was also agreed that under no circumstances was he to be taken off life support. They were to do everything humanly possible to sustain him.

During the fifth week he showed signs of semi-consciousness. There was no conversation, no opening his eyes and looking at them. Their only indication had been when he occasionally stirred. During all this, Tony's family had remained strong in their belief that somehow he'd recover.

Nearly two months passed before he was removed from Mass General to a rehabilitation center in Salem, Mass. There he would continue the road back from yet another near death experience. He drifted in and out of consciousness; people came to see him, offering him outside stimuli by way of familiar voices, music, memories, holding his hand, and companionship. At the best of times, unfortunately, the most he could do was moan. People saw what they needed to see, said what they needed to say, anything to bolster both his courage and theirs. Many left in tears.

Billy was the one who undertook the massive responsibility of caring for him. Even after they discharged him to home nursing, Billy was the one who looked after him. Billy, the brother who was so often misdiagnosed as living in Tony's shadow, now stepped up and shouldered the biggest responsibility either of them ever had. Family and friends did what they could, but they had lives to live and households to maintain. Eventually, the financial strain of Tony's healthcare got to be so much that his insurance policies were nearly exhausted and were almost at the end of their lifespan. Most of the family's financial resources had also been drained. The costs were astronomical, and they were working class people.

It was then that the Red Sox and the entertainment industry stepped up to do their part. Tony hadn't been forgotten, and the people he had touched wanted to do whatever they could to help. In early June, 1983 *'An Evening With Tony C'* was held at Symphony Hall, and it was literally a star studded event. Frank Sinatra, Dionne Warwick, Marvin Hamlisch, Ted Williams, Bobby Orr, Joe DiMaggio, Willie Mays, Oakland Raiders owner Al Davis, Ben Davidson, and many Red Sox former players teamed up to raise nearly a quarter million dollars to offset Tony's four thousand dollars per week medical expenses. Two months later, *'Tony C Night'* was held at Fenway Park, and another hundred thousand had been raised.

People hadn't forgotten, his memory hadn't faded, the dream had been fulfilled, and now those who cared and loved him had committed to remain in his life, no matter what the circumstances.

- Chapter Forty-Six -

Late in 1983, of necessity, Tony had been moved to his parents' home. His heart was no longer in danger, but the rest of his condition required round-the-clock medical attention. There was always someone there caring for him, which would have been much easier to take if he'd been getting better. But he wasn't. In time he had returned to consciousness, but his motor skills were extremely limited as was his ability to speak. He was given physical therapy, and even the most basic actions required enormous effort, often leaving him winded and sweating profusely.

And yet, despite the crushing burden it added to their lives, his family never relented, nor gave up on him. Everyone participated, trying hard to maintain their spirits. Visitors, whose numbers had fallen off, would also offer encouragement. In response, Tony would do his best to force a smile of appreciation. Though difficult as it may have been, they were a testimony to the depth and loyalty of his friendships, and though it too had trickled, the mail never stopped.

1986 brought with it another medical emergency, this time to Sal. The stress he endured through Tony's ordeal had taken its toll on him. He'd gone through another round of chest pains. Ironically, as the one who had driven him to Mass General, Billy now retraced his steps with Sal, all the way from home to the hospital, using the same route and the same entrance to the same hospital he had taken Tony. The rigors of everything he'd endured with 'Choo' had worn him down, and he wasn't getting any younger. After meeting with doctors, he was put on medication and told to take it easy. But Sal was an intense and passionate man, and what greater passion was there than 'Choo'?

****

It had been nearly a year since Sal had gone back under the doctors' care, and he'd done everything humanly possible to comply with their requests. It was bothersome at times, but he felt compelled to follow their guidance. His family needed him, and he needed them. And there was Tony. Seeing him was difficult, and at times he wondered if he was being selfish by not wanting to let Tony pass. But Tony was his child, his first-born. How does a father let go of that?

Still, he'd had to back off and rest and focus on another of his passions: horses. He was at Suffolk Downs, a well-known Boston area racetrack, where he maintained several horses. It wasn't so much them winning or losing as it was being in the company of animals that were loving, and demanded nothing of him other than the same respect he'd grant any other living thing. They were like children; they represented unconditional love. All he had to do was feed them, treat them well, show them some love - an increasing need as he'd grown older - and in return he represented everything they needed. The other thing about the track that appealed to him was its peaceful, unstressed atmosphere, which required little from him other than financial upkeep for the horses. Most of all, it provided a place where he could sequester himself from the outside world and it clamors. That included the horrific pain and struggle that came with watching Tony's plight, standing by helplessly with no way of improving it.

One of the trainers entered the stable, an older man Sal had known for fifteen years. They'd spent many hours talking horses, business, baseball, Tony and being middle aged men who had seen the world undergo a multitude of radical changes in a very short time. It was refreshing to retreat into a friendship set in a place where the outside world couldn't intrude.

"How are you, Jimmy?" Sal asked, extending his hand.

"Doing good, Mr. C," Jimmy answered. "How's the pride of Suffolk Downs?" he asked, referring to Sal's horses.

"I don't know, sometimes I think they're doing better than I am."

"Then maybe it's time you switched from all that rich Italian food you eat to some good old fashioned oats and barley." Both men howled at the suggestion.

"You know," Sal said, "If I thought things would get better by doing that, I'd eat oats and barley for the rest of my life." But today, even in the stable, conditions were weighing on him more heavily than usual.

"Still no improvement, huh?"

Sal slowly nodded in the negative. "No, he's back in the hospital again. This time it's pneumonia and a staff infection. They're loading him up on antibiotics, but it's getting to where the medicine he gets doesn't cure him. It just puts his condition on hold for a while. I sometimes wish——I sometimes wish...I--" Sal suddenly grabbed his chest and leaned against the stall for support. His breath was coming in gasps, his face was agonized, and maintaining his feet appeared to be a monumental struggle.

"Sal, what is it? What's wrong?" Jimmy asked, his face etched with concern. "Let me get you some water."

Sal waved him off, clutched at his chest, and collapsed. He moaned, and lay still; his breath labored and heavy.

Jimmy summoned an ambulance.

****

That had been on July 5, 1987. Four days later, Salvatore Conigliaro, father to Tony, Billy and Richie Conigliaro, and husband of Teresa, succumbed to his coronary at Mass General Hospital. The family, fearing for Tony's mental and emotional health, such as it was, decided not to tell him about his father's passing.

In the midst of all that continued to befall them, Billy, Richie and Teresa, somehow managed to carry on.

****

Tony's residence was never stable for long. He was transferred from his parents' house to Billy's, to one of the several rehab hospitals he regularly needed, back to his parents', then back to Billy's. His health, though not seeming to deteriorate, never seemed to improve either. Coughing bouts, fevers, infections, heart problems, reactions to medications and myriad other circumstances always had him on the move. And with that came the constant need for close medical supervision.

Billy's home was in Nahant, right down the street from his parents'. Though it intruded on his professional and personal life, and wore him down physically and emotionally Billy never once complained about the strain. Tony was his brother, he loved him. This is what family did, and that was that. He asked for no special praise; he did it low-keyed and matter-of-factly.

Now, as Julie stood in the foyer, Billy hung her coat in the closet, then led her to the living room where Tony was seated in a wheelchair. His ability to speak had never really returned, but he could muster several words at a time albeit very slowly.

When she entered he looked at her and his expression seemed to brighten. A moment later, he smiled. She went to him, bent over and kissed him. His eyes seemed to flare with a vestige of the old fire that had been there in better days. Beyond any doubt, he was happy to see her.

As she was about to pull away, Tony glanced something that triggered a profound reaction. His hand shot out and grabbed her wrist, and he pulled it to within inches of his face. There he fixated on the ring she wore on her right hand. A broad grin passed over his face as he stared at it. He remembered that ring; he had given it to her in high school and still recognized it. There was almost a childlike glee in his eyes. It was a link back to a time when life had been more innocent and simple. It was a time he longed for, but would never recapture. Nor would Julie.

She seemed physically pained, and it took a moment for Billy to understand. In his excitement Tony, still incredibly strong and emotionally charged, was squeezing her hand so tightly as to be almost crushing it. To her it felt like it was trapped in a vice. Billy went to her and gently pried her loose from Tony's impassioned grip.

"I know," she said softly. "I remember it, too. We had some great times back then." And she remembered them well. The rides in the dream cruiser, her prom, going to see him play at Fenway on opening day. Though that had been a different era, it was good to have the memories, despite them representing all the things that might have been. His face had begun to perspire. She looked around and spotted a washbasin and towel on the coffee table. She moistened the towel and dabbed it across Tony's forehead. She dabbed it across his eyes and neck and throat in much the same manner he had kissed her that first night when they'd been alone in her parents' house. As she dabbed, the memories came back with such clarity as to feel they had happened only yesterday. What might they have given to go back to yesterday...

She pulled up a chair and sat down beside him. There wouldn't be much in the way of conversation; there never was. It wasn't about conversation; it was companionship. They seemed the only ones who filled each other's void, despite all the years since they'd ended their relationship. Some things were timeless, including lifelong relationships. They never died; they never went away.

The radio had been playing in the background. Now, as Julie sat beside him, a song by Stevie Wonder came on that seemed to sum up her entire reason for being there. *I Just Called To Say I Love You...*

It would be another hour before Julie got up, kissed him, and left.

- Chapter Forty-Seven -

<u>February, 1990</u>

Under a slate-gray afternoon sky, the New England landscape was beginning to grow dim as the winter sun prepared for its descent beneath the western horizon. The biting February wind had been gusting most of the day, sending a damp chill through the hospital. Tony had been brought there yet again, this time due to respiratory complications and a temperature of one hundred and four. It had been eight years since the heart attack, and he'd made this trip so many times it had become wearisome. At least Billy was seated beside him, holding his hand. As he lay in the stillness, he began thinking of all the things that had happened over the years.

"I wish I could talk, but I can't. All I can do is think, which is something I do now more than ever. If my friends and family only knew how much I'd love to tell them.

"When I was young my father told me I was going to find very few true friends in life, but when I did that I should be grateful for them, and to hang on to them. I've done that. Friends I've made over the years, like Alex Markakis, Frank Carey, Tommy Iarrabino, from the days of my adolescence, were always there for me. What would I have done without those guys? Anthony Athanas, my close friend and roommate who I went on safari with, did double dates, and who even came with me and sat in the audience when they invited me to be on The Dating Game. He even tried to tell me which

girl to pick. Then there's Jerry Maffeo, who's both my close friend and stalwart supporter. He was with me right after the beaning, and took time off from work to take a trip when I'd needed to just get away. He hung in with me, and made me laugh when I'd needed it most. Bailed me out of a couple of scrapes that could have gotten serious, too.

"I guess I've learned a few things over the years, and one of them is how to get along better with people. It was difficult to be nice to everyone all the time when I was a ball player, and I know I made a few people mad from time to time. Unfortunately, the pressures were always there and sometimes the papers printed things that weren't always true. Even so, baseball is my number one interest and always will be, no matter what they print. It would have been nice to get that job at WSBK, but that's gone now, and it's okay. If I'd been meant to get it, I would have.

"I remember the night I got hit by that pitch. That was the nightmare of all nightmares. It changed my life, and took a lot of the cockiness out of me. Who knows, maybe I needed that. I just wish it would have happened some other way. Getting my self-confidence back was one of the hardest things I've ever done. I guess if there's something I regret, it's not letting Jack Hamilton have his chance to say how sorry he was for what had happened that night. Maybe when I come back from this I'll give him that chance. It doesn't seem right to let a man carry a burden like that for the rest of his life. I think it might make me a bigger and better man too, and there's nothing wrong with that. Besides, everyone I ever spoke to said Jack was a good man. Surely he deserves to say his piece.

"Then there's my teammates. They were the greatest bunch of guys I could have ever hoped to play with. I think about my managers, especially Johnny Pesky. He's the one that talked them into letting me come up to the big club a year early. Eddie Popowski taught me how to play at the professional level. What a great mentor. Mike Ryan, Tony Horton, Jerry Moses, George Scott, Mike Andrews, Jim Lonborg, Reggie Smith, Elston Howard, Rico Petrocelli, Joe Foy, Jerry Adair, Dick Radatz, Louie Tiant, and Yaz. Huh, Yaz... Now there's something I wish we could straighten out with the public. Carl and I always had a competitive relationship, but never had it been malicious or hateful. Indeed, we had our differences, but who doesn't? Some time after he retired from baseball, I heard he'd been asked what he would say if we could meet again. They told me he'd

thought for a minute, and had said that I was a player very similar to him in a lot of ways. He said I never left anything in the locker room. I brought it all onto the field. He said I trained as hard as anyone he'd ever seen, and practiced as many hours as they would let me. He said I gave everything I had every time I stepped onto the field, hadn't taken any shortcuts, and had never been a lazy player. He said no one could ever say that I hadn't given all I had to the game. Even though I can only lay here in my bed, unable to speak, I hope that someday someone will convey to Carl my own similar praise for him, too.

"Then there's Dick Williams, my former manager, who guided us through the year of The Impossible Dream. I really resented him for never coming to see me, or at least sending me a card. Now that I'm older and wiser, I think what Williams did was maybe all he could have done. Later on, he'd tried to give me small demonstrations of compassion and acknowledgement of my injuries; maybe I had set my expectations higher than what he was capable of giving. One thing's for sure, especially now that I look back after all these years: no one, absolutely no one else could have driven that team to the glory we attained that year. He'd been tough, but that's what it had taken; he had driven us relentlessly, even ruthlessly; but that's what it took to bring a team from 72-90 one year, to an American League pennant and the World Series one year later. It took what it took, and now the record will stand forever; the Boston Red Sox came within one game of the 1967 World Series Championship. I'd love to have played, and maybe I would have made the difference between winning and losing. I'll never know now, but at least I was there.

"And then there's Julie, my first love. I sometimes wonder if she was my only real love. I regret what I did, breaking up with her like that, and I've second-guessed myself about it a million times. It's been one of those private things that I've always kept to myself, just like I did when I wrote her those two hundred letters during the Instructional League, and when I was in the minors and spring training. Those were the most romantic, fulfilling and happiest days of my life. I know I had a lot of fun dating lots of women, but none of them ever made me feel the way she did. Even now, all these years later, I've never forgotten those days. Or her. I'm grateful for the times she's come to visit me after my heart attack. I wonder why she never got married, and neither did I. If

we'd gotten married, she would have had to endure all this, and maybe it's better that she's been spared that. I always want to be faithful to whoever I marry, and with all the dating I did it might have been hard to live up to that. The last thing I'd ever want would be to hurt her. I want a family to be held together by the same ideals I was raised on: prayer, love and respect. Maybe it was better having things go the way they had, maybe not. It takes time to change, and maybe I'm on the right track now. It'll make me a better man. I'll never know for sure what might have been best, but one thing I'm absolutely sure of: she was the crowning jewel of any girl I ever knew.

"I remember Uncle Vinnie, who sacrificed hundreds of hours training me, and teaching me how to play baseball. He laid a foundation for me that carried me through high school and into the pros. I owe Vinnie more than I could ever repay him. He always claimed that what I made of myself was payment enough, but that was only a small installment.

"Aunt Phyllis also did her part. She never tired of seeing me, was always kind to me, and she never complained about all the time Vinnie and I spent together. I thank God it had been for a worthy cause.

"Then there's my brother Billy, sitting here beside me, holding my hand to comfort me. And it does, it comforts me a lot. It's great not having to be alone, especially at a time like this. He never gave up on me being here, and he never complains. I wonder if he knows how much I appreciate all the things he's done for me, and how much I love him for it. It's unbelievably frustrating for me to be aware of so much, yearn to say so many things to so many people, and not be able to express them. I've heard everything my family said, even though they didn't think I could hear them. I hear them; I just can't express myself to them in return. At least it doesn't diminish my love for them. I've reveled in their limitless outpouring of love and support, their inspiration, their consolation and their encouragement. If only there was some way I could tell them. It weighs so heavily on me.

"I thank God for my parents. I love them. I more than love them; without them I'm nothing. Having them behind me has been the most important thing in my life. Yet, I wonder where my father is. It seems like it's been a long time since I've seen him. How I love that man, and I know how much he loves me. 'Choo', that's what he called me. He

gave me that name before I could even walk, and it's stuck with me all my life. It's something special, just between him and me. I wish I could hear him say it again, just once.

"I hate the hospital. It means I won't get to hear the sound of my mother's voice as much as when I'm home. Even though I'm forty-five, there's still something musical about it. I know this is a terrible emotional burden to her, yet I've never heard her complain. Not even once. She's loved me from before I left her womb, and has spent the rest of her life sharing in the joy of me simply being her son. I remember the times I skipped school, and disobeyed her. I hope she forgives me for that. She must know how much I love her, and that I'd never act like that toward her now. I remember her home cooked meals; she always wanted to make sure I was healthy and strong. I couldn't have had a better mother, and wouldn't trade her for anyone else in the world. And that's how I feel about my father. I'm grateful to have him for my mentor. He was always firm of hand, but fair and gentle in his ways. And he imparted to me all the best values that a man could possess. He made me the man I became. And it went a lot further than just baseball.

"I hope Richie knows what a great kid brother he's always been. I couldn't have asked for a better one. I remember all the times I took him along for the ride. I love Richie, and I hope I've been able to pass something along to him that can help him in his own life. Richie was my pal, the one who never judged or criticized me. I could always be myself with him. He's always been there. He even washed and waxed my cars. Not for money, but because I was his older brother and he loved me. Whenever I was ready, so was Richie. We did a million things together, and I love him deeply.

"That's how I feel about Billy. I know how much he's sacrificed to look after me. If it weren't for the paralysis that restricts me from speaking, I'd tell him so. We hung out together, chased girls together, and we did something else together that rarely happens: we were brothers on the same professional baseball team. And it wasn't just any team; it was the Boston Red Sox, our home team. For now I'll have to content myself by letting Billy hold my hand, even if I can't speak or tell him how important it is to me that he's here with me.

"All these people have done so much, giving of themselves the way they have. I doubt I'll ever be able to thank them enough. This is my family, and they're a gift from God. Maybe some day I can tell my grandchildren about them.

"From all the things that have happened to me, I have to feel like I'm some sort of special guy. I still can't understand why I've never been able to see well enough to read for very long, but at least I could see the ball when I stepped to the plate those last couple of years in '69 and '70. That was a miracle. I believe that the support people gave me was necessary, and I think God's the one who made it possible. And that's why I say I must be some special kind of guy. God has always been good to my family and me, and this time I think He went out of His way.

"I'm starting to feel tired now, and my mind is beginning to drift. I think it's time for me to go to sleep..."

Tony Conigliaro passed away on February 24, 1990 with his brother Billy still holding his hand...